CASE STUDIES IN
CULTURAL ANTHROPOLOGY

GENERAL EDITORS
George and Louise Spindler
STANFORD UNIVERSITY

THE MARDUDJARA ABORIGINES

Living the Dream in Australia's Desert

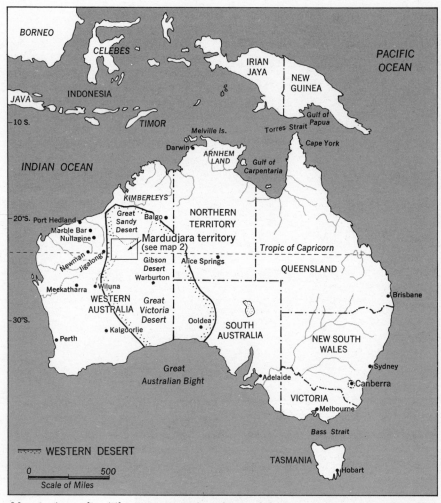

Map 1: Australia. The approximate boundaries of the Western Desert are indicated by the dotted areas surrounded by the heavy gray line.

THE MARDUDJARA
ABORIGINES

Living the Dream
in Australia's Desert

By

ROBERT TONKINSON

University of Oregon

HOLT, RINEHART AND WINSTON

NEW YORK   CHICAGO   SAN FRANCISCO   DALLAS   MONTREAL

TORONTO   LONDON   SYDNEY

For Gogara and the Jigalong Mob
and for Myrna

Library of Congress Cataloging in Publication Data

Tonkinson, Robert
  The Mardudjara Aborigines.

  (Case studies in cultural anthropology)
  Bibliography: p. 141
  1. Mardudjara (Australian people)   I. Title.
II. Series.
DU125.M32T66   301.29'941   78-46

ISBN: 0-03-039821-5

Foreword

About the Series

These case studies in cultural anthropology are designed to bring to students, in beginning and intermediate courses in the social sciences, insights into the richness and complexity of human life as it is lived in different ways and in different places. They are written by men and women who have lived in the societies they write about and who are professionally trained as observers and interpreters of human behavior. The authors are also teachers, and in writing their books they have kept the students who will read them foremost in their minds. It is our belief that when an understanding of ways of life very different from one's own is gained, abstractions and generalizations about social structure, cultural values, subsistence techniques, and the other universal categories of human social behavior become meaningful.

About the Author

Bob Tonkinson is a West Australian who received his B.A. and M.A. from the University of Western Australia and his Ph.D. in Anthropology from the University of British Columbia. He is an Associate Professor of Anthropology at the University of Oregon, and is currently holding a Senior Research Fellowship at the Australian National University (1977–1979). He has done extensive field research in the Western Desert of Australia and in the New Hebrides, and his publications include a monograph, *Maat Village; A Relocated Community in the New Hebrides* (1968), and a book, *The Jigalong Mob* (1974). He is at present an active member of the executive board of the Association for Social Anthropology in Oceania and is serving on the National Humanities Faculty. His anthropological area interests are Aboriginal Australia and Oceania; his subject interests include religion, social organization and change, and film. He and his wife, Dr. Myrna Ewart Tonkinson, who is also a social anthropologist, will be spending much of 1978 doing further research in the Australian Desert.

About the Book

This case study about the Mardudjara, a people of the great western desert of Australia, rivals the best of science fiction in interest. Some forty thousand years ago adventurous migrants from the mainland of Asia found their way into the subcontinent. Others came later, but the largest portion probably came early. For thousands of years these people have elaborated their culture less disturbed by outsiders and outside influences than in any other land mass of comparable size. What they created, the adaptations they made to the different ecological circumstances afforded by Australia, with its thousands of miles of seacoast, its tropical areas, and its vast deserts and semi-arid zones, can be described with accuracy in some instances. These can be so described because some of the peoples survived the first stages of the terrible onslaught of the western world with their ancient cultures intact. In the case of the Mardudjara, the ancient adaptations continued in relatively unchanged form, with the people living free in the open desert, pursuing a hunting and gathering existence into the mid-sixties, when they were studied in that state by Dr. Tonkinson.

This study is the result of both his fieldwork with the surviving nomadic groups and his work with the peoples who had come in from the desert and settled around places where they could enjoy some of the benefits of an industry- and agriculture-based economy. Though these groups work for wages, wear clothing, want health and welfare benefits, and are increasingly literate and aware of the larger world, they try hard to keep the "Law," given to their ancestors in the Dreamtime by the beings who made their geography and gave them their original rituals, rules of conduct, and beliefs. It is rare in anthropological experience that one fieldworker should study the people both in their native habitat, with their traditional culture substantially intact, and under circumstances so radically changed, away from their natal territory and living under the direct influence of western culture.

The culture of the Mardudjara, like all aboriginal Australian cultures in some degree, is characterized by an outstandingly simple technology and material culture and an equally outstandingly complex religious and cosmological system. This fact immediately challenges everyday assumptions about the nature of civilization and its complexities. It is a beginning lesson in anthropology. It should change the reader's conception about the nature of complexities in his or her own society and challenge assumptions about the nature of human life, human thinking, and "progress."

Of particular interest to students of anthropology will be the analysis of how rituals and beliefs change in a seemingly unchanging society. Anthropological as well as lay conceptions concerning aboriginal societies in Australia have tended toward the notion of the static, timeless culture. In contrast, the Mardudjara, and probably most other aboriginal cultures, welcomed change—so long as it fit the predetermined forms of permanence. There is no notion of progress in aboriginal cultures, but there is change. Readers with some background in anthropology will find Tonkinson's analysis of the reality of everyday life and its tensions and conflicts, in his chapter on living the dream, particularly interesting. For all readers, the analysis of ritual and religion, of kinship and social structure, will prove informative and challenging. This case study will stand out in the series both because it is about a most interesting people and set of circumstances and because it is written in a perceptive, sophisticated, but engaging manner.

GEORGE AND LOUISE SPINDLER
General Editors

Stanford, California

Preface

This study describes the traditional culture of some Australian Aboriginal groups living in a remote part of the interior of the continent. It begins with a brief account of the peopling of Australia to provide the reader with some necessary background information about the Aborigines and their culture in time and space. This chapter also introduces the Mardudjara and their desert setting, and concludes with some comments about what it is like to do fieldwork with Aborigines in this part of Australia.

Chapter 1 outlines the religious fundamentals of the Mardudjara worldview, for no proper understanding of their culture is possible without an appreciation of its intellectual foundations. The aim of the second chapter is to convey a feeling for the desert habitat and daily life of these hunters and gatherers as they ingeniously cope with an extremely tough environment. The ways in which they structure their social order are the subject of Chapter 3, which details the complexities of kinship and other categorizations that stand in marked contrast to the uncomplicated material technology of the Mardudjara. Chapter 4 examines the life cycle of the desert people, with particular attention to the long and complicated progression of young males through initiation into full adult status. This subject leads naturally, in Chapter 5, to a detailed consideration of their rich and varied ceremonial life and its inherent dynamism, which allows for excitement and change despite a very strong ideology proclaiming that nothing changes. Chapter 6 contrasts the ideal society, as laid down by the ancestral heroes of the Dreamtime, with the realities of a life in which some conflict is inevitable. To conclude, Chapter 7 presents a brief sketch of the contemporary life of the Mardudjara, who now live in contact with whites and face problems of maintaining their strong traditions under considerably altered social and economic circumstances.

Acknowledgments

The writing of this book was begun in Eugene, Oregon, and completed in Canberra, Australia. I am grateful to the Department of Anthropology, Research School of Pacific Studies, Australian National University, for allowing me to devote my entire attention to getting the manuscript finished.

This study is dedicated to the Aborigines of Jigalong, particularly Gogara, who decided in 1963 that I needed help and since then has been a true friend and teacher; my debt to him and to many other members of the Jigalong mob is profound. This book is dedicated also to my wife Myrna, whose sustained support and encouragement made the task of writing seem easy, and who, in her careful reading of the draft, provided invaluable comments and insights derived from her research among the women of Jigalong. To Drs. Kirk Endicott, Richard Gould, Nicolas Peterson, and

George and Louise Spindler, I offer grateful thanks for many helpful and constructive suggestions which together have done much to improve the book.

The fieldwork on which this study is based was financed from a variety of sources: the University of Western Australia, Australian Universities Commission, University of British Columbia, Australian National University, and the Australian Institute of Aboriginal Studies. My thanks go to the Western Australian Native Welfare Department (now Department of Aboriginal Affairs), particularly Mr. Frank Gare, who made it possible for me to participate in several desert expeditions. To Professor Ron Berndt, who first interested me in anthropology and Aborigines and gave me a great deal of assistance and encouragement, my gratitude is immense. To my former mentors, Professors Peter Lawrence and Ken Burridge, whose friendship and advice I continue to hold dear, I owe a considerable intellectual debt. To Professor Roger Keesing, many thanks for first suggesting that I write this book.

Besides the Aborigines, many staff members at Jigalong provided assistance, friendship, and hospitality over the years: Trevor and Peggy Levien, David and Gloria Goold, Terry and Lorraine O'Meara, Ernie and Edie Jones, and Graham and Jenny Wilson all assisted in many ways. Joe Criddle, formerly of Walgun station, has been a colorful host and good friend.

For assistance with photographs, thanks to Ian Dunlop, Film Australia, and A.I.A.S., Canberra.

Canberra, Australia   Robert Tonkinson
September 1977

Contents

Introduction / The Australian Aborigines

The full saga of the first discovery and colonization of Australia, which dates from at least 40,000 years ago, will doubtless never be accurately known.[1] Thanks to the continuing efforts of prehistorians, biogeographers and other scientists, however, more and more is being revealed about the physical setting for the island-hopping epic that led eventually to the peopling of the world's largest island continent. It appears that the Australia of the Pleistocene era (Ice Age) was somewhat cooler than now, and certainly much larger because of glaciation's effect in lowering sea levels. The immigrants must have been originally Asian and possessed of seaworthy watercraft of some kind. Despite the lowered sea levels, they had to cross open ocean in several places—deep-water passages of the kind that had once formed barriers to the eastward movement of large Asian carnivores and other fauna and flora. The first settlers must have arrived somewhere on the north coast (or the northwest, since at that time Australia and New Guinea were joined), but their motivations, the routes taken, the accidental or purposeful nature of their voyaging, and the location of their first landfall can only be guessed at.[2]

Like the rest of humanity in that era, the pioneers were hunters, fisherfolk, and foragers who probably utilized a stone, bone, and shell toolkit and lacked domesticated plants and animals; unlike almost all the rest of humanity, the people now known as the Aborigines were to retain their hunter–gatherer adaptation into modern times. To date, we have no clear knowledge of either the speed or the strategy of their colonization of the new homeland. They may have clung to the marine adaptation they knew best and diffused via the coastal periphery, relying mainly on seafoods and freshwater resources, supplemented by foods hunted and gathered inland, until all the marine frontages were occupied and groups eventually moved inland (Bowdler 1977). Alternatively, unimpeded by either high mountains or savage beasts, they may have adapted to inland subsistence quite early on and then spread through the interior to the far reaches of the continent—which at that time included Tasmania, whose inhabitants were eventually isolated when rising sea levels made it an island about 12,000 years ago (R. Jones 1977).

Either way, all major ecological zones, with the possible exception of the desert, were occupied by at least 20,000 years ago. By this time the giant marsupials and flightless birds of the Pleistocene were long extinct, but there is as yet no clear evidence to suggest whether Aborigines had a hand in this or whether climatic changes caused their disappearance. Desert conditions in the central area predate the arrival of

[1] See Mulvaney (1975) for a recent, comprehensive account of Australian prehistory.
[2] See, for example, papers by Birdsell and other contributors in Allen, Golson, and Jones (1977).

1

the first Australians, but Mulvaney (1975) suggests that at times during the Pleistocene regional climatic conditions were more favorable than they are now, so climate, like landform, would not have presented barriers to movement in much of the continent.

The relatively late arrival of the dingo (a type of wild dog) during the post-Pleistocene era (that is, probably within the past 10,000 years) appears to be linked with the extinction of some native species and raises important questions concerning outside influences reaching Australia in more recent prehistoric times. The dingo must have been brought to Australia because it came in an era when sea levels had risen close to their present levels. Its appearance is paralleled by that of a new material technology, consisting of an array of small, flaked stone tools. These were grafted onto an earlier kit of larger, heavier hand-held cores and flake-scrapers on the mainland. The separation of Tasmania, however, precluded the arrival there of the dingo, and, it appears, the diffusion of the small tools as well as other items of mainland technology, such as the boomerang, spearthrower, shield, axe, and adze. The more recent small tool technology may well have been developed within Australia, but resolution of this question, like so many others, awaits further research in a field that has seen its most rapid development in the past decade or so.

Further excavations and research in Australian prehistory will almost certainly push the time of arrival of the first settlers beyond 50,000 years. From what is already known, however, it is clear that the early Aborigines were subjected over millennia to significant changes in sea level that must have necessitated considerable adaptation, to climatic changes and some floral–faunal extinction, to environmental changes brought about by their extensive use of fire, and to a host of innovations and changes of greater or lesser regional significance. The culture of the early Australians could never have been static, but in most areas stability and continuity probably became the norm many thousands of years before Europeans arrived and the old order was shattered.

The Europeans were not the first foreigners to establish cultural contacts with Aborigines and affect their lives. In northern Australia, Macassan traders (from Celebes in present-day Indonesia) established seasonal camps on the Arnhem Land coast for the gathering and processing of the prized sea slug (trepang or beche-de-mer), and Papuans made contacts with the Aborigines of Cape York via the Torres Straits islands. These influences from the north had clearly discernible effects on both material and nonmaterial (for example, mythology, songs, and art forms) aspects of the lives of Aborigines in both areas. But this exposure to traders and horticulturalists and their very different behaviors and technologies must have been either too brief or insufficiently impressive to make converts of the coastal Aborigines, whose basic life style and adaptation to their environment remained substantially the same. Also, the effects of such culture contact, for perhaps the same reasons, were little felt in areas away from the coast. As Mulvaney (1975:49) notes, "While ceremonial and material borrowings enriched the Aboriginal life style and gave it a distinctive pattern, as well as increasing seagoing efficiency, they did nothing to alter drastically the Aboriginal economic orientation or social structure." That development had to await the onset of permanent white settlement, dating from 1788 on the southeast coast, where most of the Aborigines soon succumbed to contact influences while their more fortunate brethren in the tropics and the interior went about their lives, unaware of what lay ahead.

VARIATIONS AND COMMON THEMES

Physical   As members of the species *Homo sapiens,* Aborigines are as modern as the rest of humanity, but when "racial" classifications were in vogue, the inability of scientists to fit them into the three major subdivisions earned them the separate status of "Australoid." However, physical variations among them are such that there is clearly no single archetype. Recent archeological evidence suggests that there may have been two distinct types in the past (Thorne 1977), but there is no firm evidence to support the theory of Birdsell (1967) who suggested that three physically different peoples entered Australia at different times during the Pleistocene.

Birdsell bases his theory on what he considers to be significant regional variations in Aboriginal physical types. Given the very long period that Aborigines have been in Australia, the marked regional differences in their skin color, hair color and texture, body build, nose shape, cranial profile, and so on are more convincingly accounted for by factors of diet, climate, subgroup genetic isolation, cultural practices, and other ecological and environmental differences (Mulvaney 1975). From his intensive work on Aboriginal genetics, Kirk (1965) concludes that the Aborigines are a genetically distinct group with considerable internal diversity, which could have been attained in about 10,000 years, presuming that the present population stems originally from a genetically homogeneous group. As yet, no final answers are possible concerning the racial homogeneity or heterogeneity of the Aborigines, but despite the physical variation that exists among them, virtually all are recognizable as distinctively Aboriginal.

Ecological In a country as large as the continental United States (excluding Alaska), considerable variation in vegetation and climate is inevitable. The range includes monsoon savannah woodland in the north, dense tropical rainforest in the northeast, an arid interior, southern prairies of grassland and mallee (*Eucalypt*) scrub, temperate forest in the southwest and southeast corners and Tasmania, and patches of alpine country in the latter two areas, where the snow cover lasts several months. Adding to the basic difference between seacoasts, riverine areas, and the interior, each major ecological zone has a characteristic range of flora and differing patterns of seasonality. For example, in parts of the north, monsoons create distinct wet and dry seasons, while in the desert the rainfall is irregular and nonseasonal. In the southwest there is a "Mediterranean" climate of hot, dry summers and mild, wet winters. Under trade wind influences, the east coast receives more uniform rainfall, and the island of Tasmania experiences a cooler maritime climate.

Such marked differences are reflected in Aboriginal population densities, extractive activities, and associated regional technologies. The more favorable areas for human exploitation, such as the north and east coasts, the southwest and the riverine areas of the southeast were all characterized in precontact times by much higher population densities (perhaps two to eight square miles per person, as against more than thirty-five square miles per person in parts of the desert), more complex technologies, and a more sedentary society than in the arid interior regions.[3] Both rainfall, in its amount and seasonal reliability, and evaporation rates vary greatly throughout the continent, and relatively few rivers flow all year round. In combination these factors are a major determinant of Aboriginal adaptive strategies. Nowhere is this more evident than in the Western Desert area; but over most of the continent, water, or lack of it, looms large in the lives of the Aborigines.

Despite these regional variations, it has not been possible to establish a close correlation between ecological zone and distinctive cultural elements in Australia. The continent is geologically very ancient, with the result that the forces of nature have reduced topographical contrasts and have worn it down for so long that there are very few areas over 2000 feet in altitude. Also, while the number of plant species declines as rainfall decreases, two principal genera, *Eucalypts* ("gums") and *Acacia* ("wattles"),

---

[3] There are estimated to have been between 250,000 and 300,000 Aborigines at the time of first European settlement, living in a continent of just under three million square miles.

show remarkable persistence in all regions. Most ecological zones are thus not at all sharply defined, in contrast to North America, for example. When these natural factors are considered along with important cultural considerations (for example, Aboriginal mobility, widespread cultural diffusion, and the exploitation everywhere of several different ecological areas in the course of the food quest), the lack of close fit between ecology and cultural characteristics is understandable. Regardless of climate or richness of marine resources, for example, no Aboriginal group subsists entirely on marine foods, however important a part these play in their diet some of the time (see Meehan 1977).[4]

Linguistic–Cultural   Prior to European settlement, there were something like two hundred different, mutually unintelligible languages spoken throughout Australia, each language having a number of distinct dialects.[5] Aborigines looked upon linguistic differences as a major factor distinguishing themselves from their neighbors. Most

[4] Peterson (1976b) has recently postulated a broad division into culture areas on the basis of drainage basins (except in the case of the Western Desert which lacks coordinated drainage patterns). There are 12 such basins, but Peterson recognizes at least 17 culture areas on the basis of general knowledge of differences in language and culture. To illustrate, he presents evidence from three different regions in Australia. He suggests that since there will be a tendency towards culture area endogamy, validation of his scheme may come in part from biological data on genetic marker distribution. However, a difficulty remains in that culture areas based on drainage basins cut across ecological zones, with the result that there are several different zones within a given drainage area.

[5] I am indebted to Professor Bob Dixon for his assistance with information on Australian languages.

Aborigines were multilingual, being equally at home in several tongues. It was often the case that a child's parents would come from different language groups; a boy might use his mother's language most of the time during his childhood but switch to his father's tongue by puberty.

Australian languages all follow a similar typological pattern. They have from four to six nasal consonants (*m* and different varieties of *n*), but no fricatives or sibilants (that is, nothing like the English *f, th,* or *s*). Nouns take case inflections, and there are generally several verbal conjugations, much as in Latin and Greek (Dixon 1972). All of the languages, excepting a group in the central north, are closely related genetically, and descend from a single ancestor language that may have been spoken 10,000 or more years ago. It is likely that the more divergent languages of the central north are also related, at a somewhat greater time depth, making a single large Australian family.

Attempts to relate Australian languages to linguistic families outside the continent have been uniformly unsuccessful. Although there are some superficial typological similarities to the Dravidian family of southern India, for instance, it has not been possible to find cognates and systematic formal correspondences that would indicate genetic connection. Australians and their languages have been on the continent for so long that any sister languages they left behind in Asia would likely have changed out of all recognition, and genetic connection could not now be recognized.

Obviously, the persistence of distinctive dialects and mutually unintelligible languages suggests that boundary-maintaining behaviors of some kind have prevented

A man, his two wives, and two of their children en route to a new camping place.

the loss of distinctive group identity. A major cause of this group distinctiveness, which is common throughout Australia, is the existence of very powerful bonds of sentiment that unite every social group to a particular stretch of territory. This land base furnishes most of their material needs and also provides them with much of their distinctive identity, through links of birth, descent, and totemic association. At the same time, however, the Aborigines stress mutuality and interdependence with neighboring groups and others with whom they come into periodic contact. The widespread diffusion of valued objects and the universal importance of ceremonial exchange attest to the great emphasis placed on intergroup contacts.

Aborigines everywhere share the same basic economic strategy, hunting and gathering, and regardless of the particular resources and the technologies that have been developed to exploit them, this mode of adaptation promotes many uniformities. Thus everywhere the band is a basic social grouping, with a sexual division of labor and an emphasis on food sharing that together allow more efficient resource exploitation, a varied diet of meat and vegetable foods, and an equitable distribution of food. Throughout the continent, these strategies make for conservation of effort and the maximizing of leisure time (Peterson 1976). Aborigines everywhere put fire to the same variety of important uses, do their cooking in ashes and sand, employ very few food conservation or storage techniques, and use a variety of similar practices to ensure long-term population stability.

To this partial list may be added countless shared cultural elements that relate less directly to ecological adaptation but are profoundly significant: classificatory kinship, protracted male initiation, a shared conception of a creative period, concern with the separation of body and spirit after death, totemic identity with creative beings and flora and fauna, male chauvinism (including the exclusion of women from major aspects of the religious life), and so on.[6]

Everywhere, there is a wealth of local elaboration and differentiation, a playing up or a playing down of certain of these common cultural elements. But with very few exceptions they are readily discernible as variations on shared themes that signal a unique Aboriginal culture, unmistakable to any observer with at least a modicum of knowledge about it. Many of the component practices and beliefs may well have parallels in small-scale societies outside Australia, but everywhere within the continent the total constellation of traits is distinctively Australian Aboriginal.

WESTERN DESERT CULTURE

The major characteristics and homogeneous features of the Western Desert are discussed in Chapter 2, so the only question to be dealt with here is whether there exist clear differences between this area and the rest of Australia. Genetically the Aborigines of this region appear quite distinct, and the uniqueness of genetic marker patterns indicates a long period of isolation from external inputs (Kirk 1971). Evidence from prehistory suggests climatic and cultural continuities lasting at least 10,000 years. There has undoubtedly been variation in technology, economy, and settlement patterns, but this is overshadowed by compelling evidence for the persistence of both hafted and unhafted tool types, of regularities in living-surface layout, of a similar mixed meat–vegetable diet, and of long-distance transport of valued lithic materials

[6] There are of course, some notable exceptions, such as the Tiwi of Bathurst and Melville Islands in northern Australia. A study by Goodale (1971:338) shows that ". . . the basic equality of the two sexes as unique individual members of the society is stressed in the culture."

Evening camp scene: Yanindu stokes the fire; note the small brush windbreak behind them.

(Gould 1971). From his excavations at Puntutjarpa Rockshelter, Gould concludes that the lack of sharp breaks in the sequence and the absence of changes suggestive of cultural transformation suggest the existence of a stable hunter–gatherer life style in the Western Desert for virtually the entire post-Pleistocene period.[7]

The ecologically unique features of uncoordinated drainage, the lack of permanent rivers or freshwater lakes, the paucity of springs, and an extreme variability in rainfall distinguish this region as being the least amenable to exploitation based on seasonality in all of the continent. Because water is the crucial variable, Aboriginal movement is correlated most of the time with its occurrence in particular localities.

Both population densities and average band sizes would undoubtedly have been lower here than elsewhere in Australia. Yet even in this most marginal of life spaces, the Aborigines do not exploit all available resources. Among the factors that lead people to ignore edible foods are the following: individual tastes, the availability of preferred alternative foods, food tabus (although these are few and rarely apply to all members of any given group at the same time), and the inability to exploit resources because of the absence of water or because of avoidances following a recent death in that locality. A strong tabu on the skinning of kangaroos in much of the Western Desert prevents the use of skins and fur as clothing or covers (which were extensively used in cooler southern areas of Australia), or as water carriers (utilized, for example,

[7] Putting these findings in crosscultural perspective, Gould (n.d.a) compares the Western Desert case with those of the Eskimos and Polynesians, two peoples whose physical appearance, language, and culture show remarkable homogeneity despite great geographical diffusion. In both these cases this uniformity is best explained in terms of the relative recency of migration and diffusion of the Eskimos and Polynesians throughout the new homeland areas. This contrasts with the Western Desert case where the characteristic of homogeneity is shared but the explanation for it is quite different.

in parts of the central desert). Gould (personal communication) notes that in this region no use is made of either snares or traps in hunting. The desert people practice some drying and storage of vegetable foods at times, but have never developed this into a major strategy. In considering these various examples of undeveloped or ignored potential, however, it is advisable to keep in mind that considerations of mobility and portability, as well as the very low population density that is maintained, may operate to overrule those of comfort, convenience, or maximum resource exploitation.

WHO ARE THE MARDUDJARA?

Western Desert Aborigines frequently refer to neighboring groups by selecting a word that is used by speakers of the different dialect, to which the suffix -*djara* ("having") is added; for example, Bidjandjara, from *bidja* ("to come"), and Mandjildjara, from *mandjila* ("to get, pick up"). Groups so designated may or may not refer to themselves by the same term, and may not see themselves as the unity that is suggested by such language-use labels. In the same way as the desert people, I have chosen the term *Mardudjara* (*mardu*, "man, people") to refer to the linguistic groups whose home territories lie in the area surrounding Lake Disappointment on the western side of the Gibson Desert and who often use *mardu* as one of their words for "people" (see Maps 1 and 2). These groups are principally the Gardudjara, Budidjara, Guṟadjara, Mandjildjara, and Giyadjara speakers.[8]

Physical Appearance   Although the Mardudjara and their neighbors show much variation in stature and color of skin and hair, they share many typical Aboriginal characteristics: dark skin pigmentation, pronounced brow ridges, broad noses, and slender arms, legs, and buttocks—as the photographs in this book illustrate. One notable Western Desert trait common among them is blond hair and honey-colored skin, seen most clearly among children before their hair darkens to a sandy color. Women average about 5'2" in height, men about 5'6", although some are as tall as 6'. Obesity is rare, and the only plump people besides babies are some women who have had several children. Older children, men, and women have scars on their upper arms, and most men have larger scar ridges (called cicatrices) across their chests. These are either self-inflicted or put on by friends to enhance personal appearance.

---

[8] The desert homelands of these groups are now empty, following migration to settlements along the desert fringe after the coming of whites. It is therefore impossible to estimate the precontact populations of the groups here referred to collectively as Mardudjara. There are no Guṟadjara speakers left, and few Budidjara or Giyadjara. Mandjildjara and Gardudjara speakers are now numerically dominant, and together number probably 600–800. The Mandjildjara people are scattered in several widely spaced settlements whereas the Gardudjara are concentrated in one, Jigalong (see Tonkinson 1974).

The ethnographic present tense is used throughout most of this study. Although the traditional local organization of these peoples is no more, most of their traditional culture lives on (albeit in some aspects it exists in altered form). Most of the data presented here are drawn from direct observation, and some are reconstructed from informants' statements about life in the desert before contact with whites. In the case examples, fictional names are used for the people described. In accordance with the wishes of the Mardudjara men with whom I have worked, no photographs of secret-sacred objects or ritual activities are included.

With respect to the orthography used in writing Aboriginal words, there are 17 consonant phonemes: *b, dj, rd, d, g, m, n, ny, rn, ṅg, ly, rl, l, r, ṟ, w, y*. Four of these (*rd, rn, rl, ṟ*) are retroflexed, as in American English *r* sound. The vowels are *a* (as in father), *i* (sheep), and *u* (root), and the lengthened vowels, *aa, ii, uu*. The unretroflexed *r* is trilled (the Scottish *r* sound). The *ng* sound is similar to that of the *ng* sound in "singer." The interdental *ly* is somewhat like the *li* in "William," but the *y* is hardly heard.

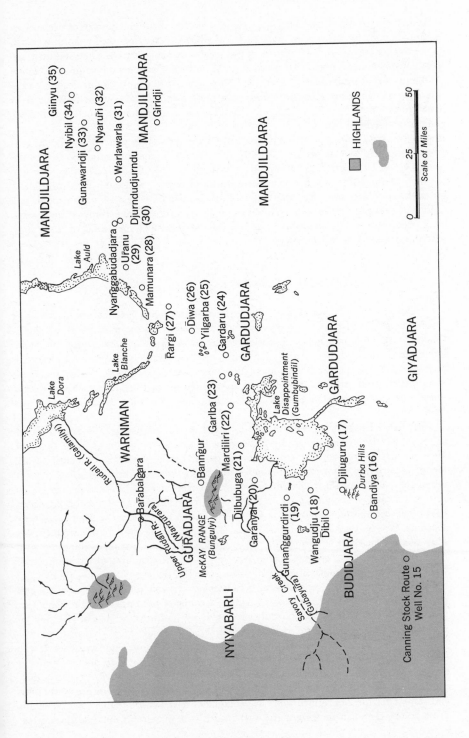

Map 2: Mardudjara territory.

9

Unless engaged in ritual activity, people wear very little in the way of decoration. A thin hair-string belt is the only male "clothing," used mainly for holding small game so that the hunter's hands are free to use his weapons should game suddenly appear. Women sometimes wear a small pubic tassel of string or possum fur, which hangs from their waist belt. Females may also wear small gum-tree nut decorations in the front of their hair. Men sometimes wear pubic pendants of pearlshell. When their hair grows long, men tie it back from their face with hair-string, which doubles as a decorative forehead band or *yagiri,* worn also in most rituals. Adults frequently anoint themselves (and children) with a mixture of fat and red ochre, which they say has protective and medicinal properties. Children of both sexes go completely naked, but like their parents, they rarely complain about extremes of heat or cold. The desert people normally wear no footwear at all. Their thickly calloused soles and heels resist most prickles, splinters, and sharp stones, enabling them to traverse all kinds of rough terrain without great discomfort. However, they sometimes make throw-away sandals that protect their feet from the fierce heat of the ground if they need to make long daytime journeys in hot weather.

DOING FIELDWORK IN THE DESERT

The exodus of Aborigines from their desert home areas was already in progress when researchers first appeared, so none could be sure that the movements witnessed among remaining nomads were patterned in the same way, or covered the same exploitative areas, as before alien influences first were felt. The earlier introduction and spread of European rabbits, dogs, cats, foxes, sheep, and cattle had profound effects on the landscape and therefore on Aboriginal adaptations. Many desert people were using metal tools and scraps of cloth and were hunting rabbits and feral cats before they ever encountered whites.

Since 1963 I have done research among desert Aborigines in both precontact desert and contact fringe situations. In seven trips a total of 26 months were spent at Jigalong settlement, and six trips into the desert proper entailed six months' work among Aborigines whose prior contacts with whites were minimal or nil. On most desert trips I accompanied government welfare patrols and had tasks to perform as an interpreter, and in every case our presence halted normal hunting and gathering activities much of the time. Even on a longer film-making trip where the Aborigines were asked to carry out many traditional activities, our presence and the requirements of film-making meant that normal life was suspended for the duration of our time with them.[9] Through this exposure to the Aborigines in their traditional environment it was possible to learn much about many aspects of the traditional culture, though not the precise nature of Aboriginal local organization. To concede this is not to suggest that a comprehensive and reasonably accurate account of precontact culture cannot be given. With this note of caution duly proferred, let us turn now to a brief expose of the delights and despair of fieldwork in the desert.

Anthropologists always speak highly of the warmth, humor, and patience of the desert Aborigines and rudely of the torments imposed by nature and by vehicles clearly never meant to be there. Coping with the desert is hard work, especially during the seven or eight months of summer, and you soon develop immense admiration and respect for the Aborigines who have conquered it and made it their own. There is great beauty there, in the bright red of the earth, the majesty of the desert oak trees,

[9] Information on the 11 films that resulted is provided at the end of this study.

the shimmering expanses of spinifex grass (which from a distance look exactly like a prairie wheatfield ready for harvest), the blue and pink hues of the sky at sunrise and sunset, and the unforgettable brilliance and clarity of the night sky—*if* you can ever get comfortable enough to appreciate it all.

Summer days are unspeakably hot; winter nights literally freezing; and the balmy winter afternoons are wonderful only if the flies are absent (a rarity). They teem in their indefatigable millions and easily beat out ants, scorpions, snakes, and other insects as the scourge of the desert, for whites and Aborigines alike. Unless kept at bay with nets and sprays, they make speaking and eating almost impossible during daylight hours, and when swallowed, have the nasty habit of sticking halfway down and refusing to budge! Dingoes, wild or domesticated, are never vicious but as raiders can wreak havoc on anything left within their reach; they jump into vehicles, eat what is readily available and carry off what is not—even canned food which they will bite into. After twice having my toilet bag stolen, ripped open, and its contents chewed up, I concluded that dingoes love toothpaste and tablets, and ruefully wished the culprits brighter than bright teeth and relief from diarrhea.

Motor vehicles are a poor match for the desert. They bog down in sandhills up to their axles. Clumps of spinifex grass jolt them and their hapless occupants unmercifully. Scrub thickets puncture even the heaviest of tires with little provocation. Spinifex seeds clog radiators and force them to boil, unless of course the heat has already beaten them to it. Dust from bush-tracks billows into the cab, covering and choking all within, but it is no problem after a heavy rain because then mud replaces it, bogging vehicles for days on end. Lumbering four-wheel-drive vehicles, with their incessant thirst for fuel and water, bring home the advantages of the Aboriginal mode of life, which emphasizes maximum flexibility and mobility, and a minimum of material encumbrances.

Although whites and Aborigines alike personify the natural environment, in the case of the desert their attitudes are very different. To the whites it is an implacable foe to be cursed at much of the time; to the Aborigines it is their home and their provider, which they amiably enjoin to cooperate. For whites, the oneness of the Mardudjara with their natural environment is a difficult thing to fully empathize with and appreciate. The Aborigines assent to its terms and embrace it, responding with fluidity and confidence to its vagaries, whereas the outsider, who fails to "see" its totemic geography and spiritual forces and has no mental maps of its water and food resources, responds to it with frustration and anger and at times fears it as a deadly opponent. With all our technology we still fare poorly in the desert, while no doubt the spirits of countless generations of Aborigines for whom it was a familiar and beloved home mock us for looking without ever seeing the environment that they transformed, through their religion, into a compliant ally—at times fickle, but never an adversary, since both they and it share descent from the same ancestral substance.

First encounters with the desert people are vividly remembered: the rapid realization, as you are touched, squeezed, and discussed, that as one of the first whites they have seen, you are at least as interesting an oddity to them as they to you; their complete unselfconsciousness about nudity (and on a winter's morning you wonder how can they be so warm in their bare skins while you're freezing in every piece of clothing you have with you); the pungent smell of grease and ochre, the matted hair, the wads of tobacco that are taken from the mouth or from behind the ear and generously offered (Will refusal offend? Is *this* what our teachers meant when they said rapport must be established regardless?); the way they constantly use their lips in indicating direction, which will soon become so habitual that you continue to do it back in "civilization," providing further proof that anthropologists are crazy (or become so, after fieldwork); and always, the rush of conflicting thoughts that beset the novice: thank God they're so good-humored . . . the flies will drive me out of my mind . . . what the hell am I doing here . . . the sunsets are beautiful . . . I'll *never* sort out that language . . . I could be out of this and back home in a week . . . shut up, it'll be a great experience to look back on in later years . . . maybe, but can I wait that long?

After the excitement of first contact has subsided and major logistical problems are overcome, the tasks of observing and recording and of interacting with Aborigines in the setting of a camp are for the most part manageable and enjoyable. The later and unavoidable bouts of culture shock produce the same kinds of reaction regardless of the outsider's personality or the foreign culture concerned. There is a growing aware- ness of the enormity of what you are attempting in trying to understand a very dif- ferent culture. Feelings of inadequacy alternate with frustration and anger according to whether you are blaming yourself or them for what seems to be a lack of progress. During periods of culture shock one's ego is easily bruised and there is hypersensi- tivity to real or imagined slights (paranoia?). You go around mumbling complaints that invariably begin: "Why wasn't I told . . . ; they could at least have . . . ; they couldn't care less if I cleared out tomorrow!" On this last score, the position of the anthropologist as uninvited guest, as needing the people more than he or she is needed by them, as virtually defenseless in the event of rejection, is a nagging reality that takes a long time to reconcile. Another major long-term problem is that of cop- ing with the realization that no matter how far empathy, understanding and commit- ment take you "inside" another culture, you remain forever an outsider, *with* but not *of* the people, since you can no more fully transcend your cultural roots than they can. The anthropological double-bind is that while understanding requires deep empathy and emotional involvement, an equally pressing need for objectivity demands dis- tance.

On the positive side, the Aborigines fit you into their kinship structures as a matter of course, and the terrors that its complexities once held abate as constant interaction and the use of kin terms make it increasingly familiar and automatic. Also, what was at first encounter an undifferentiated mass of men, women, and children gradually separates into distinct personalities, as increasing familiarity breeds compatibility and friendship with many, indifference or perhaps even dislike of a few. Children, espe- cially, are open and friendly, and their company can be a real tonic on those bad days when nothing seems to go right. They can also be keen, if not always very accurate, informants about everything from animal tracks to the latest gossip.

Once some sort of working relationship is firmly established, and your chief infor- mants have chosen you, the gathering of data is not difficult if you can retain your motivation and sense of humor, and if you are judged to have a genuine interest in learning about and respecting Aboriginal traditions. The desert people are willing and interested teacher–informants most of the time, provided discussions are kept open- ended and they are given ample opportunity to talk about what interests them in ad- dition to answering all those questions on topics they may find less than engaging. Their language and temperament demand a special style in interviewing. For ex- ample, because there is no "either–or" construction in their language, a question must be phrased in affirmative or negative terms, not as a choice. The problem with presenting the question in the affirmative is that your informant may well decide, from your intonation, that you would like an affirmation, and obliges, even though a negative answer may be a better reflection of the truth of the matter. Careful cross- checking provides a safeguard, although fortunately the desert people are not usually given to deliberately misleading their anthropologist pupils.

The Aborigines neither philosophize nor attempt objective assessments about cultural origins or evolution, and they never engage in protracted explanations of their motivations, symbols, and behaviors. Their usual response to the anthropologist who thinks out loud about deeper societal themes and possible motivations will evoke vague mutterings of "perhaps," mild agreement, noncommital shrugs, or silence if this can be managed without giving offense. The observer is certainly entitled to be carried away in flights of interpretive fancy—this is, after all, the fieldworker's task in translating the raw materials of social process into sense-making structural and symbolic patterns—but the Aborigines are not about to embark on that particular trip.

Fieldwork in a contact situation (where most of my research is done) adds new problems, such as coping with the whites, while solving some of the logistic ones that loom larger in the desert proper. The weather, flies, and dogs are much the same, but it is very easy to become involved with roles as interpreter, mediator, Aboriginal advocate, and so on. If these are of benefit to the Aborigines, so much the better, although life may then become difficult with some of the local whites. Since minimal rapport is essential with the latter, for both practical and professional reasons, there is always a balancing act to perform.

The fact that in the mission situation I invariably found the company of the Aborigines more congenial than that of most missionaries stems in part from irreconcilable philosophical differences with fundamentalist Christians, but it has much more to do with the great capacity for humor and the warmth and humanity that the desert people display in their daily life. Fieldwork is never without frustrations, anger and grief, but in the 15 years since I first arrived at the settlement, full of self-doubt and in fear and trembling of almost everyone (and the camp dogs, who turned out to be all bark and no bite), the good things have heavily outweighed the bad. Like most anthropologists, I thank the people I worked with for teaching me as much about myself and my own culture as about theirs.

1 / The spiritual imperative

INTRODUCTION

One of the most notable of the many distinctive features of Australian Aboriginal culture is the remarkable contrast that exists between its relatively unelaborated material technologies and the great richness and complexity of its social and religious forms. The Aborigines show marked ingenuity and resourcefulness in successfully exploiting a continent that is one third desert without the benefit of metal tools, domesticated animals, agriculture, and so on. This great achievement is readily appreciated by anyone who ventures into the forbiddingly barren interior. Yet the full significance of Aboriginal cultural achievement cannot be grasped without a good understanding of its nonmaterial forms and of the extent to which the nomadic life styles of these scattered groups of hunter–gatherers is itself a religious act.

For many millennia the Aborigines were insulated from alien influences that would have brought the kinds of new objects, ideas, and dogmas which lead people to question the adequacy and truth of tradition. This long isolation from potentially disruptive external forces must have contributed to the Aborigines' development of a fairly confident and secure worldview that in the desert, at least, belies the many uncertainties entailed in getting a living. Their cosmology not only accounts for the origins and form of their world, but also binds them closely to one another, to the land and all living things, and to the realm of spiritual beings who control the power on which life itself is held dependent. The sum of these bonds is to the Aborigines a logically unified order, in which all will be well if only they live according to the rules laid down by the spiritual beings who created their universe.

No one knows how or when the complex belief systems of the Aborigines developed, but recent evidence suggests startling continuities in certain cultural elements, such as the ritual use of red ochre, which dates back at least 25,000 years (R. Jones 1973). This is not to suggest that in the evolution of their culture the Aborigines locked themselves into a completely unchanging existence. No culture is static, regardless of how isolated, introspective, and tradition-bound its members may be. One major aim of this study is to reveal the genius involved in accommodating the inevitability of constant change, however minor, to a pervasive Aboriginal ideology of nonchange. In Aboriginal culture prior to European contact, most changes would probably have been small in scale and rarely traumatic, and even major events such as changing sea levels occurred slowly enough for Aborigines in the affected areas to adjust without panic.

The Aborigines ground their entire existence firmly in a conception of spiritual beings as holders of life-giving and life-sustaining power that is automatically accorded those who act out the life design formulated by these beings. The living conform to the dictates of a culture transmitted by their forefathers but attributed to

14

spiritual, not human, actions. By denying the human innovatory component in their cultural development and by cleaving to a cosmic rather than chronological notion of history, the Aborigines are in effect claiming primacy for religious conceptions of causation, being, and purpose.

This essentially spiritual basis of life, while denying people the capacity for independent creativity, does not deny them their individuality. Instead, it simply removes creativity as a criterion for assessing individual social status or worth. The measure of man becomes a continuing willingness to follow the founding design, to submit to what Stanner (1965a) calls a sacred purpose. In this way, humanity reaps the benefit of reciprocity, in the form of continued fertility of living things and the maintenance of a long-term ecological and social status quo. For a contemporary Westerner, the trade-offs required in holding to this view of life would probably seem quite unreasonable, but we have neither a limited technology nor a heritage of prolonged isolation from the rest of the world.

THE DREAMTIME

The profoundly religious view of life that characterizes the Aborigines rests on their concept of the Dreamtime, which is typically described as the period of creation (see Stanner 1958). At one level of meaning, this is an indistinct era in the distant past, a time long, long ago, well before the memories of the oldest living people, when Australia was transformed from a featureless plain by the activities of a great number of ancestral beings. The ultimate origins of these beings is unimportant, as is the timing of their creative endeavors. The heroes of the Dreamtime, who are generally conceived of as simultaneously part animal, part human, and endowed with characteristics of both, simply arrived and began their many adventures. Some, the *djilgañggadja* ("travelers"), ranged far and wide and engaged in a great many creative exploits over a large geographical area, while many others, *ñgurandadja* ("homebodies"), restricted themselves to one particular area or even a specific site. Humanlike, yet larger than life and gifted with superhuman magical powers, these beings hunted, gathered, and interacted much of the time in similar ways to the living today. But in so doing they were also creating most of the land's distinctive forms—here a winding creekbed, created by the movement of an ancestral snake; there, a gap between hills opened by a blow from the stone ax of a fighting lizard-man, and a granite outcrop made up of large oval boulders, the metamorphosed eggs of an emu ancestress. Every Aboriginal group attributes a host of physical features in its territory to the activities of the Dreamtime beings, which are embodied in myths, songs, and rituals. As they wander in their continual food quest, the Aborigines are surrounded constantly by what they regard as certain proof of the power and vitality of the creative beings. Their human forefathers who first peopled their territory must have sensed a need to ground metaphysical conceptions in the stones, sand, and streambeds of the physical world, to unite spirit and substance and in this way render much more immediate and meaningful the essential unity of the two realms.

During the exploits of the ancestral beings, the vital life essence contained in their bodies and in everything they possessed remained undiminished, but not indivisible. For wherever they went, they left behind some of this fund of power, which later animated hosts of tiny spirit-children that were ultimately born as human beings. This, then, is another vitally important way in which the Dreamtime concept is made meaningful for the Aborigines, since it extends the ancestry of every living person right back to the creative epoch itself. At the same time, it underlines the uniqueness of the individual, whose coming into being is associated with a quite distinctive chain of connections and events (see Chapter 4 for a discussion of conception totemism).

After their worldly activities came to an end, the Dreamtime beings "died" and then changed into stones, other natural features, or celestial bodies, never to be seen on earth again. However, the absence of any special beginning of the Dreamtime era is matched by the absence of any definite end. None of the ancestral beings is believed actually to have died. Their bodies disappeared or metamorphosed into some other form, but their spiritual essence remained. They and their associated spirits, some of which act as intermediaries between Dreamtime and human orders, retain ultimate control of plant, animal, and human fertility, and are thought to take a continuing interest in human affairs.

It should now be clear that the Dreamtime is a fundamental and complex conception, not only embracing the creative past and the ordering of the world, but having great relevance to present and future Aboriginal existence. For the Aborigines, it still exists, as a reality that is at the same time "out there," a vital backdrop for the culture, and an integral part of their being. A day cannot pass without their responding in some way to its presence. The Dreamtime is crucial because it is held to be the source of all power, given in response to ritual performance, but also available to individuals when they are able briefly to transcend their humanity and tap this reservoir (for example, during dance, trance, visions, dreams, and heightened emotional and ritual states). Also, the Dreamtime remains the source of all new knowledge, which may be transmitted to humans via spirit-being intermediaries. It is no coincidence that the word *dreamtime* or *dreaming* is now commonly used by Aborigines and whites to embrace this concept. Although the principal Mardudjara word for Dreamtime is *mañguny*, almost as common is the term *djugur*, which can also be translated as "dream." The analogy goes deeper, however, because during dreams Aborigines sometimes communicate with spiritual powers.

The Aborigines see their entire culture as the legacy of the Dreamtime epoch.[1] In their nomadic existence they are reenacting the wanderings of the creative beings, and in their subsistence pursuits, reciprocity, kinship behaviors, and virtually everything else within the bounds of normal activity they emulate the life design that was set for all time in the creative epoch. In common with many other hunter–gatherer societies whose adaptation demands highly symbiotic relationships with their natural environment, the Aborigines see an essential unity among the components of their cosmic order: human society, the plant and animal world, the physical environment, and the spiritual realm (see Lawrence 1964). To maintain this unity and guarantee continued harmony with the spiritual powers, the Aborigines must perform rituals regularly and obey the Law.

As humans, the Aborigines see themselves as being unique and distinct from the rest of the animal world, yet intimately related to it. This relationship is expressed and affirmed in totemism, which posits a unity of substance or flesh between people, both as individuals and members of groups, and plant and animal species and other elements, such as minerals, in the natural environment. The multiple totemic associations that characterize all humans and link them to the Dreamtime powers are enduring and indissoluble.

The existence of an intimate link between humans and animals is also reflected in

---

[1] This legacy is now connoted by their use of the English word *law*, the coining of which suggests that they see parallels in terms of obedience to a set of powerful dictates, and of punishment for nonconformity, since in both systems human agents are involved in the punishment process. In this study, the capitalized Law is used to connote the Mardudjara concept, called *yurlubidi*.

the Aborigines' conceptions of the creative beings: almost all had the ability to assume either human or animal form and behavior when the occasion demanded. The Mardudjara may be emphatic about the essential "humanness" of, say, Marlu, the well-known kangaroo creative being, yet in relating his exploits, a person will use the verb *hop* to describe his mode of locomotion.

In addition to acknowledging the superior powers of creative beings, the desert Aborigines recognize human social hierarchy, males and the elderly being generally accorded higher status than females and the young. Nevertheless, a basically egalitarian society is their model for conceptions of the great transcendental powers. Certain ancestral beings are known throughout the Western Desert because of the extent of their Dreamtime wanderings and the widespread diffusion of major rituals associated with them. But these "traveler" beings are not accordingly considered more powerful or higher in status than the many localized beings.

The creative beings, invisible yet omnipresent, are not reachable in the course of everyday mundane activities, but they or their spirit intermediaries are amenable to contact through rituals, dreams, and so on. The idiom for any such attempted communication is kin-based. As relatives, the ancestral beings are thought to be receptive to appeals or requests on the part of their human kin. But the Aborigines do not pray, prostrate themselves, or offer sacrifices. If ritual appeals are properly made, the ancestral powers, as co-residents of the same cosmic order, are obliged to respond positively by supplying the rain, babies, flora, and fauna that guarantee life's continuance.

RELIGION AND MORALITY

It is true that human society is founded on that of the Dreamtime beings, but many of these beings, as if mirroring human propensities for both good and evil, were often guilty of what would be heinous crimes in human society. Perhaps these immoral examples are there, safely locked into the world of myth, as bad examples that harmlessly accentuate the immoral in order to highlight what is moral (see R. Berndt 1970). In myth, immoral and amoral acts are often, but not necessarily, followed by the kinds of unfortunate consequences that suggest punishment and thereby reflect a moral element. But many acts, especially killing, have no dire consequences for the Dreamtime perpetrators, and the possible motivations for them are not commented upon by either the characters themselves or the human narrators. The Dreamtime beings lived very similar lives to humans, with the same potential for kind or antisocial acts. But as superpowers living in a creative milieu where they sought to impose themselves indelibly on one another and on their natural environment, they are permitted the luxury of unpredictability and perversity.

Yet an examination of Mardudjara mythology suggests that much Dreamtime behavior would be considered moral in contemporary terms and reveals a concern for the instituting of a Lawful way of life to be adhered to by their living descendants. When bad things happen, and especially when these go unpunished in a myth, it will end with a statement affirming that what has happened belongs *only* to the Dreamtime. In contrast, when the event involves the instituting of a behavior or a condition that is to endure forever, it is often stated as such by one of the characters concerned. For example, one myth that ends with a fierce spear and boomerang fight between some dingo-men and a group of strangers has the men turning into dingoes and saying as they snap at one another, "We will remain dogs forever now; we are finished as men. As dogs, men will keep us. We will bite kangaroos and keep giving the meat to men. Truly we will remain dogs, and men will always be taking us hunting."

Their Law tells Aborigines which Dreamtime behaviors are to be copied and which are to be avoided. Fully aware of human imperfections, they rely on informal but effective socialization processes to inculcate notions of right and wrong. Yet, if some break the Law, as is bound to happen, it must be people not spirits who punish the offenders. The spiritual powers do not exist to uphold the laws of society by punishing transgressors. They have long since withdrawn, leaving the all-inclusive blueprint that guarantees normal operation of human life if faithfully followed, and relying on a human sense of mutual obligation to see to it that offenders are not permitted to threaten the status quo. Where supernatural sanctions exist, human agents are essential for their execution, and such sanctions are limited to specific ritual infringements (R. Berndt 1970). The great power or life essence that is believed to reside in sacred objects and in certain songs, dances, and localities is extremely dangerous for females and the uninitiated. If men reveal such objects to women or if women trespass into sacred areas, they will sicken and die, but this belief is supplemented by an imperative: these offenders should be killed if discovered because of the grave nature of their crime.

ENSURING CONTINUITY

Every human society faces the problem of ensuring that its cultural heritage, traditions, and values, are successfully and effectively transmitted through time so that for each generation the existing way of life is rendered relevant, fitting, and "right." In small-scale societies lacking in specialized institutions for the accumulation and transmission of knowledge, virtually the entire nonmaterial culture must be carried in people's heads. This great burden is borne by adults, particularly the men in Aboriginal society, who control the religious activities on which survival is held ultimately to depend. The superstructure of Aboriginal society rests firmly on a religious basis. Although an outsider would no doubt view the ecological imperative as primary, the Aborigines in fact take their skills in exploiting the environment very much for granted, as knowledge gained almost incidentally in the normal process of maturation. They stress instead the imperative of conformity to Dreamtime laws, for what use are survival skills (themselves said to have been developed in the Dreamtime) if neglect of the Law results in a withdrawal of reciprocity by the spiritual powers, such that people and the land become infertile and rain ceases to fall? In the worldview of the Aborigines, it is spiritual rather than ecological imperatives that have primacy in guaranteeing their way of life.

Aborigines come to understand and share in the Dreamtime heritage largely through the media of myths, rituals, songlines, and so on. All the notable marvels of the Dreamtime are embodied in one or more of these elements. Creative and world-ordering acts of the first beings are narrated in myths, acted out in dance, condensed into song, and proven by a host of landforms of all kinds, as well as by portable stone objects intimately connected to the beings themselves. Landforms weld the Dreamtime solidly to territory; song and dance provide the means by which communication with the spiritual realm is enhanced and reciprocity is guaranteed; the mythology reveals the nature of the founding design and of its creators; and totemic beliefs complete the synthesis by providing vital linkages between individuals, groups, specific sites, and ancestral beings. The resulting unity is fundamental, not incidental, to the Aborigines' cosmic order.

It remains only to reiterate that the Aborigines are certainly heavily indebted to tradition, but they are not at all passive, unimaginative imitators who live on the spiritual capital of their forefathers, as a few writers have implied (see Strehlow 1947). Maddock (1972) notes that tradition must be allowed to be varied and vivified, and as will be seen, there is a strong element of internal dynamism in the religious life that contrasts markedly with their dominant ideology of nonchange. Through processes of cultural transmission that assume great importance in the Western Desert, through revelations of new lore by spirit intermediaries, through variations in mythology that allow for individual embellishment and the incorporation of new knowledge, through "the appearance of ordinarily experienced and conventionally interpreted signs of the powers" (Maddock 1972), the religion is revealed as a vibrant and vital force in the lives of the Aborigines. In this study of the Mardudjara I hope to show how they accomplish the very tricky task of accommodating dynamism within a culture predicated upon its denial while at the same time coping with one of the world's harshest environments.

2 / Subsistence in a
most marginal habitat

This chapter describes the physical and ecological setting for Mardudjara culture and provides an overview of the technology and subsistence behavior of the Aborigines as they go about the business of getting a living from their desert homeland. A brief glimpse of what the desert looked like to some of the early white explorers is also included to highlight the contrasts between alien and Aboriginal perceptions of the same environment.

ECOLOGICAL SETTING

The Aboriginal groups that comprise the Mardudjara live on the western side of the Gibson Desert, in the area of the Tropic of Capricorn between longitudes 122°E. and 125°E. The Gibson merges with the Great Victoria and Great Sandy Deserts to form what is commonly called the Western Desert, a plateau about 1000 feet high that covers an area of about 500,000 square miles, almost all of which lies in the state of Western Australia (Map 1).

Owing no doubt to the influence of movie epics in their formative years, most Westerners carry an image of desert which consists either of rugged cactus and sagebrush country or endless expanses of huge, rolling white dunes that totally lack vegetation save for an occasional palm-lined oasis, complete with camels. There are some camels in Australia's interior too, a legacy of early explorations, but the rest of the image must be drastically reworked: the rocks and soils are bright red, the sandhills do not move, and on almost all of them some kind of plant life exists. Also, these dunes share the desert with several other kinds of landforms, so there are several different ecological zones scattered throughout.

The most obtrusive but least economically important landform in Mardudjara country is Gumbubindil (Lake Disappointment), a huge salt lake that covers about 650 square miles. Like the many other salt lakes that dot the desert, Gumbubindil is dry most of the time and useless as a source of drinking water. Local drainage channels may fill such lakes after heavy rain, attracting a large variety of water birds which are then hunted by the Aborigines. In the case of Gumbubindil, however, no Mardudjara ever set foot in it or on its shores, because it is believed to be the home of the dreaded cannibal beings, Ṅgayunaṅgalgu ("will eat me") who dwell in their own world beneath the lake and emerge to attack human trespassers. These ancestral beings are of mythological and totemic importance to the Mardudjara and are involved in certain curative magical activities (see Chapter 5), but a strong fear of them keeps Mardudjara well away from their habitat.[1]

---

[1] For a detailed description of these beings and associated mythology, see Mountford and Tonkinson (1969). Figure 2–1 shows a carved wooden figure depicting a Ṅgayunaṅgalgu cannibal-being.

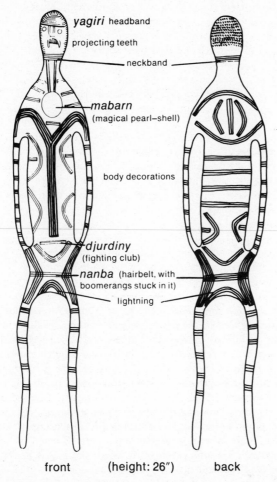

yagiri headband
projecting teeth
neckband
mabarn
(magical pearl–shell)
body decorations
djurdiny
(fighting club)
nanba (hairbelt, with
boomerangs stuck in it)
lightning

front   (height: 26″)   back

Figure 2–1. Carving depicting a Ñgayunañgalgu cannibal-being.

In terms of the total area covered, the dominant landform in Mardudjara country is the sandhill. Averaging about 50 feet in height, these long, parallel ridges tend roughly west-northwest–east-southeast in orientation and are separated by relatively flat areas (about 100–400 yards wide) of sandplain dotted with grasses, shrubs, and a few trees. Several different varieties of plant life favor the ridges, but the hardy, prickly spinifex grass is the most common. The different hues of green in the vegetation and the many colors of flowers that appear briefly after rain contrast vividly with the red of the ridges, rocky outcrops, and low, rugged breakaways (flat-topped, stony hills) that also occur throughout much of the desert. Stands of dense mulga scrub (*Acacia aneura*) sometimes surround hilly areas, as do flat, stony plains that at times resemble wheat fields when the ubiquitous spinifex is in seed. The distinctive and stately desert oak tree (*Casuarina decaisneana*) occurs widely, but favors sandy inter-dunal areas.

Creekbeds of various dimensions, which contain water only after heavy rain and for brief periods of runoff, radiate from the hilly areas and are distinguished by the growth of large gum trees (*Eucalypts*), *Acacia* shrubs, and grasses along their banks. Claypans, shallow depressions of varying size, fill with rain via surface runoff and underground drainage. At such times they become valuable water sources for the Aborigines and the wildlife which the men hunt (usually from brush blinds set up near pads leading to the water). In the hilly areas, which rise 100–300 feet above the plateau, there are often rugged narrow gorges which have distinctive vegetation and sheltered catchment pools, often long-lasting and therefore very important when less reliable water sources dry up. Some of these gorges, such as Djiluguru in the Durba Hills, south of Lake Disappointment, are quite spectacular. They contain huge gum trees, deep pools, sheer high rock faces of brilliant red coloring, and many tropical ferns and plants that seem totally out of place in the desert interior. These gorges and surrounding rough, stony breakaway country are the haunt of the incredibly agile rock wallaby and its larger cousin the euro, which can go for more than a week without water. They and the larger plains-kangaroo (*marlu*), which prefers open country, are all hunted by the Mardudjara.

Both daily and seasonal temperature ranges are considerable in the desert. In summer, shade temperatures range from about 80°F. to 130°F., but the very low humidity makes conditions bearable unless clouds associated with thunderstorm activity block the heat in. Winter temperatures can range daily from below 25°F. at night and in the early morning, to about 80°F. after midday when cloudless skies allow the sun to make an impression. The air is rarely still; breezes or winds blow from varying directions most of the day and sometimes also at night. Whirlwinds, called "willy-willys," are frequently seen in the desert, as thin columns of dust, ashes (of spinifex and other vegetation burned by the Aborigines), and plant debris that career erratically about and wreak minor havoc when they blow through a camping area. Most of the time the air is remarkably clear and the quality of light is correspondingly strong and sharp, producing clear outlines of distant landforms, but playing tricks with their color as the day wears on. In summer, a more heartless trick is the frequent appearance of mirages, which beckon and shimmer with false promise of pools of blue. Sunsets feature vivid pinks and blues, and the clear dry air ensures that night skies are always spectacular, with stars in great profusion and the moon visible in incredible detail to the naked eye. The immensity of the night sky is matched by the seemingly limitless panoramas of the land that are gained from any point that is elevated above the plateau. The desert seems to stretch away forever in all directions, overpowering the observer who feels reduced to a near nothing. For the Mardudjara, however, there is security in knowing both what can be seen and what lies beyond, and in the certainty that other groups, of kin and friends, are out there, perhaps visibly manifested by their hunting or campfire smokes, which can often be seen from distances of up to 50 miles.

By any standards, this is an extremely arid land, with an average annual rainfall of somewhere between 5 and 10 inches—a statistic that conveys little, since falls of rain are quite uncertain and erratic. Some areas may receive no significant falls for two or three or more years, then in one cyclonic disturbance or violent thunderstorm, several inches of rain are dumped onto the parched earth in a matter of hours, turning an area into one huge lake and causing short-lived but frighteningly powerful torrents in the waiting creekbeds. In most years there is a summer rainfall maximum, caused principally by thunderstorms in December and January, but in May and June winter rains may also occur, especially in the southern parts of the desert. Winter rain is less welcome to the Mardudjara because it often takes the form of light drizzle, which wets them and makes them miserably cold when the wind is blowing.

Because of the patchiness and unreliability of rainfall, the Aborigines rarely depend

Nyungala getting water from a small rockhole catchment.

on surface water that lies in abundance for short periods after heavy rains, but look instead to established and well-known sources, such as sheltered rockholes, creekbed soakages (called soaks in Australia), wells (found in both sandhill and rocky areas), springs (some of which are probably permanent), and a few unusual sources such as the forks of large gum trees, the roots of certain trees (which are dug out, cut into foot-long pieces, and drained into wooden dishes), and even dew. The reliability of creekbed soaks, which have to be dug down into until water level is reached, varies with previous runoff into the creek, so that after a heavy flood, a lot of water seeps down and the soak will remain usable for a much longer period than after a light water flow. In sandy or clay areas, the Aborigines watch for certain small herbs that signal the presence of water close to the surface. True wells, which must also be dug out, often dry up, but a few are far more reliable because their supply issues from deeper subterranean sources, such as fault lines that cross aquifers and allow water to move upwards under pressure along the crack.

Most wells have small surface openings and there is nothing in the surrounding vegetation to suggest their presence, so their location must be definitely known, not intuited from generalized knowledge. Some are so deep that the Mardudjara insert ladders (notched poles) to reach the water, which may lie 20 feet or more beneath the surface. They scoop the bottom mud out with their hands or digging dishes, then pack it against the walls, which helps reinforce them in some cases. Small and shallow catchments are sometimes covered with sticks, stones, grass, or boughs, possibly to cut down evaporation, but when several such holes occur together, the blocking of all but one is part of the Mardudjara's emu hunting strategy. Grasses and sand are used to filter water, which can be extremely smelly and "full-bodied" (for example, dead rats, lizards, and birds) after prolonged drought. Such is the extreme localization of most rainfall that bone-dry wells and rockholes can be found just a few miles from full ones, and huge freshwater lakes and deep rockpools that give every indication of being permanent can disappear in a few short weeks or months of summer heat, victims of the astronomical evaporation rate in the Western Desert.

Considering its low and unpredictable rainfall, the desert is surprisingly rich in insects and birds, and to a lesser extent marsupials. Besides flies, ants, and a host of different flying insects, snakes, centipedes, spiders, and scorpions also compete for attention. In daylight hours a few relaxed kangaroos, sunbathing lizards, or the odd skittish kangaroo rat may be spotted, but most of the animal life is shy and nocturnal, rarely seen but known to be present because of the many tracks that crisscross the sandy ground. Most noticeable, because of their movement, noise, and bright colors, are the many varieties of bird life, ranging from the tiny finches that cluster noisily in shrubs close to water to large eagles and tall, flightless emus. A favorite target of hunters because of its large size, the emu frequents mulga thickets and can run at speeds of over 30 miles per hour—which is faster than they should travel because they sometimes trip when distracted and sprawl headlong in a mass of ruffled feathers and red dust, after which they quickly regain speed but never their dignity in the eyes of laughing human onlookers.[2]

Each distinctive area, be it sand ridge, claypan, mulga flat, or whatever, has certain plant and animal life that favors it. But neither the flora and fauna nor the Aboriginal hunters and gatherers are great respecters of physiographic boundaries, and all areas generally contain a mix of trees, shrubs, grasses, and tubers. The territory of the Mardudjara contains about fifty edible plant species, which variously provide seeds, berries, tubers, fruits, and nectars.[3] Of these, several play a major role in their diet at times. A variety of grass and tree seeds are ground into flour, which is made into a paste and eaten raw or cooked in ashes. Several varieties of the hardy bush tomato (*Solanum* sp.), which grows abundantly in good years, are staples. The skins are eaten raw or sun-dried and skewered on sticks; they are eaten later after being soaked in water or ground into a paste. Both the skins and the paste will keep for many months. In wooded areas, yams (*Dioscorea* sp.) may be found; the creeper is easily spotted because its light color stands out against the duller color of the host tree. Women look for hairline cracks in the ground which signal the presence of tubers some 12–18 inches beneath the surface; or they tap the ground with their digging sticks, listening for a change in sound that reveals the presence of a yam below. The tubers are very moist and tasty when eaten raw or roasted in ashes. Blackish berries (*Canthium* sp.), wild figs (*Ficus* sp.), and quandong (*Santalum* sp.) are fruits that bear heavily at certain times and are usually eaten raw.

Over fifty different kinds of animals, including reptiles, birds, and introduced mammals (rabbits, mice, feral cats, camels, and foxes) are hunted for food by the Mardudjara. Of these, several kinds of lizards, small marsupials, kangaroos, and emus are regularly hunted, although the presence of plains-kangaroos and emus depends a lot on favorable water and feed conditions. The Aborigines know intimately which zones produce or contain which food resources, so the major uncertain element is rainfall—and this, of course, is the crucial one because plant growth and animals depend on it.

THE DESERT THROUGH EXPLORERS' EYES

How did the desert interior look to the few hardy souls who, with horses or camels, ventured there late last century hoping to find wealth of one kind or another: gold, inland seas, rich pastures, and so on. None was successful in attaining such goals, several perished, and all at some time suffered terribly, thinking themselves lucky indeed to get out with their lives. All at various times encountered Aborigines, whose reactions ranged from friendly, after an inevitably nervous beginning, to downright hostile. The Aborigines were in some cases doubtless provoked, by the practice of

[2] For readable and concise information on bird and animal species, see Sadleir (1970).
[3] Gould (1969b) lists 38 plant species and 47 named varieties of meat and fleshy foods that are hunted and collected by the Ngatjatjara Aborigines in an area southeast of the Mardudjara.

A hunter poses with two major desert staples: lizards and bush tomatoes; he carries his spears and thrower also in his left hand. Note the use of his hair-twine waistband as a holder for one of the lizards. (Photo by Ian Dunlop.)

running them down for capture so that they would eventually become thirsty and lead the explorers to water. They would have been angered also by the unwitting trespass of whites into sacred sites and their removal of sacred objects. What follows are some of the "unfavorable reviews" given by explorers who survived to tell of their desert adventures.

Colonel Peter Egerton Warburton   In 1873, Warburton led a large expedition from central Australia to the west coast, passing to the north of the Mardudjara. The following excerpts come from his 1875 account of his journey:

. . . ants swarmed over everything, and over us; indeed they wanted to take away the cockatoos we had for dinner but we rescued them (p. 165).

. . . deepened last night's well but with no better results than yesterday. Started in a north-westerly direction and sunk another . . . no water; . . . dug three more wells . . . same unsuccessful results . . . last known water already 50 miles away (p. 183).

The heat is now very great and the camels are suffering from travelling during the day over hot sand and steep hills (p. 209)

. . . my riding camel has completely broken down . . . and we could only get her on her legs again by lighting some spinifex under her tail (p. 211).

. . . master bull camel has eaten poison, and is very ill (p. 213) [It later died, as did many of the explorers' camels after eating poisonous plants.]

Our position is most critical in consequence of the weakness of the camels (p. 256).

God have mercy upon us for we are brought very low. . . . Our miseries are not a little increased by the ants. We cannot get a moment's rest night or day . . . (p. 258–259).

John Forrest   Forrest passed to the south of Mardudjara territory, heading east, in 1874. The excerpts below are from Forrest (1875):

. . . most miserable country, thickets and spinifex . . . (p. 173).

We have not seen any permanent water for the past eighty miles. . . .it is very risky going on . . . (p. 176).

. . . the most wretched country I have ever seen; not a bit of grass, and no water . . . spinifex everywhere. (p. 200).

. . . it is a most fearful country. . . . We can only crawl along, having to lead the horses, or at least drag them (p. 202). [All this party, too, survived].

Ernest Giles   Giles, an intrepid adventurer, made several trips through the desert 1872 and 1882, one of which took him and his party through the southern part of Mardudjara territory, heading eastward. In his later writings, Giles, who had more than one very close brush with death, shows a propensity for the humorous turn of phrase; for example, his description of the cursed, needle-sharp spinifex as ". . . porcupine, triodia . . . Festuca irritans, and everything-else-abominable, grass" (1889,I:191). Several times in his account he waxes most eloquent on flies:

It was impossible to get a moment's peace from the attacks of the flies; the pests kept eating into our eyes, which were already bad enough. This seemed to be the only object for which these wretches were invented and lived, and they also seemed to be quite ready and willing to die, rather than desist a moment from their occupation. . . . they scorned to use their wings, they preferred walking to flying; one might kill them in millions, yet other, and hungrier millions would still come on, rejoicing in the death of their predecessors, as they now had not only men's eyes and wounds to eat, but could also batten upon the bodies of their slaughtered friends (1889,II:303).

David Carnegie   Carnegie, son of a Scottish nobleman, made many astute and valuable observations of the Aborigines and their environment, and his book *Spinifex and Sand* (1898/1973) is a remarkable account of his Australian adventurers. In 1896 he led a small party northward along the eastern edge of Mardudjara county:

[Crossing what he describes as "The Great Undulating Desert of Gravel"] In this cheerless and waterless region we marched from August 22nd until September 17th seeing no lakes, nor creeks, or mountains; no hills prominent enough to deserve a name, excepting on three occasions. Day after day over open, treeless expanses covered only by the never-ending spinifex and strewn everywhere with pebbles and stones (p. 208).

As for animal life—well, one forgets that life exists, until occasionally reminded of the fact by a bounding spinifex rat, frightened from his nest (p. 209).

[Further north] A vast, howling wilderness of high, spinifex-clad ridges of red sand, so close together that in a day's march we crossed from sixty to eighty ridges, so steep that often the camels had to crest them on their knees. . .(p. 249).

Words can give no conception of the ghastly desolation and hopeless dreariness of the scene which meets one's eyes from the crest of a high ridge (p. 251).

Carnegie's party spent almost a year in the interior before seeing rainfall. He attributed their survival to the capture of Aborigines to lead them to water. Carnegie and many other explorers were very well served by Aboriginal guides, who, although strangers to the regions traversed, were invaluable because of their greater knowledge of bird and animal habits and their superb tracking abilities.

THE WESTERN DESERT AS A CULTURE AREA

Except for the presence of higher hills in the southeastern area, the same range of landforms, vegetation, and fauna occurs in all the contiguous deserts that comprise the Western Desert, and none of these areas is a well-defined or clearly demarcated region. Climatic features also show only minor variations throughout, because neither altitude nor latitude has much bearing on weather or seasonal conditions. This striking uniformity of climate and landform is paralleled by a high degree of cultural homogeneity among the hundreds of Aboriginal groups that inhabit the area, such that anthropologists speak of a "Western Desert culture" that is distinguishable from other Australian Aboriginal subcultures.[4]

All Western Desert people speak mutually intelligible dialects of the same basic

[4] There is ample evidence of this homogeneity. For instance, compare the following songs, collected at Jigalong in 1963, with those recorded 22 years earlier by R. and C. Berndt (1945) at Ooldea, a thousand miles to the southeast:
(a) a song sung by featherfeet killers (see Chapter 5):
    Jigalong: *baba ṅganana garli bambuna burnu gadi*
    Ooldea: *baba naṅgana gani maṅguna burna gaadi* (p. 179)
(b) a chant sung over a love-magic object (see Chapter 5):
    Jigalong: *madagi na ṙurubuṅgu diili lilinyba na wirubuṅgu*
    Ooldea: *madagi na rereibuṅga maieli lilingba rereibuṅga* (p. 167)
Although there are differences in the translations given for these songs, the overall meanings are quite similar.

language, characterized by four classes of verb stems, very few irregular verbs, dual pronoun forms (for example, -*li*, "we two"; *nyubali*, "you two"), extensive use of verbalizing suffixes (for example, *galyu*, "water"; *galyurini*, "becomes water"), and a paucity of conjunctions. It is a suffixing language, and whole sentences can consist of one verb stem and a string of suffixes; for example, *wagal-djagu-ladju-djananya*, "spear-might-we [plural, exclusive, subject]-them [third-person plural, object]"— that is, "We-all [excluding the person being addressed] might spear them."[5] All Western Desert forms of social organization are basically similar, too, and in the structure and operation of the kinship systems and marriage rules, the range of variation is not great. This is true even of the northeastern region where social categories of the subsection type are operating (see Chapter 3).

Significantly, it is in the realm of the religious life that the most striking continuities exist throughout the desert. For many millennia the diffusion of religious and other lore to and from constituent groups and sometimes even beyond the culture area has ensured the retention of homogeneous sociocultural forms. Most of the major rituals performed by the Mardudjara are also part of the ritual life of groups elsewhere in the desert, and show remarkable similarities in structure over time and space. Some of the Kangaroo dances captured in Spencer and Gillen's remarkable 1902 film taken among the Aranda of central Australia are virtually identical to those being performed by the Mardudjara and their neighbors today.

The Mardudjara constitute, numerically and geographically, a small part of this culture area, and are in some respects indivisible from the rest because boundaries, even dialectal ones, do very little if anything to impede the free flow of people, ideas, and objects across the face of the desert. Lacking what most peoples would view as essential elements for survival, the Mardudjara have lived in their desert home for many thousands of years. This raises a major question: how have they achieved success in exploiting an environment so limited and acutely susceptible to the vagaries of rainfall that its only certainty seems to be uncertainty?

COPING WITH THE DESERT

It has been customary in discussions of human societies to characterize the Australian Aborigines in negative terms, in a sense putting them down because they lack such features as metal tools, crops, domesticated animals, the wheel, villages, chiefs, a market economy, and so on. A fairer and more rewarding approach would be to focus instead on the positive aspects of the culture of a remarkably resilient and resourceful people whose dominant mode of adaptation precluded the development or adoption of many technological and organizational forms common to the rest of the world.

Mobility and Flexibility   The Aborigines have responded to the challenge of scattered food and water resources by evolving a highly mobile adaptation that enables them to exploit different resource areas at different times, but demands spacing into small, scattered groups as a prevailing condition of life. The maintenance of a very low and stable population density is most essential in the desert, and the need for mobility and flexibility is also greatest there. The size of the basic exploitative group, the band (discussed in Chapter 3), varies according to local conditions and food availability, just as its movements vary in large part according to the occurrence of rain. The

[5] For further information on Western Desert language structure, see Glass and Hackett (1970); Marsh (1969); Hansen and Hansen (1969).

desert people have an extensive vocabulary for cloud and rain types and weather phenomena, and are experts in judging where, when, in what amounts, and for what duration rain falls anywhere in their territory.

The rhythm of desert life is one of irregularly alternating aggregation and dispersal of social groups, but neither these demographic changes nor the patterning of a group's movements is strictly seasonal (see Gould 1968:103). The explorer Carnegie must have been one of the first observers to comment that the best water sources in the desert are the least used, and to intuit a basic adaptive strategy whereby the small wells are used first, and only when these are emptied do Aboriginal groups resort to more permanent waters. After good rains promote plant growth and replenish surface and rock catchments, bands fan out rapidly toward the edges of the affected area, then hunt and gather as widely as possible until obliged to begin a retreat.

In comparing the subsistence behavior of the desert people with that of the Kalahari Bushmen of Africa, Gould (1969b:267) notes that whereas the !Kung Bushmen typically occupy a camp for many weeks and eat their way out of it, the Aborigines:

> . . . eat their way into a camp by first exploiting all the food resources near the surrounding waterholes whenever possible before settling at the main waterhole. Then they consume staples between a five- and 10-mile radius of that waterhole before beginning the trek toward (but not always *directly* toward) another reliable waterhole.

Camp scene: while Yanindu mends a cracked wooden dish with spinifex-resin, her son Djambidjin plays nearby, while his pet lizard rests on his head; although fierce in looks, the thorny devil lizard (Moloch horridus) *is a harmless insect-eater. The smaller dish in the foreground is made of bark.*

The direction of subsequent movements depends of many factors, the most important of which would probably be the location of known or predicted supplies of staple foods at that time of year, the direction of recent rainfall and the position of known chains or "lines" of water sources that will accord with the first two factors (Gould 1969b). Except in extreme drought conditions, the many small groups cover the same general area of the desert year after year, but for reasons that are both ecological and cultural (see Chapter 3), no group would ever repeat its specific round of movements exactly over time.

Ecological necessities keep people dispersed in small groups most of the time, but sociability is highly valued, and under normal circumstances neighboring bands, on seeing one another's smokes, will make contact. They may then camp together until food or water shortages, differing travel plans, or perhaps rising tensions lead to a separation as each goes its separate way. Periodically, when a relative abundance of some food staple can be predicted for a given site, and plentiful water is available, large numbers of people from widely separated areas assemble in response to invitations sent by the local group in whose territory these favorable conditions exist. This temporary aggregation or *djabal* ("multitude") is the high point of the Aborigines' social calendar.[6] It facilitates, among many other important things, the maintenance of a shared religious life and of cultural diffusion, which to the desert people are their lifelines of survival.

Despite the necessary fluidity of their nomadic life, the Aborigines are not rootless wanderers who lack territorial attachments. As individuals and group members, they maintain strongly felt and enduring bonds to certain stretches of territory, and within this home area, to particular sites of totemic and religious significance. Under normal conditions, they are physically present within their homeland, but if separated for some reason, strong sentiments of belonging persist.

The mode of adaptation of the Mardudjara involves a continuing dialectic between the ecological constraints that push people apart and the cultural pressures that draw them together. Although the resulting synthesis favors dispersal, it is important to understand that the Aborigines see this condition not as one that is dictated by the physical environment, but rather as ordained by the Dreamtime. They wander in small bands because that is how the ancestral beings lived.

Attitudes Toward the Environment   For countless generations of Mardudjara, the evolution of their culture has entailed a maximizing of the exploitative possibilities of the natural environment. This has taken place within the limits set by ecology and technology, but it has not necessitated any radical disengagement or alienation of the Aborigines from their environmental surrounds. They attribute neither superiority nor autonomy to the forces of nature, since to do so would suggest an *opposition* between nature and humanity. On the contrary, the Mardudjara see both as elements of a wider cosmic order, a totality that must include the all-powerful spiritual beings of their Dreamtime. They postulate a harmony among its component parts, yet egotistically they regard their actions as essential for its maintenance.

The most visible impact made by the Mardudjara on the land is the burning of grassland, a continuous practice. They also dig holes, cut down trees, uproot shrubs, clear campsites, place sticks and stones in forks of trees (which warn of something sacred and/or dangerous nearby), dig out wells, and so on. Yet because they are few in number and highly mobile, their total impact on the physical environment is slight. The resulting impression is one of "environmental awareness" to the observer, yet this

---

[6] Henceforth, this will be referred to as the "big meeting," a term now commonly used by Aborigines in the contact situation to describe such assemblies.

may well be an illusion, merely a product of ecological imperatives. Even if significant alteration of landforms was possible with their existing technology, however, such activity is precluded by religious convictions. Creativity is the sole prerogative of the Dreamtime beings, whose life design is set and immutable and leaves no room for human transformations of the landscape. The blueprint is clear, and as embodied in the culture of the living, it demands only assent and the fulfilment of ritual responsibilities.

Knowledge   Flexibility of movement and in the size of the exploiting group does not in itself guarantee survival, which depends also on the possession of an extremely detailed and comprehensive knowledge of environmental resources and their utilization. Children begin accumulating this fund of information and skills from a very early age. Because their lives are so closely attuned to the natural environment, the Mardudjara must develop a great ability to "read" correctly the multitude of signals that constantly impinge on their consciousness. To take just one prominent example: the amount of information encoded by tracks and other markings on the ground is enormous, so knowledge of how to decipher them accurately is not only enormously time-saving (as when a mere glance tells the hunter that the marsupial he seeks is not in its burrow) but in very bad times can perhaps mean the difference between life and death.

For adult males this intimate knowledge of the physical world is supplemented by what they regard as an equally pragmatic and necessary ritual technology through which they claim to exert a measure of control over resource production and weather conditions (see Chapter 5). Through ritual acts they communicate with and co-opt metaphysical powers in order to change things in their favor. As a mode of exploitation, the act of spearing an emu and the performance of a rite that will ensure the presence of large numbers of emu each year are considered by the Mardudjara as equally real and effective productive activities. Unlike the Melanesians, for instance, who tend to surround their fishing, horticulture, and pig raising with a host of ritual acts aimed at protecting and promoting success and fertility, the Mardudjara rely on occasional small rites to ensure continued supplies of needed plant and animal foods, but pay much less attention to the particulars of exploitation.

Tools   Nomadism and a lack of beasts of burden impose considerable constraints on the volume and weight of tools, weapons, and other possessions that can be carried by the desert people. Gould (n.d.b.), who adopts an activity-oriented view of Aboriginal technology, suggests that the artifact inventory of the Western Desert people encompasses three kinds of tools: multipurpose, appliance, and instant. This classification is used in the following discussion.

Virtually all multipurpose tools are lightweight and portable, and most are made of wood. The essential kit of the woman is the digging stick, a wooden rod about four feet long, with fire-hardened points that are often chisel-shaped. In digging out small game and tubers, it is sometimes supplemented by small wooden (or bark) digging dishes, which double as containers or scoops. Another major artifact of the women is the wooden dish. This and less durable bark containers are carved by men from large gum trees, and most are 2 to 3 feet long, a foot wide and less than a foot deep, carried under the arm or on the head (supported by a pad made from grass, string, or feathers) and used to carry foodstuffs, water (with grass usually added to lessen splashing), and on occasions, small babies. The other essential woman's tool is a small, smooth stone, used together with large, flat base stones or flat rock surfaces for grinding seeds and other foods.

The inventory of men's portable artifacts is greater. Spears are mostly of the throwing type, 8 to 10 feet long, straightened shortly after cutting and stripping (from trees or roots) by heating over a fire then manipulating by the use of hands, feet, and teeth while the wood is still supple. They are smoothed and sharpened with stone adzes and flakes, with a fire-hardened tip at one end and at the other a small depression which engages the tip of the spearthrower's barb. Most are left plain, but some have barbs either carved into them or attached by means of sinew taken from the legs or tail of a kangaroo. This sinew is chewed until thoroughly softened, then tightly bound around the small sharpened wooden barb and the spear tip; the sinew contracts and tightens the joint as it dries. In the same way, the nesting barb for spears is attached to the spearthrower. A second kind of spear is the shorter, thicker stabbing variety, which is used to inflict thigh wounds in fights.

The spearthrower best exemplifies the multipurpose nature of Aboriginal artifacts. The Mardudjara version is 2 to 3 feet long, 4 inches wide, with a concave, containerlike shaft (some are much flatter, and these usually have a geometrical snakelike design carved onto them), a barb at one end, and a stone flake set into the other with a lump of spinifex resin.[7] Besides its primary use as a spear launcher, which enables a man to throw a spear 80–100 yards and hit a target with force and accuracy within about forty yards, it has many other uses: as a tray in which to mix native tobacco and ashes or ochres used in body decoration;[8] as a fire-making tool; as a scraper and knife for woodworking and preparing and butchering game; as a percussion instrument, when tapped in accompaniment to singing; and as a hook for reaching fruits, berries, or other objects that are out of reach.

The returning boomerang is about 2 feet long, cut and carved from suitably bent mulga trees, and used for fighting and as a musical instrument but not for hunting. With its sharp edges and susceptibility to wind gusts, it makes a vicious and unpredictable weapon, thrown so that it bounces short of an opponent and ricochets up into the body, unless deflected with a parrying shield. Shields are 2 to 3 feet long and 6 inches wide; they are used with marvelous dexterity by men to deflect incoming missiles, and they double as clubs in fighting at close quarters. Boomerangs, shields, and wooden fighting clubs (2 or more feet long and cut from heavy wood or roots) are not usually carried during hunting activities.

The selection of suitable trees from whose trunks or roots tools will be manufactured requires considerable skill, for a man has to visualize what the finished shape will be like. After "seeing" the completed tool in a tree of the right shape, he must remember the spot so he may return some time later when the need for that particular tool arises, if he decides not to make it immediately.

Men carry a limited assortment of small flake knives, used for a variety of cutting and scraping tasks. Most are hand-held in use, but favorite blades may have a small resin handle attached. The use of larger hand-held axes has ceased since the acquisition of metal tools and objects that can be made into tools. The Mardudjara converted to these in most cases long before they first saw any whites, since such highly valued items entered the desert from fringe settlement areas and were soon diffused throughout.

[7] Resin is found in tiny globules at the base of spinifex stalks, most often in rocky areas. These are collected by beating clumps of the grass, which is then winnowed; fire is used to fuse them into a ball, which is soft when heated but is rock-hard when cooled. It is used to mend holes in dishes and for hafting.

[8] Tobacco (*Nicotiana* sp.) is chewed by men and women, after mixing with ash (made by burning leaves of an *Acacia* shrub or river gum bark. As a narcotic it produces little observable effect, but in hot weather especially, it keeps the mouth moist (Gould 1969a:9). It stains the teeth and the roof of the mouth.

Appliances, the second category of artifact, are left at a site and reused on subsequent visits. Large base stones used in grinding are quite heavy and so are left at sites close to seed-producing areas. In areas of granite outcrops and at sites where suitably flat rock surfaces occur, these are used as grindstones. Large stone pounders, used for mashing bones to extract marrow, and formerly, hand axes (which weighed 4 to 8 pounds), are left at sites that lack rocks, and a supply of stone suitable for flaking may also be carried to such sites to form a reserve for future visits.

Instant tools, the third category, are implements fashioned from raw materials available close at hand when a particular need arises, then later discarded. Stone axes, pounders, and flakes are often made in this way, as are grass circlets made by women as head cushions when carrying dishes, and some of the objects used in fire making. The side of a spearthrower is the main fire-making tool, but other materials are also needed: a split piece of dead wood into which a mixture of tinder-dry grass and powdered kangaroo dung is rammed, soon to be ignited as the thrower is sawed rapidly across the open crack. It usually takes only a couple of minutes of hard sawing to produce fire.

Another instant tool is the spindle, a thin stick about 18 inches long, with two small crosspieces at right angles to each other and several inches down the shaft. Human hair is the source of most twine used by the Mardudjara, although strips of possum fur and bark are also used. Hair is spun by men or women, who roll the spindle up and down the thigh to produce the spinning motion that twines the hair, which has been mixed with fat and red ochre to bind it and help retain its suppleness. A ball of string is built up around the crosspieces along the shaft, and when the task is completed, the sticks are removed and discarded.

Shelters and Camp Layout   The shelters of the Mardudjara are of simple construction and require little effort. They sweep or scrape the site clear and burn the surrounding area to discourage unwelcome scorpions, centipedes, and such. The summer camp (*buṟi*, "shade") is a semicircle of leafy shrubbery or branches stuck upright in the ground, with grass sometimes added to thicken the shade. The simple winter shelter is really only a windbreak of uprooted grass or shrubbery, with a slight depression dug out on the leeward side for each family member. A small fire is set on each side of every depression, with a length of wood placed parallel to the sleepers, ready to be pushed into the coals throughout the night so as to keep the fire alive.

Simple storage platforms, made by shoving grass into shrubs close to the camp (if no tree forks are close enough to be used), hold leftover meat and other food beyond the reach of dogs. Bones and other refuse are tossed in any direction outside the cleared habitation area. A cooking pit may be made close to a camp, but the cooking of most large animals is done close to where they are killed rather than back in camp. The men carry large hunks of butchered cooked meat into camp threaded on their spears like a huge shish kebab.

Each family group camps separately and has its own cooking fire. Boys and young men camp separately in bachelor shelters but eat with their respective families. The distance between camps varies between about ten and fifty yards, depending on the nature of friendship and kinship ties, current amity or tension, and felt needs for a measure of privacy at night. When different bands camp together, the spatial orientation of their camps is such that each group sites its camping area on the side closest to its home territory. All campsites are located some distance from a water source, rarely closer than 100 yards, so as to allow game undisturbed access to water, and sometimes because a site is sacred and therefore dangerous to all but initiated men. In sandhill country and when winds are not too strong, the tops of high ridges are preferred as

campsites because they provide a good vista. In fact, the desert people choose campsites in most cases that afford a clear view in all directions. The Mardudjara do not
like to camp in hilly country or any partly enclosed areas.

Subsistence Activities   The food quest of the Mardudjara is not as time-consuming as
might be expected in view of their resource-poor homeland.[9] Their "harvesting" entails no real sense of urgency, no battle against time and the elements. Activities connected directly with getting food occupy rarely more than half a day, and much less if
there is an abundance of easily harvested fruit, berries, or grass seeds nearby, or if the
men are successful in spearing large game close to camp. In summer, especially, people hunt and gather food very early in the day, before it becomes too unbearably hot
in the open. Whatever the season, there is normally ample leisure time to be enjoyed,
for sleeping, playing with small children, chatting idly, or engaging in some ritual
activity, which for the men is a consuming passion.

Each new day necessitates decision-making by band members as to which foods to
seek and where, and eventually, about when to move camp and in what direction to
travel. These decisions are reached informally and depend on factors such as weather
conditions, the amount of leftover food in camp, individual inclinations, and so on.
Whatever the decisions made, no two days' routines are ever identical, but the patterning of sex role allocation remains much the same: men and youths seek large game
while women and children collect plant foods and smaller game that make up the
bulk of the diet. The women's contribution to the food supply has been variously estimated at between 60 and 80 percent of the total weight among desert Aborigines
who exploit similar areas to those of the Mardudjara (Gould 1969b:258; Meggitt
1964). The vegetable foods and small game they obtain are more reliable resources
than those commonly exploited by men. Plant foods are either there or they are not,

*A satisfied group after a successful day's gathering; note Manggadji's hair-twine necklet, and
the use of emu-feather head pads by both women.*

[9] See Gould (1969a) for a detailed account of subsistence activities and other aspects of the
Western Desert culture.

Ending a long and tiring dig after the rapidly burrowing rabbit-eared bandicoot (Macrotis lagotis), *Minma finally secures his quarry.*

whereas large animals are less certain food sources because there is always a measure of unpredictability and luck in the hunt. However, men often hunt lizards and smaller game with greater likelihood of success. Both sexes engage in hunting and gathering activities at times, and they are quite capable of maintaining themselves independently when the occasion arises; for example, if ritual concerns take men away from the band for a prolonged period, as sometimes happens.

Women usually gather food in groups if possible, because the nature of their activities allows them to be sociable and share child-minding as they work. Men are more likely to hunt alone or in pairs, since few of their hunting techniques require the cooperative efforts of a large group. However, several men may sometimes join forces to ambush game after they are driven into a cul-de-sac. Many desert animals are skittish and easily panicked, so great skill in stalking and considerable patience are required to get close enough to spear them. Men do not take their sons with them until the boys are mature enough to cover long distances and endure the tension of stalking game without detection.

During hunting, a man's encyclopedic knowledge of the behavior of animals is tested. Kangaroos, for example, have such acute smell and hearing sense that they can detect the presence of humans a long distance away. Should this happen, the hunter does a perfect imitation of appropriate response behavior, including sounds. If the animal is thus reassured, the hunter can continue to close in until he launches a spear. If he is fortunate, the wounded animal will not go far before collaspsing.[10] After gutting it and closing the incision with a sharp stick, the hunter sets a large fire and throws the kangaroo in long enough to singe off its fur. Later, when the fire has died

---

[10] Dingoes are not heavily relied upon as hunting dogs, but they are useful in corraling wounded game animals to prevent their easy escape.

While Mimma prepares a large fire to cook a plains-kangaroo (Macropus rufus: marlu), sons Nun and Djambidjin play with it.

down, the animal is placed on its back in the pit and covered with hot ashes and sand. Mardudjara tastes in large game run to the partly cooked, and these are eaten quite bloody most often. Kangaroos are always butchered into the same cuts, each of which is designated as belonging to particular kin if they are present in the camp. Large game is always shared with other families in the band.

In most cases, the hunter receives one of the least choice cuts, with the dogs getting the inedible scraps and bones, unless they can steal something more appetizing. Meat is usually consumed within a day or so, before the rotting process is far advanced, although this does not deter people from eating it. With sharing, generalized reciprocity prevails, for regardless of differences in skill and determination that exist among hunters, there is an unstated conviction that everything evens out in the long run. In any case, the fulfilment of kinship obligations is a primary responsibility and, in terms of an individual's status in the group, it is one of the most significant measures of social worth.

Most sharing of vegetable foods, on the other hand, occurs within the family, sometimes called the "hearth group" in recognition of the importance of the cooking fire as the locus of each family in a band. Sharing of foodstuffs does occur, especially when older women whose gathering activities have been curtailed by infirmity are given food by their daughters, daughters-in-law, and other younger female relatives in the group, so that they and their husbands are adequately nourished.

Although as a rule the Mardudjara eat only one main meal a day, in the late afternoon, everyone snacks from time to time while hunting or gathering. The most com-

Djambidjin displays his haul of edible grubs before devouring them.

mon snack foods are fruits, nectars (sucked from flowers or mixed with water to make an infusion) and berries, tree gum, eggs, fungus (an edible trufflelike variety grows in sandhills), lerp (a white sweet secretion left by insects on leaves), honey ants (first dig out the nest; hold the ant's head; bite off distended honey-filled abdomen; discard head; repeat), and edible grubs, an important desert food source. High in protein and prized for their taste, edible grubs are the larva of a genus of woodmoth, and are dug from the roots and base of shrubs and small trees. Each kind is named for the plant in which it is commonly found. Eaten alive or cooked very briefly, these "witchetty grubs" (which are 1 to 3 inches long) have a pleasant nutty flavor.

Children generally eat all that they hunt or gather on the spot. They frequently hunt small lizards, and at an early age boys become skilled in throwing sticks and stones at small birds. These are roughly plucked, then—as is done with lizards and mice (common in the desert)—the birds are thrown into a small fire for a brief period before being taken out and rapidly consumed. Like their elders, children share food with one another, and sometimes play at distribution. They climb trees to get eggs and live young birds, which are also prized food. Some birds and animals may be kept as pets, but children are so rough on them that they usually die in a very short time. Tame dingoes are incredibly patient in this respect, allowing children to perpetrate all sorts of indignities on them without protest, just as they allow adults to abuse and kick them at times. On the positive side, they are also fondled, petted, and kissed by both young and old, who also sleep with them, so it is not entirely a dog's life. Besides their status as pets, dogs are valued by the Mardudjara because they are believed to be excellent detectors of the presence of evil spirits or strangers with homicidal intentions.

For women, the preparation of food is usually a simple and quick task, with the exception of grass seeds. These are harvested into wooden dishes, then taken back to camp, where they are wind-winnowed and finally separated from the chaff by an

Manggadji harvesting seeds from woolybutt grass (Eragrostis eriopoda); *her digging stick and emu-feather head-pad lie nearby as she "milks" the grass-seeds into her wooden dish.*

ingenious and efficient panning method. The dish containing seeds and chaff is rhythmically shaken in such a way that the separation occurs and the waste is easily removed. The seeds are then ground up and mixed with water to make a paste, which is usually cooked. Men cook large game and prepare secret ritual feasts at times, but the bulk of cooking is done by women. Firewood is usually readily obtained, so cooking entails little more than the preparation of a suitable quantity of hot ashes and sand, in which the food is baked. Cooked food has the sand and charcoal fragments dusted and picked off it before it is eaten. Nevertheless, considerable grit is chewed and ingested with food, and contributes to a wearing down of teeth in later life, although in other respects the teeth of the Mardudjara are excellent. Teeth are used for a lot of tasks besides chewing; for example, men sometimes use them to flake and sharpen stone blades.

Besides its obvious uses for cooking and heating in cold weather, fire plays a major role in subsistence in Aboriginal culture. Whenever they shift camp, the Mardudjara always carry firesticks, and in their traveling and hunting they set fire to the vegetation en route. Firesticks carried close to the body provide a surprising amount of warmth, and burning spinifex gives out intense but short-lived heat. The abundant smoke that results indicates not only a group's presence but also its direction of travel, making the chances of meeting up with like groups much greater, although there is no message inherent in the pattern of smoke. The firing of vegetation flushes out small game such as marsupial rats, snakes, mice, lizards, and such, which can then be easily tracked and caught. Also, the burning of spinifex, in particular, promotes the growth of grasses, herbs, and bush tomatoes that are more useful as food resources, since spinifex seeds only for a short time and is laborious to harvest.[11]

Manuba grinds woolybutt grass-seeds into flour while daughter Nyanyawa plays by her side. (Photo © *Film Australia from the film* Desert People.)

[11] For a brief account of the significance of fire in Aboriginal culture, see Jones (1969).

A hunter fires spinifex-grass as he goes on his way.

"Trade"   Most material goods needed for subsistence can be obtained within the home territory of every group, but a few scarce and valued resources necessitate exchanges of some kind so that they become available to people in areas that lack them. The small amount of trade that exists takes place within the framework of ritual activities during big meetings, incidentally as gift exchange between friendly kin when small bands meet, or as part of obligations owed to certain close kin and affines. These more scarce resources, such as red ochre, stones prized for toolmaking, and pearlshells (from the northwest coast) diffuse through countless such exchanges, but there are no markets and no set standards of value for such items. Trade, as usually understood, is in the case of nonsacred material objects a peripheral element in desert culture. In gift exchange the most commonly exchanged objects are foodstuffs, which are categorized simply as *guwi* ("meat") and *mayi* ("vegetable food"); for example, a man gives meat to his parents-in-law and receives vegetable foods from them. The significance of exchange lies far less in the nature or value of the items than in the act of reciprocity itself, which is an affirmation of a continuing bond. The alliances so forged promote an interpersonal and intergroup harmony that is essential in an environment as marginal as the desert.

Nutrition and Health   No detailed nutritional studies have been made of the Western Desert Aborigines, but several medical surveys have been carried out among people who have had little prior contact with whites (for example, Elphinstone 1971). These studies are in agreement that the desert people seem adequately nourished and that their diet is well balanced, with no notable vitamin or protein deficiency detectable. In addition to game animals, particularly lizards which are the most reliable source of animal protein, many of the grass and tree seeds that are desert staples have protein contents in excess of 20 percent, and the many varieties of edible grub are very high in protein. When ripe, most bush tomato varieties (*Solanaceae*), which are important staples, are very high in Vitamin C (Peterson 1977).

Their nomadic life style in small scattered groups, as well as the dry desert air, must contribute to the physical health of the Mardudjara, who suffer few serious ailments and probably have an average life expectancy of 50 or 60 years. Trachoma, an eye disease that can cause blindness, is probably the most widespread serious affliction, especially among old people, some of whom become completely blind. Boils are common, and so are periodic intestinal upsets, brought on most often by eating large quantities of fatty meat, such as emu. Many people get burned while asleep, when they thrust an arm or leg, or they roll, into the fires that burn close beside them in winter. If burn sores develop, they are treated with mudpacks. If children survive the first year or two, they will probably continue to be healthy. Many children have distended bellies, but among the desert people this is not symptomatic of malnutrition or parasitic infestation, and the fat bellies disappear in adolescence as stomach muscles develop.

Head lice are endemic, and their removal is a frequent grooming activity of adults and children alike. A novel treatment for this condition is to catch a snake lizard (a four-inch, pink, two-legged creature) and put it on one's head, where it proceeds to feast on the lice. People sometimes suffer from headache, which they treat most often by binding hair-string very tightly around the head. This kind of hair-string, called *yulydja,* is soaked in a mixture of fat and red ochre and is frequently used to alleviate all kinds of aches and pains.

Illness that lingers or is considered serious is treated by a native doctor (see Chapter 5). Few herbal medicines are used by the Mardudjara. Cooked and pounded quandong nut kernels are rubbed in to treat headaches. For fever or chills, a grass with a very strong menthol smell is chopped finely or pounded and mixed with water to make a liniment. Sickness caused by eating toxic substances or plants is rare, because the Mardudjara know and avoid these, but they do make some use of poisonous plants, such as a *Duboisia* species, in hunting emus.[12]

In terms of mental health, it could be assumed that since these people live in what is probably the world's most marginal environment for human survival, they are tense, morose, and anxiety-ridden because of all the uncertainties created by the capricious nature of rainfall in the desert. In fact, nothing could be further from the truth, as was indicated in the Introduction. Since personality factors will be discussed later (Chapter 6), all that needs to be said here is that the Mardudjara seem to be very well-adjusted people. They are every bit as complex and given to behavioral idiosyncrasies as any other peoples, with the same capacity for exultation and despair. Because sharing, humor, and harmony play such an obvious role in their daily lives, the abiding impressions that outsiders have of them are most often quite positive.

CONCLUSION

To conclude this brief overview of Mardudjara habitat and subsistence, it should be noted that although their most marginal environment may test them severely in times of prolonged drought, it almost never tries them beyond the limits of their considerable ingenuity and endurance. They have adapted to an irregular rhythm of life by imposing their will intellectually rather than physically on the desert. In the chapter that follows, their social organization is examined to show how vital is the part played by kinship, social groupings, and categories in the imposition of order and pattern on their lives, which are played out in their seemingly disordered and unpredictable habitat.

[12] Choosing a site with more than one water source, the men block all but one with sticks and other materials, then put crushed leaves of the poison shrub into the uncovered pool. Upon drinking the water, an emu (or birds or other animals) quickly become drugged and unsteady, making them an easy target for the hunters, who watch from a nearby blind. The guts of any animal thus poisoned are never eaten, and the water is not drunk until a long time after.

3 / The social imperative

The Mardudjara Aborigines view their kinship system, marriage rules, social categories, and so on as givens, left behind for them by the creative beings of the Dreamtime—and also as imperatives, because it is only by conformity to them that people can realize the good life. Since their culture produces neither revolutionaries nor sceptics, it seems fair to assume that the fit between social organization, spiritual directives, and ecological adaptation is for the Mardudjara a satisfying one.

This chapter examines the structural bases of behaviors that constitute the world of social relationships among these desert people.

KINSHIP

As a system of social relationships that are expressed in a biological idiom, kinship provides a kind of blueprint for almost all interpersonal behavior among the Aborigines. In small-scale, familistic societies of this kind, where sex and age are the only major determinants of status, virtually no relationship of dominance, deference, obligation, or equality exists separately from considerations of kinship. The moral universe of the Mardudjara is populated with kin. All people with whom a person comes into contact are classified and known by a particular kin term, and most interaction is modeled on an ideal set of behaviors that characterize the kin relationship involved.

A basic feature of all Aboriginal kinship systems is that they are classificatory; the kinship terms used between people who are consanguines (blood relatives) are also applied to more distantly related, and unrelated, people. Classificatory kinship is based on two major principles. First, in reckoning kin relationships, siblings of the same sex are classed as equivalent, so that my father's brothers are classed together with my father and are all called by the same term, which in Mardudjara is *mama;* likewise my mother's sisters are called *yagurdi* ("mother"), and therefore my parallel cousins on both sides of my family (MZChn and FBChn) I classify as "brother" and "sister" because they are children of people I call "mother" and "father." [1] In turn, I class the children of my male parallel cousins "son" and "daughter," since any woman my "brother" calls "wife" I will also call "wife." Secondly, the classifying principle can be applied to a theoretically infinite range; the web of kinship thus extends far beyond consanguineal and local group limits to include the most distant of kin and former strangers.

The social universe of the Mardudjara includes "kin," "strangers" (who are suf-

---

[1] Quotation marks are here used to distinguish classificatory kin from consanguineal; "Z" is used for "sister" and "S" for "son"; for example, "MZS" is "mother's sister's son". "E" and "Y" are "elder" and "younger"; "W" is "wife."

ficiently like them to be incorporated into the category of "kin"), and "distant people," that is, those who are never encountered and who are thought to possess many less than human characteristics and behaviors, such as long teeth, cannibalistic habits, huge sexual organs, and depravities to match. When strangers are met, their kin relationship to only one member of the group they contact need be known for all other group members to be able to categorize them correctly in kin terms. If not even this much is known, their social category (see below) is used to help designate them adequately.

The central place of kinship in Aboriginal life is underlined by R. and C. Berndt (1977:90):

> . . . kinship is the articulating force for all social interaction. The kinship system of a particular tribe or language unit is in effect a shorthand statement about the network of interpersonal relations within that unit—a blueprint to guide its members. It does not reflect, except in ideal terms, the actuality of that situation; but it does provide a code of action which those members cannot ignore if they are to live in relative harmony with one another.

All normal interaction occurs among "kin," and as a rule Mardudjara make constant use of kin terms of address and reference. Since every term connotes a complex of ideal behaviors, kinship is dominant as a framework for action, particularly between people not well known to each other. It provides them with a ready-made, mutually understood interactional code, and thus eliminates the need for any tentative period of negotiation of suitable behavior. A kin term is simultaneously a status term, so it encodes a great deal of information that is useful for framing interaction between individuals. Whether some other person is loved or hated, admired or envied, patterned kin behavior allows both actors at least minimal expectation of a measure of predictability in their encounters.

Within the limits set by these ideal patterns of behavior, there is always scope for variation. In other words, the Aborigines are not so rigidly imprisoned by their kinship system that the free expression of feelings and emotions is stifled. Enmeshed they certainly are, by the fact of birth and the impossibility of opting out of the system, but the Mardudjara appreciate individual differences and the need to make allowances for differing personality and temperament.

Many factors make for variations within the broad limits imposed by kin categorization. For one thing, no terminological distinction is made between close blood relatives and distant kin, so while, for example, a person generally behaves toward all those women termed "mother" in a similar patterned way, the emotional component in the behavior will be very different for one's physiological mother (genetrix) and for those other "mothers" who were part of his or her early socialization, than for distant "mothers." [2] The kin terminology, then, gives no clues to the intensity of feelings that exist within a given relationship. Except for terms that distinguish older from younger siblings, the classificatory system ignores relative age, so that in every category there will be a range of individuals from infants to very old; that is, some of one's "mothers" will be infants and young girls, and some of one's "sons" will be middle-aged and old men, and so on. Frequently, then, the relative ages of the two people concerned will modify the nature of their interaction. Close friendship, especially if it dates from childhood (which among the Aborigines is free

---

[2] Should the need arise, the term *walydja* ("own") is used to distinguish consanguineal from classificatory kin, but this is not an infallible guide because people sometimes use the term in reference to other relatives with whom some special bond is felt but no close blood tie exists.

from the restraints of patterned kin behavior), motivates people whose relationship ideally entails restraint to relax the rules a little.

People possess a fund of information concerning the personality and behavior of their relatives, which provides a reliable guide to the expected actions and reactions of these kin in given situations. People's personal likes and dislikes of others are obviously important in motivating decisions to seek or avoid contacts. The physical setting, and a person's emotional state, general disposition, and felt needs can also influence conduct. Knowing only the kin categories involved, an outsider should be able to predict with some success the kinds of interpersonal behavior that will obtain. But the factors just enumerated would also need to be taken into account to understand just what is going on—unless the patterned behavior requires total avoidance, which is mandatory and operates regardless of personality factors or sentiment.

The relatively restricted and patterned behavioral field that is set by the nature of Aboriginal kinship has advantages for interaction. As a facilitator, it allows for a good measure of prediction of expected behavior, but also, it gives people a strong sense of security and well-being that stems from their envelopment within a universe of kin, with all of whom some feeling of mutual obligation and responsibility ideally exists. People know mainly what their culture and culturally conditioned senses tell them is real, relevant, and good. I have never heard Mardudjara express resentment or frustration at the restrictions that their kinship system places on them. Instead, people talk with satisfaction about the good feelings that come from being surrounded by so many others who are "one family" and "one people" with them.

The Mardudjara, realistically, do not expect children, especially small ones, to conform to the kinship system. Children's lives in the desert are remarkably free from restraints and very little pressure is put on them in their socialization. But they are born into a world of kinship statuses; they hear kin terms in constant use; and as soon as they are considered capable of assimilating knowledge, they are taught the shoulds and should-nots of behavior towards various kin. They see the system in action and thus learn both the ideal and actual patterning of social relationships as part of growing up. They absorb the system effortlessly, learning the primacy of kin category as a behavioral guide. People of the grandparent generation, in particular, who teach them songs and dances and tell them stories, also tell them much about the proper behaviors and obligations associated with kinship and may jokingly scold them for "improper" behavior. Having learned the system, children begin conforming to it in early adolescence without any specific directives from their elders. Conformity is prompted by the development of feelings of shame and embarrassment as they become increasingly self-conscious about their behavior.

The several linguistic units that are here referred to collectively as the Mardudjara share basically the same kinship system, and there is no kin category that is found in one and not the others.[3] There are some differences in vocabulary, however, so the terms given below are those of the Gardudjara speakers. (Many of these terms occur widely throughout the Western Desert, though not necessarily in reference in the same category.)

Table 3–1 lists the terms of address, from both male and female perspectives, and the kin categories to which each refers, plus the reciprocals of each term.

From Table 3–1 it can be seen that males and females share most terms and each sex uses 17 different terms of address (umari is not an address term because men and women so related completely avoid one another, the rare exceptions occurring during

[3] Mardudjara kinship contains elements of two key Australian types: Kariera and Aluridja (see Elkin 1954; Tonkinson 1974).

TABLE 3–1   KINSHIP TERMS

	Male Ego			Female Ego	
English	Mardudjara	Reciprocal	English	Mardudjara	Reciprocal
SPOUSE	marduñgu	[same]	SPOUSE	marduñgu	[same]
EB;FBS;MZS	gurda	marlañgu	EB;FBS;MZS	gurda	marlañgu
EZ;FBD;MZD	djurdu	marlañgu	EZ;FBD;MZD	djurdu	marlañgu
F;FB	mama	gadja;yurndal	F;FB	mama	gadja;yurndal
M;MZ;WFZ	yagurdi	gadja;yurndal	M;MZ	yagurdi	gadja;yurndal
S;DH;ZS;ZDH;BS	gadja	mama;gaga	S;BS;ZS	gadja	yagurdi;gurndili
D;ZSW;BD	yurndal	mama	D;BD;ZD;	yurndal	yagurdi;gurndili
FZ	gurndili	gadja	FZ;HM	gurndili; ñgunyari	yurndal;ñgunyari
MB;WF;MMBS	gaga	gadja	MB	gaga	yurndal;ñgunyari
WM (some FZ;MBW)	umaři	[same]	DH	umaři	[same]
WB;ZH;MBS;FZS	yuñgguři	[same]	BW;ZH; MBD;FZD	djuwaři	[same]
some MBS;FZS	wadjira	[same]	some MBD; FZD	wadjira	[same]
some MBD;FZD	yingarni	[same]	some MBS; FZS	yingarni	[same]
ZD	ñgunyari	gaga			
FF;MF;SS;DS; ZDS;FMB;MMB	nyamu	[same]	FF;MF;SS;DS; BDS;FMB;MMB	nyamu	nyami
FM;MM;SD;DD; ZDD;FMZ;MFZ	nyami	nyamu	FM;MM;SD;DD; BDD;FMZ;MFZ	nyami	[same]
some MBDS;FZDS; MBDD;FZDD	bunyayi	[same]	some MMBS; MMBD;MFZS; MFZD	bunyayi	[same]

certain rituals and in the event of a serious dispute). It can be seen how the system lumps several different categories of kin under a single term in many cases; for example, all a person's relatives in the grandparent and grandchild generations are merged under two very similar terms, differing only for the sex of the person addressed. Whenever identical reciprocal terms are used, as between most same generation members and their grandparents, the relevant patterned behavior is predominantly symmetrical or egalitarian. On the other hand, when two people address each other using different reciprocals (for example, "father"–"son") this suggests a difference in status and asymmetrical behavioral norms; that is, one person will defer to the other, as in most relationships between adjacent generations, but also between older and younger siblings.

Besides the many address terms listed in Table 3–1, the Mardudjara make extensive use of reference terms, which derive partly from the single terms, but are usually used in the dual case when a person refers to two different relatives, one of whom is being addressed, or to many relatives standing in the same relationship. This large set of dual terms adds considerable complexity to the system of kin terms—to say nothing of the headaches it causes for the struggling anthropologist! But for the Mardudjara who are continually using them in reference, the dual terms simplify the identification of people they are talking about. Another set of terms also in common use is *murgañgunya* ("first-born"), *malyurda* ("middle"), and *nyirdi* ("last-born"), which as address and reference terms may persist long past a person's childhood (as in our society when young adults are referred to as the "baby" of the family).

The kinship system of the Mardudjara is bilateral insofar as male and female descent principles are accorded about equal stress, even though the patriline is more important in relation to "residence" preferences. The bilaterality of kinship is well illustrated in cases where a person is confronted with a choice in reckoning relationship to the children in a single family; in many cases the person calculates through the father in allotting terms to some of these children, and through the mother for others. This kind of choice making shows the egocentric nature of kinship reckoning, which makes it possible even for full siblings to use different terms for the same person; for example:

Rali calls Nyingudja "mother" but her husband Djiin happens to be related to Rali as "sister's son." He follows Djiin ("ZS") in calling two of their three children "grandchild," but in reckoning his relationship to their older daughter he follows Nyingudja ("M") and thus calls the girl "sister."

Once a choice is made in situations such as this, the decision is stuck to because there is a strong emphasis on keeping kinship alignments stable, both in the terminology used and in maintaining the relevant patterned behavior. But some changes can and do occur, resulting in modifications in behavior between certain people. This is best seen in connection with ritual operations (see Chapter 4) when new relationships are activated between a novice (and some of his close relatives) and the men who perform the operation on him, such that restraint and avoidance become the new norms.

Although the Mardudjara themselves do not describe kinship patterning in terms of a continuum, it may be helpful to consider the different gradations of patterned kin behavior as falling between two extremes: complete avoidance and uninhibited joking. Table 3–2 shows the approximate range of behavior exhibited between a male Ego and other kin categories to give some idea of what kinds of behavior are expected between which categories of kin and to show the range of variation involved. The two extremes are usually easy to detect. Avoidance relationships, typified by the "WM"—"DH" affinal link, necessitate the taking of rapid evasive action if either party seems likely to come within 20 or 30 yards of the other. Joking relationships, which generally obtain between certain same-sex relatives, involve rowdy exchanges of sexually explicit epithets and mock abuse, with much body contact and sexual horseplay, which amuse onlookers at least as much as the joking pair.

Whenever an element of restraint figures in the relationship, it is accompanied by the presence of "shame–embarrassment" between individuals so related. Restraint signals also an asymmetry of status that calls for a measure of deference, respect, obedience, authority, and so forth. Restraint relationships are exemplified by restrictions on behaviors such as touching, joking, the direct passing of objects hand to hand, sitting together, visiting another's camp, calling by name, looking directly at another while talking, and arguing with or physically assaulting any members of certain kin categories. A pervasive fear of shame or embarrassment, rather than threats of punishment, is what regulates this system most of the time.

The Mardudjara are mindful of the status differences that exist between members of adjacent generations, and they show restraint in their interaction unless extreme anger motivates them temporarily to ignore the norms—in which case they will be upbraided as *gurndabarni* ("having no shame"). With fairly unrestrained relationships, on the other hand, it is up to the pairs concerned to decide how familiar and physically close they want to be, according to factors such as personality compatibility and individual inclinations.

In general, women enjoy a greater number of relatively unrestrained relationships with one another than do men, and most can talk and interact freely with most other female kin. This freedom may well relate to the fact that they normally spend much more time together in groups than do the male hunters. As Table 3–2 indicates, Mardudjara men interact openly with a few categories of male relatives and with certain individuals in others, but a man's behavior toward most close consanguineal adult kin is marked by various degrees of restraint. As might be expected, spouses ideally enjoy

TABLE 3–2   KIN BEHAVIORAL PATTERNS (MALE EGO)

Avoidance	Restraint	Moderation	Lack of Restraint	Joking
umaři (WM;"WM")				

gurda (EB)
djurdu (EZ)
yingarni (cross-cousin "Z")
yurndal (D;"D")
yagurdi (M;"M")
gurndili (FZ;"FZ")
yuňgguři (WB)
←——— mama (F;"F")———————→   *
←——— gadja (S;"S";ZS)———————→

gurda ("EB")
marlaňgu ("YB";"YZ")
djurdu ("EZ")
gaga (MB;WF)
ňgunyari ("ZD";"SW")
wadjira (some MBS;FZS;"MBS";"FZS")
bunyayi (female; see Table 3–1)
←——— yuňgguři ("WB")———————→
marduňgu (W;"W")
←———————————gadja ("ZS") ———————→
←———————————gaga ("MB") ———————→
nyamu (FF;"FF";SS;"SS"; etc.
nyami (MM;"MM";DD;"DD"; etc.)
bunyayi (male)
djira (cross-
cousin "B")

*Arrows indicate approximate range of behavioral variation occurring within these categories. Note the difference between consanguineal and classificatory kin in some categories (for example, B, Z, and MB) and sex differences in others (for example, cross-cousin "sibling" and *bunyayi*) (see Table 3–1).

a relaxed relationship, but men generally show considerable restraint in their dealings with their parents and with siblings of both sexes.

The fact that a terminological distinction is made between older and younger siblings reflects a status difference based on relative age. Older siblings share an obligation to discipline younger ones who make trouble, but they should also speak for them and defend them against verbal and physical attack. The mechanics of wife selection are such that brothers rarely compete for the same women, so sexual jealousy is not usually a factor in their relationship. However, the ambivalence inherent in the chastiser–defender roles that older brothers must play no doubt leaves a residue of resentment among some younger siblings, which must be controlled because open conflict is untenable between brothers.

Marriage Rules   The prescribed form of marriage among the Mardudjara is between cross-cousins; that is, a person marries a classificatory cross-cousin ("MBD" or "FZD" for a male; "MBS" or "FZS" for a female) who is called by the term "spouse"; some cross-cousins are classed as if they are siblings and therefore not marriageable. A person enjoys a very relaxed familiarity with same-sex relatives in this category, but shows the same restraint toward an opposite sex relative as if the other were a sibling. Also, most consanguineally related cross-cousins call each other spouse, but marriage between them is uncommon because a "spouse" comes ideally from groups that are both genealogically and geographically distant.

There are some differences in interpretation of marriage rules between different Mardudjara subgroups. Among the Mandjildjara and Warnman speakers, marriage sometimes occurs between actual cross-cousins, particularly between a male and his MBD, and a man ideally marries any daughter of a woman he refers to as *umari* ("WM"), but never the daughter of any *gurndili* ("FZ"), who is regarded as similar to "mother" and whose daughter is therefore *yingarni,* cross-cousin "sister", not "spouse." Among the Gardudjara and other southern groups, however, the mother of a man's spouse is most often *umari* but is sometimes related to him as *gurndili* (here a distant "FZ"); in this case there is an important behavioral difference in that a man does not have to avoid his *gurndili,* although the pair should show mutual restraint.

Sister exchange, in which two men from different groups who classify each other as "B" exchange their sisters in marriage, is possible within the Mardudjara system, but in fact is quite rare. Instead, they prefer long-term reciprocity. There is an expectation that the sons or sons' sons of a family which gives one of its females in marriage will eventually receive a wife from the recipients when circumstances permit this. The bestowal of infants or little girls is closely linked to the initiation/circumcision process; the distant "MB" or "FZH" who is chosen to remove the youth's foreskin, thus symbolically "killing" him, must in compensation offer a daughter to him by bestowal. Circumcision not only marks the beginning of a prolonged series of gift exchanges between the families of initiator and novice, it also sets up relationships of strong restraint and avoidance. This inconvenience is offset, however, by advantages derived from close alliances with distant families, whose territory could be a welcome refuge in times of food or water shortages in a family's home area.

Wrong Marriages   Unlike some groups to the northeast of them, which favor marriage between second cousins (that is, between pairs whose parents are related as cross-cousins), the Mardudjara allow both first and second classificatory cross-cousin marriage, thus giving an individual a wider selection of spouses. This is perhaps one reason why there is such a low incidence of "wrong" marriage; that is, a union between two people who are not related as "spouse" (see Sackett 1975). For a couple who are not so related to cohabit would in almost all cases be considered incestuous, *regardless of genealogical distance;* a "sister" is a sister, whether consanguineal or classificatory, and should therefore be treated like one, with restraint that is devoid of sexual overtones.

The only non-"spouse" sexual relationship that is not considered incestuous is that between a man and his "ZD," which is favored by a few people as a "lover" relationship. Marriages between such *nyagadji* ("wrong") pairs are rare, however; judging from extant marriages and genealogies collected, they constitute less than 3 percent of all marriages (there are no known "incestuous" unions). If children are born of *nyagadji* partners, other people follow the mother in reckoning their kin relationship to the offspring, ignoring the father's affiliations and thus "straightening" the system of kin reckoning and section membership.

LOCAL ORGANIZATION

The social and spatial arrangement of Mardudjara groups involves two different but closely related elements: kinship and territoriality, which are impossible to consider apart from subsistence requirements and religious concerns. A major feature of Mardudjara local organization is its flexibility and fluidity—thus the absence of concern with boundaries and exclusiveness of group membership.[4]

[4] Aboriginal local organization has been the subject of considerable debate among anthropologists; for example, Hiatt 1962, 1966; Stanner 1965b; Birdsell 1970; Peterson 1972, 1976a,

The following description of the significant kinds of groupings is based on a distinction proposed by Stanner (1965b) between the *estate* and the *range*. The estate is the traditional heartland of what is most often some kind of patrilineal descent group. It consists of a limited number of important waterholes and sacred sites to which the members of the group are intimately related through bonds that imbue them with strongly felt sentiments of attachment and belonging. Whereas the tie to the estate is primarily a religious one, the relationship of social groups to their range is principally economic. A range is the large area exploited by bands during the food quest, and it normally includes within it an estate which a majority of members of the bands concerned think of as their *manda* ("main place"). Although severe drought sometimes forces bands to move far away from their estate, a strong longing for "home" and, among men, a major religious commitment draw them back to the heartland as often as ecological and social circumstances will permit. In the desert the ranges of neighboring estate-groups invariably overlap, and it is possible for individuals to develop strong allegiances to more than one estate in the course of their lives, which further adds to the openness of local organization.

The Linguistic Unit   As noted earlier, the unity implied by the term "Mardudjara" is not recognized by the people so designated, for they belong to several differently named linguistic units (see map 2). I refrain from calling them "groups" for several reasons. Individual speakers of the Gardudjara, Giyadjara, or other dialects sometimes use the language label when identifying others, but when identifying themselves they more often use the name of a waterhole in their estate, usually a site that is widely known because of its mythological significance. They can identify territorial boundary zones between themselves and neighboring linguistic units, but their conception of territory is one of clusters of points in space rather than enclosed or bounded tracts (O'Connell 1976). Therefore boundaries are often vague, especially between water sources and where prominent landforms are absent.

Speakers of the same dialect never congregate as an exclusive group or act in concert in any way. The largest aggregation that occurs is the *djabal* ("multitude") which gathers for big meetings once or twice a year to engage in ritual and other activities. This assembly invariably includes members of several different dialect units, *and no two meetings will have an identical or nearly identical membership*. Between one meeting and the next all sorts of factors intervene to prevent some groups from attending and allow others who missed the previous gathering to attend.

In the normal round of life, member groups of the same linguistic unit are bound to interact more often and have closer kinship and friendship ties to one another than to distant groups, but they have no reason to make linguistic boundaries coincide with exclusive, on-the-ground assemblies. Such a condition would be quite impossible, given the nature of marriage arrangements, kin networks, the mixing of dialects by groups whose estates lie near linguistic unit boundaries, and the many other factors that stress wider homogeneity and cooperation.

The Estate-Group   Each linguistic unit is composed of a number of estate-groups whose members are normally dispersed in bands throughout and perhaps beyond its

---

and other papers in *Tribes and Boundaries in Australia* (Peterson 1976). The task of definition is complicated by several factors: Aborigines and outsiders have different conceptions of unity; Aboriginal conceptions of "belonging" vary with respect to geographical and social boundaries; and their nomadic life style makes groupings larger than bands difficult to isolate in many cases. In the Western Desert, the term *tribe* is ill-suited to characterize any of the groups found there (R. Berndt 1959); it connotes a corporateness of economic, political, and boundary-maintaining activity that is absent there. Recently, Barker (1976) and Myers (1976) have done much to clarify the nature of the estate-group and of local organization in general.

territory. The Mandjildjara, who occupy the largest area, traditionally had more estate-groups than, say, the Guradjara, whose territory is much smaller (though ecologically more favorable) and probably contained only three or four such groups. It is
impossible to estimate with any certainty the size, population range, or number of estates in each unit, partly because of dislocations and migrations resulting from European influences, but also because estate-group boundaries are not always clearly
defined. The estate-group can be elusive to identify because its members never assemble en masse to the exclusion of other like groups. Membership criteria are not
rigorously defined, and although most men maintain a primary allegiance to one
group and secondary allegiances to a number of others, options always exist and are
sometimes exercised.

The following description of a Mandjildjara estate-group whose "main place" is
Giinyu (now Well No. 35 on the Canning Stock Route; see Map 2) is included to illustrate the nature and functioning of estate-groups. The Mandjildjara speakers are almost all Diṅgari, a generic term for the many different mobs of Dreamtime beings
who left the Manjildjara behind on their eastward travels.[5] Prominent among them
were the Possum and Native Cat people, and the Minyiburu women and their pursuer
Nyiru, a man with a huge penis and an insatiable, rapacious sexual appetite. In the
end Nyiru tried to follow them up into the sky but the Minyiburu pushed the ladder
down, and he has remained beneath them ever since—as three stars that represent his
knees and penis, in an intercourse position facing the Pleiades, which are the
Minyiburu. According to the Dreamtime myth, when the Minyiburu were camped at
Giinyu, they spotted Nyiru in the distance, headed in their direction. The women
fled in panic, leaving behind two of their number, whom Nyiru caught and raped to
death, and also a big hairless dingo bitch called Giinyu. The bitch later gave birth to
hundreds of pups of all kinds and colors, which dug themselves nests all around their
home area, thus creating the holes that are a distinctive feature of the site (pitted sedi-
mentary rock patches, in sandhill country). The dingoes remained there forever, and
composed the Yiniṙari ritual so that people would know of their exploits. The group
of people who identify themselves as Giinyumardadji (-mardadji, "belonging to that
place") are known to others as the "dingo mob." Many of them have dingo as their
djugur ("ancestral totem")—that is, they believe that they were left behind by the
dingo beings—but some identify Minyiburu or Nyiru as their djugur and a few have
other Dreamtime beings associated in some way with the Giinyu estate.[6] This use of a
major totem as a convenient label regardless of individual totemic associations is common in other parts of Australia; for example, Strehlow (1965:140) notes that among
the Aranda, men of the same estate-group may call themselves "honey-ant" people,
yet for many this group of Dreamtime beings is not a personal totem.

Most men who head families that comprise the several bands whose estate locus is
Giinyu are related in the male line. This situation comes about because of a strong
preference for children to be born somewhere in or near the estate of their father so that
both will share the same ancestral totem. When adverse conditions force bands away
from the Giinyu estate for long periods, some children are born elsewhere. In this case
the father may try to arrange a birthplace that is associated with one of the Diṅgari
mobs, but again, this may not be possible.

It follows, then, that birth on the estate is not the only criterion for membership; a
person can be a member by virtue of having been conceived there, or because of his or

[5] For accounts of the Diṅgari beings and the significance of the associated ritual complex, see
R. Berndt (1970) and Myers (1976).
[6] The conception totem is the plant, animal, or mineral form that the spirit-child (left by the
ancestral beings in the form of life essence) assumed at some later time (see Chapter 4).

her father's membership of the estate-group (and through the mother to her natal estate, though this linkage is less often stressed). For males, there are other important avenues which exist through the religious life. The estate in which a youth is circumcised becomes "his" (some men, when asked for their ancestral totem, give the name of their circumcision site rather than that of a Dreamtime being), and he is thus entitled eventually to learn all the secrets of the estate-group elders provided he returns periodically for ritual activities there. Obviously, the more of these criteria that coincide, the stronger the primary attachment, but because full congruence is rare, every individual is entitled to membership in more than one estate-group through bonds of shared spirit and substance (discussed in Chapter 4).

Many of the sisters of Giinyu men are living elsewhere, having joined the bands of their husbands sometime after marriage. But their sentimental attachment to the Giinyu area and to relatives there draw them back from time to time. During these visits, their husbands use the opportunity to hunt meat for their in-laws in continued fulfilment of affinal obligations. This is one reason why men are periodically absent from their estate-group bands, but they also leave from time to time when religious business takes them elsewhere.

The blood ties that link many of the members of the same estate-group are less important as bonds to the estate than are the religious ties, which are of course shared with others who may not be related consanguineally to them. The recognition of blood ties is not carried back great distances in time (the genealogical depth of recognized ties is rarely more than three or four generations in the desert), and because of a strong tabu on uttering names of the dead, ancestors are soon forgotten. Because wealth and status are not acquired through inheritance and there are no human ancestor cults of any kind, there is little to be gained by tracing biological descent far back in time; totemic affiliations to Dreamtime ancestors are of far greater significance to the Mardudjara.

The initiated men who comprise the Giinyu estate-group as the landholders, or more aptly the caretakers of the sacred sites and objects in the estate, share important religious responsibilities. They collectively "own" the Yiniřari ritual left for them by the human–animal dingo beings, and periodically they must organize its performance at or close to Giinyu. For this event they invite men of neighboring groups, and because most visitors will have long since been initiated into the Yiniřari, they will participate fully, with the Giinyu leaders acting as planners and directors of the various ritual activities. On every occasion, there are novices present, so they must be initiated into the Yiniřari and will receive instruction from the Giinyu men who, as dingo people, are best qualified for this task.

Performance of the Yiniřari is believed to stimulate the supply of dingoes throughout the desert. In addition, the Giinyu estate men must at some time each year perform increase rites (see Chapter 5) at Giinyu and Girbin to the east, to ensure that plenty of pups will be born, and at two other sites within the estate area, one for mulga seeds and the other for a variety of bush tomatoes, both of which are important food staples at certain times. The older men most closely associated with these sites carry out the simple increase rites there, assisted by others whose bands are somewhere in the vicinity at the time.

Perhaps the greatest responsibility of the Giinyu men rests with the care of the cache of sacred objects that are kept hidden close to the waterhole and with the performance of Mirdayidi rituals (see Chapter 4) and feasts there. All the secret-sacred carved wooden boards and stone objects associated with the Yiniřari and other initiatory activities of the group are kept there. Besides being regularly checked and anointed with protective fat and red ochre, these sacred objects are revealed to novices—from Giinyu as well as those who are brought from other areas—when they undergo the very important initiation stage of Midayidi (see Chapter 4). This ritual activity is of great importance because it entitles initiates not only to full access to the territory and resources of the Giinyu estate-group, but also to active participation in any religious activities that take place there. The bond to Giinyu and its people that is forged through the Midayidi is as strong as that of having been circumcised there.

Because of the existence of multiple criteria of attachment to estate, no two Giinyu people name exactly the same set of sites when asked for their *manda* ("country"). Every individual imbues some places with special meanings and significances that are not shared by many others.[7] The tie to the land is extremely strong for everyone because one's home territory is the locus of social identity and of "belonging" in a spiritual as well as emotional sense. When, through choice or necessity, Giinyu people move beyond their normal range area, their travels are facilitated by these various individual attachments that extend far from Giinyu itself, as well as by a multiplicity of kinship and marriage ties, and the bonds of shared language, religion, and values. It is not necessary for them to obtain permission to hunt and gather there because the males have already ritually "paid for" rights of entry (see Chapter 4). Besides, how self-defeating it would be for any group to refuse others access to its resources and thus invite later retaliation when, as would inevitably happen at some future time, drought conditions force it to evacuate into the territory of other groups.

The Band   The band is composed of one or more families whose male heads are more often than not patrilineally related. This land-exploiting group varies in size from perhaps as few as six or eight people to more than thirty according to ecological and social factors. Various other people will come and go, including, for example: visiting in-laws who come to spend time with their daughters or sisters and their children; intending sons-in-law who spend varying periods hunting meat for their future wife's parents while at the same time giving the girl concerned the opportunity to become accustomed to them prior to marriage; patrikin of the males; and young men and their guardians who are following the path of ancestral beings in fulfilment of initiation requirements. If times become bad, in that water or food shortages occur, a band may be forced to atomize into single-family groups. At other times, when conditions are favorable, bands may disappear for a time through the fusion of two or more neighboring groups. The only name given to bands is *gabudur* ("small group").

The family, or hearth group, is the smallest identifiable group in Aboriginal society. If its male head is middle-aged or older, it is typically polygynous; that is, the man has two or more wives at the same time. Few Mardudjara have more than three wives at any given time, and many, especially younger men, have only one. The family loses the services of its daughters when at the age of about twelve they are given in marriage. But loss of the considerable productive capacity of these girls as food gatherers is offset by their father's acquisition of wives from other groups. The family is rarely isolated from like groups, because people enjoy the increased sociability that results from living in bands.

Flexible in size, movement, and membership, the band is prevented from becoming a free-floating amorphous mass by its attachment to an estate, with kinship and "descent" as important factors. The preference for children to be born and raised in their father's country and for women to live in the bands of their husbands after marriage, as well as the ritual responsibilities of the male landholders of the estate-group,

[7] Myers (1976) in a valuable study of the Pintupi, whose territory lies to the east of the Mandjildjara, concludes that their social organization is the outcome of individual decisions and affiliations, so that there is considerable overlap in membership of estate-groups, which are therefore unbounded. He suggests that these are not unilineal descent groups, but are best viewed as bilateral kindreds.

ensure a measure of territorial attachment and the presence of patrilineally related men in the several bands that habitually exploit an estate and surrounding range.

The difficulties of defining local groups, especially in the desert, point to a fact of great importance: except for facets of the religious life, which in any case crosscuts spatial and social groupings, exclusiveness and narrowly defined ethnocentrism are potentially destructive sentiments in such an extremely marginal environment.

SOCIAL CATEGORIES

In common with many other small-scale societies, Aboriginal social organization is replete with duality: the categorization of objects, animals, people, or whatever into two opposing but complementary groups. But among the Aborigines, dualism is most clearly seen in varying combinations and permutations of social categories or "classes" whose degree of elaboration is unparalleled anywhere in the world. A deeply felt urge to oppose the vagaries of a hunting and gathering life with intellectual constructs that impose order, system, and predictability may well underlie such dualism. Dual organization of some kind is so universal that it has been attributed to some characteristic of the functioning of the human brain (see Lévi-Strauss 1962). For the Australian case, Burridge (1973) offers an alternative suggestion. He links this duality to the polarity of Aboriginal life, the rhythm of dispersal alternating with aggregation. In this sense their life does swing between two extremes: the predominant condition of peaceful, rather monotonous, and low-keyed life in the small band contrasting with large gatherings, which are brief but always highly charged, tense, exciting, and eventful interludes.[8] However, the Mardudjara do not describe the two phases of this oscillation as a dualistic opposition.

Few Aboriginal societies lack a division into two, four, or eight categories, but this is not to say that those lacking in them are somehow deficient in their functioning. Where four-category (section) and eight-category (subsection) systems exist, they are based on dual organization, whether or not this is explicitly recognized or exemplified in named subgroupings. The distribution of these various category systems is geographically uneven and is not correlated with ecological differences.[9] Whereas moieties (division into two categories) may or may not be named sociocentrically, sections and subsections always are.

All these social categories have certain common characteristics. Because membership is ascribed by birth, it is impossible for individuals to change categories. Moieties indicate intermarrying divisions and, by the same token, divisions into which marriage is forbidden, but they do not regulate marriage, because this follows prescriptions that are expressed in terms of specific kin relationships. So, although the categories are exogamous, they are not "marriage classes." Nor do they exist individually as actual on-the-ground gatherings of people, which is why they are not "groups," although at certain times and for specific purposes members of paired categories may assemble in discrete groups. In both section and subsection systems, a child's category is always different from those of its parents. These categories crosscut estate-groups and the kinship system, and are of a different order from kinship, which is an egocentrically defined network of relationships, whereas categories are sociocentrically ordered. Social categories are obviously much less important than kinship in

[8] Durkheim (1915) was one of the first scholars to discuss this polarity and its implications for Aboriginal society and religion.

[9] Service (1960) attempted to derive such a correlation, without conspicuous success; see R. and C. Berndt (1977) for criticisms.

everyday life, but there is a significant correspondence between the two. The categories, by lumping together sets of kinship terms within each, do provide individuals with rough guides to the kind of patterned behavior expected of them.[10]

Meggitt (1962) has observed that, as a mode of classification or a guide to specific action, social categories are too broad and ambiguous a referent. Nevertheless, in a society like the Mardudjara, who possess a four-section system, section labels are in constant use as terms of address and reference. The Mardudjara make little use of personal names, which are such an intrinsic and inseparable part of the self that they should not be bandied about indiscriminately. Rare is the adult who will say his or her own name or will reveal the names of any members of kin categories toward whom restraint must be shown. Adults sometimes resort to teknonymy (the practice of referring to other adults by the name of one of their children, of either sex), but more commonly use section terms to label others. Since there are only four such terms, and the same term is used for male and female members of each section, their use is imprecise and sometimes confusing to the outsider, as the following typical exchange shows:

Informant: That Banaga [section name] saw a big snake-spirit yesterday.
Anthropologist: Which one?
  I: I don't know . . . it could have come from Linbul [a waterhole associated with two ancestral snake-men].
  A: No, I mean who saw it?
  I: That old one [*djirlbi* can refer to an old person of either sex]
  A: Woman?
  I: No! Old man! That one, over there—see!
  A: Which one? There are three Banaga sitting in that camp.
  I: The one with the beard.
  A: Two of them have beards; do you mean Buyu or Wadagaba?
  I: Yes, him [Mardudjara has no equivalent of "or"].

Of course, the anthropologist soon learns quicker ways of arriving at the needed information, but the Aborigines are in no confusion regarding section name usage because the conversational context generally tells them the sex and identity of the person alluded to.

Although the kinship system is dominant in patterning behavior, reference to sections provides a useful general guide. Once a stranger's section is known, people can immediately reduce the possible kinship relationship to a finite number. However, no interaction will occur until others present have ascertained the stranger's kinship connection and then formally introduce him or her to the other local people present. This necessity to know the kinship link prior to interaction is a major reason why incoming strangers always remain at some distance from a camp. Even if known to all, they always await a signal from an older male to join the group. This is especially important when avoidance relationships are involved between certain individuals.

The diagrams following are of the Mardudjara section names and their arrangement, and are intended to help the reader better understand the working of the system of social categories. In Figure 3–1 the symbol = indicates intermarrying pairs of sections, and the double-ended arrows connect the sections of a mother and her children (siblings are *always* members of the same section).

The system works this way: taking, for example, a Garimara female as Ego, or

---

[10] Myers (1976:420) notes that at a more abstract level section and subsection systems synthesize ". . . the relationships of the egocentric kinship terminological system into a sociological model organizing *social categories.*"

Figure 3–1

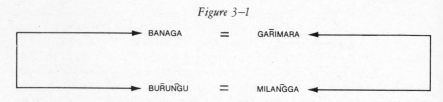

starting point, she will marry a man of Banaga section whom she calls by the term for "spouse." She cannot marry just *any* Banaga man because his section contains her real and classificatory mother's fathers, son's sons, and certain cross-cousins who are classed as "brothers," all of whom are nonmarriageable relatives (see Figure 3–3)—for this reason the section system considered alone does not regulate marriage. The sons and daughters of this Garimara woman will be in the Milangga section and will eventually marry Burungu spouses. Her daughter's children will belong to Garimara, her own section, but her son's children will be born into Banaga section, eventually to take their spouses from among the Garimara.

Continuing with the same Ego, it is possible to derive the sections to which all one's relatives belong. It can thus be seen that the section system groups together certain categories of relatives into each of the four divisions, as shown in Figure 3–3. (Remember that "Z" symbolizes "sister" and "S" is "son") Many of the relatives listed in Figure 3–3 are grouped together and are called by the same kinship term, so the system is not as complicated as it looks.

Figure 3–4 shows the three possible forms of dual organization that are inherent in

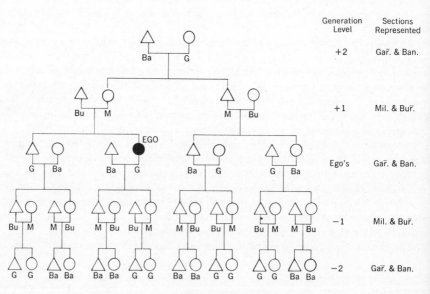

Figure 3–2.

Figure 3–3

BANAGA	GAṚIMARA
H;ZH;HB;HZ;BW; MF;FM;MBS;MBD; FZS;FZD;ZSD;ZSS; SD;SS; and so on	*Ego*;Z;B;FF;MM; FFZ;MMB;HMF;HFM; DS;DD;ZDS;ZDD; BSS;BSD; and so on
BUṚUNGU	MILANGGA
F;FZ;HM;BS;BD; DH;SW;MMBS;MMBD; FZDS;FZDD; and so on	S;D;ZS;ZD;M;MB; HF;FMBS;FMBD; FZSS;FZSD; and so on

the section system: mother–child pairs of sections, called matrimoieties (Banaga–Buṟungu and Gaṟimara–Milangga); father–child pairs, or patrimoieties (Banaga–Milangga and Gaṟimara–Buṟungu); and what are called merged alternate generation levels (Banaga–Gaṟimara and Buṟungu–Milangga), which are the intermarrying pairs of sections.

Nowhere in the Western Desert are matrimoieties found, and there are neither corporate groups nor social entities based on this kind of dual division. At large gatherings, the Mardudjara group their camps into two patrimoiety "sides," also used in the seating arrangements for certain men's rituals and seen in intergroup gift exchange. But the most important division is the merged alternate generation levels, which figure prominently in many religious activities. Both kinds of division, but particularly the latter, are useful because they separate into opposite groups some kin categories between whose members restraint or avoidance relationships exist.

Neither division is named sociocentrically; that is, has a single name that all members of society can use to label it. Individuals identify them only egocentrically, as *marndiyara* ("my patrimoiety"), *yarigira* ("other patrimoiety"), and *maṟira* ("my generational side) or *yinaṟa* ("other side"). In other words, the choice of terms used depends on which division the speaker belongs to. Figures 3–2 and 3–3 (above) indicate why this third dual division is termed "merged alternate generation levels." One's "own side" comprises not only all members of the same generation, but all grandparents and grandchildren on both sides of the family. This merging of own, +2 and −2 levels into one is paralleled in some merging of kin terminology; for example, the use of only two terms for all +2 and −2 members. From an individual's perspective, the "other side" consists of all +1 and −1 members (parents, children, MB, FZ, ZS, ZD).

As noted earlier, a person's "own side" (own generation plus +2 and −2 levels) has a majority of kin with whom relatively unrestrained interaction is possible, whereas

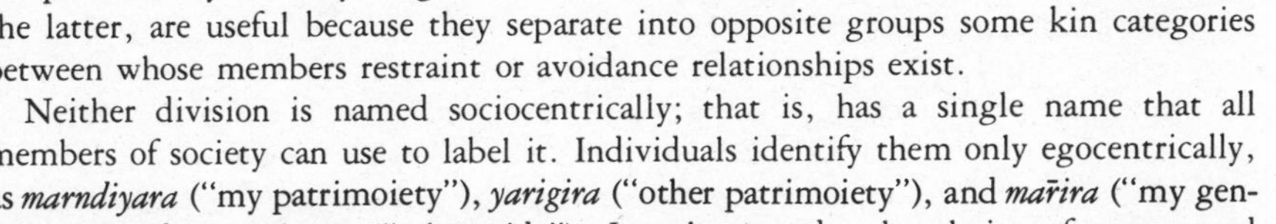

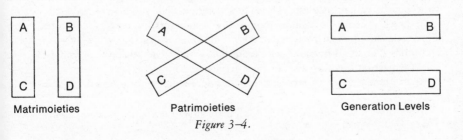

Matrimoieties   Patrimoieties   Generation Levels

Figure 3–4.

"other side" (+1 and −1 levels) is composed mainly of people with whom one interacts asymmetrically; that is, either owing or receiving respect and deference, generally in a somewhat restrained manner. In most ceremonial activities involving division into two "sides" the groups sit a short distance apart and engage in verbal jousting with each other during the proceedings in loud and light-hearted fashion. These exchanges, which engender great amusement from an appreciative assembly, can occur between members of the same or opposite sex, most often people of kin categories that are related as wife-bestower/wife-receiver. Their themes focus mostly on reciprocal obligations and marriage arrangements and involve joking offers of, or demands for, gifts of meat or vegetable foods, or for women as wives, and accusations of stinginess in the provision of wives.

These expressions of good-natured ritual opposition always enliven an already exciting and joyful atmosphere that is a universal feature of religious activities which bring together all members of the various groups in a shared experience. At times when the two sides are most actively opposed, good-humored banter is directed en masse at the opposition group, or at all "other side" members of the one sex, and comments dwell on shortcomings such as poor hunting ability, laziness, a lack of generosity, and failure to live up to promises. But interpersonal opposition, which in some rituals involves mild forms of physical aggression (for example, in rainmaking rituals, the throwing and spitting of water), is directed only at "other side" members who stand in specific kin relationship(s) to Ego, and most *milyura* "poking fun" has members of these kin categories as targets.

Another kind of dual division that is very important as an organizing principle in some religious activities, particularly male initiation and those associated with death and burial, is quite similar to the generational division. Members of the *djindjanuñgu* group are predominantly a person's "own side" group, but with the exclusion of all close consanguineal kin—"B" and "Z," some "cross-cousins," and any other kin who as members of the same or neighboring bands feel an emotional bond to that person—all of whom side with the opposing group. The *djindjanuñgu* group is active in the mechanics of actually organizing and carrying out the appropriate ritual tasks. Members of the large *garngu* group, which consists of "other side" members plus those listed above, minus Ego's "S" and "D" who join the *djindjanuñgu*, make most of the preliminary plans and are consulted on the conduct of activities, but play no active role during the proceedings because its members are too "sorry" for the initiate or deceased to do anything more than express grief through crying and wailing.[11]

Figure 3–5 summarizes for easy reference the important categorical dual divisions in Mardudjara society.

The *djindjanuñgu–garngu* division may be involved in complementary or ritually opposed behaviors and activities. Certainly there are occasions when ritual protests associated with the seizure of a youth for his initiation erupt into hostile accusations of unseemly haste and insufficient prior consultation with the close *garngu* relatives concerned, or when relatives who arrive after a death aggressively accuse the deceased's close kin of callous neglect. These confrontations, although expected and usually short-lived, usually necessitate intervention by others to prevent bloodshed. Yet among the Mardudjara there is an overriding emphasis on the values of cooperation and unity that in all but unusual circumstances transcend whatever divisions exist in the organization and execution of their activities.

Apart from the use of section terms in address and reference, the categories and

---

[11]For convenience, members of this dual division are henceforth termed "Activists" (*djindjanuñgu*) and "Mourners" (*garngu*).

Figure 3–5

Division	Type	How Defined	Mardudjara Term	Major Cultural Referents
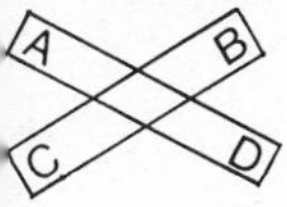	Patrimoiety (A+D;B+C)	egocentrically	mandiyara ("own"); yarigira ("other")	some camping arrangements; some rituals; some gift exchange
	Merged Alternate Generation Level (A+B;C+D)	egocentrically	mařira ("own"); yinara ("other")	many rituals
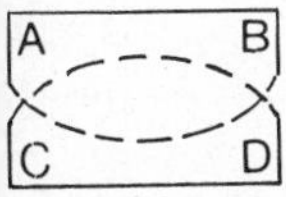	Activist–Mourner (modified A+B;C+D)	egocentric basis, but sociocentrically named	djindjanuṅgu ("Activist"); garngu ("Mourner")	initiation rituals; activities and rituals following a death

divisions just discussed have little relevance to the mundane hunting and gathering activities of the Mardudjara band. At this level kinship provides the medium of articulation for much of the interaction that occurs. But whenever larger gatherings occur, and when any kind of ritual performance is envisioned, social category and dual group membership inevitably become relevant to some of the resulting activity. It is clear that both kin and category idioms, as two different but interrelated usages, are important because, as Maddock (1972:94) notes, each ". . . enables Aborigines to make statements to which exact expression cannot be given in the other." This is undoubtedly true, but it cannot alone resolve adequately the puzzling question of why the Aborigines have evolved such a unique and complex categorical system in imposing order on their world. Munn (1973) points insightfully to a significant transformational aspect of the categories, which are of a higher level of sociocultural order than the egocentrically based system of kin reckoning: sections and subsections provide a generalized sociocentric grid onto which kin relationships are projected and thus locked into the overall social structure.

What does the imposition of a seemingly unwarranted level of complexity mean at the level of the individual who must live with all this? As noted above, the burden, if one exists, is not felt by the Aborigines, who see sections as a useful idiom and labeling device as well as an essential preliminary guide in establishing relationships with strangers. Burridge (1973) sees the Aborigines' elaboration of different sets of rules and conventions as connected to two major themes in their social organization. First, these many classificatory schemes crosscut one another so thoroughly that:

> No category which groups people together for particular purposes contains persons exclusively of that group and no other; and each category groups together those who, in other situations, will be differently grouped. Rivalry is balanced by cooperation, opposition by complementarity. There is no group of persons whose relations with the features of the natural environment are precisely the same, each category contains those whose particular relationships with, and responsibilities for, particular features of the environment are different (p. 133).

Secondly, these schemes operate to separate out and individualize people rather than the natural world. Through them, the Aborigines ensure that each individual emerges as unique in relation to the sum of the many different categorizations. But this uniqueness, what Burridge calls the "unitive" function of these interrelated modes of classification, is embedded within a broader cultural framework that stresses cooperation and unity. As Burridge summarizes it:

. . . a sufficient number of modes of classification on the one hand stimulates—even demands and demonstrates—perceptions of a complete integration of the self with otherness, and on the other hand points to the individual as unique and separate from all else. At all levels of Aboriginal organization categories of sameness, aggregation and cooperation are accompanied by others, which, in evoking situations of rivalry and opposition, revealed uniqueness in being (pp. 133–134).

The foregoing discussion of the ritual functioning of merged alternate general level groupings among the Mardudjara illustrates the kind of tension that exists between these individualizing versus unifying pressures that are simultaneously exerted in the desert culture. This dichotomy is exemplified in the religious life (Chapter 5), and particularly in the activities and rituals that surround male initiation, which is described in some detail in the following chapter.

4 / Life cycle and male initiation

Like many other peoples, the Mardudjara have myths that explain the beginnings of human mortality, following an earlier state wherein everyone lived forever. Here is one such myth:

A Dreamtime man died . . . no one knows why . . . and Wirlara the Moon-man, who was traveling with his large pack of dingoes, found the body and decided to try to save the man. He dragged him along by the hand but the body was rotting and pieces of it began dropping off, whereupon the Moon-man, being a clever magician, would stick them back on again. Some people saw him doing this and burst into laughter, ridiculing him for dragging a smelly corpse around. He was very angered by this, and embarrassed, so he scattered the pieces of the body far and wide, saying to the people, "From now on you will die and stay forever dead." Had these people not ridiculed the Moon-man in the Dreamtime, human beings would never have to die.[1]

However, this kind of death is physical only. Just as the creative beings of the Dreamtime grew tired and eventually died, yet live on in spiritual form, so does every Aborigine live on after bodily death. Life is cyclical in that it begins and ends with a spirit which is indestructible because it is of the same essence as the Dreamtime powers. The Mardudjara have no beliefs in reincarnation; the spirit returns to the place from which it originally came and lives on forever there with other spirits of the dead.

SPIRITUAL PREEXISTENCE

The Mardudjara have no one word for *power* or *life essence,* yet it is clear from their conceptions of the Dreamtime that all creative beings are limitless reservoirs of power, which is immanent in everything they have touched, possessed, transformed, or have themselves been transformed into. Just as the Dreamtime beings left at certain sites spirit reservoirs of particular plant and animal species, they created along their routes similar homes for *djidjigargaly* ("spirit-children") in various locations, and left them behind in small numbers wherever they traveled.

Despite individual variations in beliefs, the Mardudjara are generally agreed that spirit-children are very small and humanlike except for webbed feet and a very hairy body, and very clever and dangerous to anyone trespassing close to their favorite haunts (usually caves, rocky hills, large sand dunes, and big trees). A stranger who comes too close to the home of a spirit-child may be sorcerized, and women who trespass may become instantly pregnant. The spirit-children, who wander far in search of

[1] No doubt because of its regular cycle of "death" and "rebirth," the moon is frequently associated with death in Western Desert culture (see R. Berndt 1974).

nectar from flowers and dew for their sustenance, take on the form of a particular animal, plant, or mineral before first encountering their human mother; this manifestation is later identified as the baby's *djarin* or *nyuga* ("conception totem"). The spirit-child magically enters its mother through her stomach, mouth, or loins or under the nail of her thumb or big toe, and once inside is usually quite protective of her. Sometimes, however, it causes her to behave in an uncharacteristic and excessive way. Because the spirit-child is generally thought to have its own food and to be self-sustaining in the womb, the mother is in a sense a passive host who plays no role whatsoever in its prenatal nurture (see Montagu 1974).

Although in some cases a woman's husband plays a part in the spirit-child's finding of its mother, either by seeing its approach in a dream or by hunting and catching it in animal form, the intercession of the husband is not essential because the spirit-child is so clever that it locates its mother easily. Occasionally, though, it chooses not to enter its "proper" mother, but goes into the womb of one of her "sisters" instead. The example that follows illustrates the independence of action of the spirit-child.

A middle-aged Mardudjara woman, whose only child, a son, is now an adult, periodically cares for a small girl, the physiological daughter of a younger "sister" who agrees that the child is indeed the older woman's "own." In spirit-child form the girl was a kangaroo, hunted down and clubbed to death by the older woman's husband. When buried in hot ashes, the animal would not cook through properly, and when the younger "sister" ate some of the meat she later vomited—both signs that it was probably a spirit-child in kangaroo form. When the baby was born, she carried marks on her head and chest which "proved" her to be the older couple's child, who, for reasons known only to the spirit-child, had been born from the wrong mother.

In discussing the topic of maternity and paternity, the Mardudjara talk only in terms of spiritual powers, never physiology.[2] When questioned, they deny the relevance of semen or intercourse to procreation. A child's "real" father is the husband of its mother. Given the prominence of the social father role in everyday life, and the markedly spiritual Mardudjara perception of cosmic order and its creative and life-ordering processes, the idea of the male as responsible for the creation of life, or even as a catalyst, is contradictory and superfluous. Spiritual explanations are paramount and fundamental; belief in spirit-children gives every person a life-sustaining and virtually direct link to the great powers of the Dreamtime.

In identifying conception totems, people view any unusual characteristic or behavior of objects in the natural world as suggestive of the presence of spirit-children. Here are three typical examples:

Marnagal, a young man; ancestral totem, Two Men; conception totem, wallaby.[3] His father Djadurda was hunting one day when a wallaby suddenly appeared ("from nowhere") and instead of fleeing, hopped toward him, and "allowed itself" to be easily speared. When a short time after his wife Minu realized she was pregnant, he knew that the wallaby was really a spirit-child, and when Marnagal was born, on his shoulder was the mark of his father's spear. Djadurda's EB Gagubanya told him that Two Men had been hunting at that place in the Dreamtime and one had thrown a club at a kangaroo and lost it. It later became a spirit-child which turned into the wallaby that entered Marnagal's mother after Djadurda had killed it.

---

[2] This example of the autonomy of the spirit-child has important implications for the long debate that has raged about whether Australian Aborigines are ignorant of, or deny, physiological paternity and maternity. This is discussed in Tonkinson (1977c), and other examples of "wrong" mothers are given.

Mulila, a little girl; ancestral totem, Minyiburu women; conception totem, yam. Her mother Nibala was digging for yams with several other women of the same band near a Dreamtime campsite of the Minyiburu. She found a huge tuber of unusual shape, and when roasted, it would not cook through. She vomited after eating it, and later found out that she was pregnant. When Mulila was born, her left leg bore the mark of her mother's digging stick where it entered the tuber.

Rabudji, a man in his sixties; ancestral totem, Ngayunangalgu; conception totem, snake. A Ngayunangalgu Dreamtime being left a beard-hair in the bed of Savory Creek (Map 2) where a large mob of them were camped. The beard-hair became a snake, which Rabudji's mother speared with her digging stick. She vomited after eating some of it, and later realized that it was really a spirit-child, not an ordinary snake. [The carved wooden figure shown in Figure 2.1 was carved by Rabudji to show me what a Ngayunangalgu cannibal-being looks like. His crayon drawing of the Lake Disappointment area and associated mythology, shown in Figure 5.2, includes himself in beard-hair-become-snake form]

When asked to identify their conception totem, Mardudjara often point to a birthmark or blemish in telling the story of how they found their parents. Although everyone has a conception totem and is frequently named after it, the Mardudjara do not therefore feel a special bond with the species or object that was chosen by the spirit-child in finding its parents, and if it is an edible food, few have qualms about eating it. The medium itself seems less important than the message of a personalized link between each individual and a spirit-child that was left behind by some Dreamtime being. This message also explains why people who share the same conception totem feel no emotional or spiritual oneness on this basis, in contrast to Aborigines in areas of Australia that have totemic clans, where shared descent is claimed from a common ancestor or ancestress and is symbolized in terms of spiritual sameness or "shared flesh," and the clan totem is not eaten by clan members (Elkin 1954).[4]

BIRTH

There are no food tabus associated with pregnancy, for either the Mardudjara woman or her husband. When a woman feels that she is about to give birth, she removes herself to a secluded spot away from camp and is attended by one or two "own side" female relatives; for example, "Z," "grandmother," who act as midwives and massage her if labor is prolonged. She crouches over a small depression in soft sand, perhaps near a tree whose trunk she can use to bear down on. The midwives sever the umbilical cord with a sharp stone or their teeth, cover the afterbirth, and clean off the baby with sand or ashes. Some of the cord may be made into a necklet which is worn by the baby as protection against sickness. The mother and baby remain in seclusion for four or five days, warmed by a constantly burning fire.

If the baby is deformed or otherwise visibly abnormal, if it comes too soon after an older sibling (that is, if the latter is still too small to walk long distances without being carried), or if the mother is in a weakened condition, the baby may be killed at

[3] I have termed this *ancestral,* not *cult* totemism because among the Mardudjara who share the same substance—that is, were left by the same being(s)—there are no cult lodges. They do not form corporate groups on this basis or carry out exclusive and secret rituals centering on the exploits of the shared totem (see Tonkinson 1974; Elkin 1954).

[4] Nor does the conception site itself assume great importance by entitling an individual to active membership in a "conception clan," as occurs among the Aranda (Spencer and Gillen 1899; Strehlow 1965).

birth by smothering it in the sand. Women say that infanticide is only practiced when considered necessary, is uncommon, and must be done at the moment of birth lest the mother see the child's face or hear its cries and thus become so overwhelmed by compassion that she will not allow its death. It is impossible to assess the incidence of infanticide among the desert people with any accuracy, but given the tremendous attachment felt between parents and their children, it must be assumed that it is resorted to only when absolutely necessary.[5]

It is customary for "grandmothers" of the baby to come and scold it, saying, "Bad! Bad!," probably to dissuade malevolent spirit-beings from taking an interest in it. It will not be given a name until quite some time after its birth; grandparents or other relatives usually name it. The most common criteria for naming are place of birth or conception totem; whichever is chosen, the name obviously reinforces the link that is implied. During the postnatal seclusion period, the father and all other close consanguineal relatives keep their distance. The married couple resume sexual intercourse a month or two later. Birth is not celebrated ritually, and there is no elaboration of either postpartum tabus or magical measures to protect the newborn from harm.

CHILDHOOD

The Mardudjara use many labels, based on physiological maturation stages, to cover the childhood phase of life; for example, there is a separate term for newborn, unable to sit up, able to crawl, walking but only just, walking properly, no longer breast-fed, no longer carried. Then follows a long period known simply as *ñgulyi* ("child"), until for girls their breasts begin to swell and they are termed *durndurn* and are ready for marriage. These labels, like kin and section terms, are frequently used in address and reference as substitutes for personal names.

Within a few days of birth, the infant becomes the center of attention in the camp, surrounded almost continuously by siblings and older relatives who shower it with affection. Adults show extreme indulgence toward children of all ages, and a crying child can be sure of a quick response from its mother and others nearby, who pacify it by acceding to its demands. Parents who allow their small children to cry for long periods risk criticism from others for not looking after them properly. Small children are breast-fed on demand, which usually pacifies them. They continue to suckle for several years, even after the birth of a younger sibling or when the mother is no longer producing milk. Most children wean themselves eventually, since mothers see no point in deliberately or traumatically ending the practice.

Given the nature of their shifting outdoor life, it is not surprising that toilet training of small children is casual. Small children are encouraged, and occasionally scolded, to leave the immediate vicinity of the camp to defecate, and later to cover their feces. The onus for this and other early training lies with the mother and other adult females of the same band, some of whom will also suckle the child if it so desires. In toilet training, older siblings and other children of the group sometimes contribute by lighthearted scolding or ridicule, but they are careful not to offend the little one too much, lest it begin screaming.

Temper tantrums are tolerated with great patience and resignation by adults—and

[5] Individuals who are, or who become, partly crippled, blind, or senile or who are later found to be deaf-mute or mentally deficient, are in no way ostracized or shunned, and only unmanageable, homicidally deranged persons would be put to death, according to the Mardudjara, who add that no such maniacs have ever existed among them.

less so by older siblings. The offended child is rarely disciplined unless it is jealously threatening violence against a younger sibling or one of its parents at a time when they feel unwell. If the adult loses patience, the child is slapped—a self-defeating act, though, because the child then continues the tantrum with renewed vigor. Screaming, writhing on the ground, hurling whatever it can lay hands on at the offending adult, the child, if able to talk, also lacerates the alleged oppressor with foul language, drawn from a large supply of obscenities that children master very early in their speaking careers. It amuses other members of society, victims included, to hear children who barely know which is what using epithets such as, "Crooked penis!," "Stinking vagina!," "Hairy anus!," and so on *ad nauseum*. In pain or anger, they also blaspheme, screaming the names of sacred objects, without ever knowing what they are; in fact, everyone uses such words in exclamation, but men never comment on the practice.

The usual adult reaction to temper tantrums is to cover the face and other vital parts as best one can while the assault continues, and laughingly protest until the child gets what it wants, or forgets and goes away. Mardudjara society is child-centered in the sense that children almost always get their way, except when they want to accompany their father (or, less often, their mother when she is similarly involved) when he is going away to discuss or perform ritual with other adult males of the group, or when the child wants to go in a direction that would lead it anywhere near "men's country."[6]

Minma, with son Djambidjin watching, shapes a new spearthrower with his metal ax. (Photo © Film Australia from the film series People of the Australian Western Desert.)

[6] This term is used here to denote any site or locality which, through mythological significance, ritual use, or the presence of sacred objects is considered sacred and dangerous to all but

Djambidjin launches his toy spear by hand; he holds a toy thrower in his other hand.

Children are free to do very much as they like most of the time, and are given very few concrete directives or instructions from any of their elders. Elderly people, particularly those who are too old or infirm to participate actively in daily hunting and gathering activities, spend much of their time in the camp as guardians and entertainers of the small children. As tellers of stories and singers of songs, and as "grandparents," they normally enjoy a really affectionate and unrestrained relationship with the children. From these elders children learn much of the lore of their people, but a great deal is also learned from their observation and emulation of peers and older members of the small community that constitutes their social universe for the greater part of the year.

The children play—and sometimes fight—at many different kinds of games, few of which are competitive, and their few toys are simple and easily gleaned from the local environment. Much of their play emulates aspects of the lives of adults: boys or their older male relatives make toy spears, shields, clubs, and bark boomerangs with which they "hunt" and "fight," whereas girls prefer to play *milbindi,* in which they draw lines in the sand to represent hearth groups and make up stories about family life and people's various exploits. For the first half-dozen or so years of their lives, the children usually play in mixed-sex groups and their games sometimes include "making camp" and "mothers and fathers." This at times includes attempts at sexual intercourse and

fully initiated men and is therefore tabu to all others. Most areas so designated owe their sacredness to Dreamtime events and are therefore permanently tabu; some, however, may be only temporary, and once sacred objects are removed, they revert to open areas and the sticks, stones (stuck into tree forks), and broken branches which indicated their boundaries are removed.

the staging of adultery, elopement, and so on. This amuses adults, who turn a blind eye to such erotic play, although an older relative may mildly scold them if the couple concerned stands in an "incestuous" relationship, as a reminder about the correct behaviors they will have to observe as adulthood approaches.

The children learn about sexual intercourse when they are quite young and still sleep in the same camp as their parents, and since it is not a forbidden topic of conversation, by hearing about it. The sex act itself, although ideally a private concern, is as normal an activity as any others in daily life and is treated as such by everyone. However, it is never separate from concerns about kin relationships, and this is the arena where for adults considerations of morality are always involved. The desire of married couples for privacy or lack of interruption in their conjugal sex life is no doubt a factor in the separation of band families into spaced camps. It may also influence growing children in their decision to sleep somewhere else.

Any time from about the age of 7 or 8 onward, boys go to join their peers and older unmarried males in the *giridji* ("bachelor") camp and girls begin sleeping at the camp of grandparents or other old female relatives. This is about the time that the sexual dichotomy of play groups becomes more pronounced. Boys are increasingly likely to go off in their own groups, playing and food-getting away from the women and younger children. They are not yet old enough to go out with the men, but their growing realization of the separateness of men's and women's lives is no doubt a factor influencing them to disengage themselves somewhat from the females and from identification with the activities of women. By now they have learned the skills of gathering and of tracking and hunting small animals and lizards, and much of the time they use these skills to obtain food for snacks. In this respect there is an important difference between the older boys and girls; boys are not expected to contribute to the food consumed by the family as a group, whereas girls are increasingly regarded as providers. For females, the transition from their family of orientation into an early marriage is one of essential continuity in daily activities. A girl's change of status to wife and then mother goes largely unheralded, in marked contrast to a boy's long path to full social adulthood.[7]

Sometime around the age of 11 or 12, the fortunes of boys and girls begin to take a markedly divergent course. A girl will soon be given to her husband. Considering her tender age and attachment to her natal group, her husband might decide to remain with his in-laws for some time after being given his new wife, especially if he is a young man and she is his first wife. This arrangement allows her to adjust to the status of wife in the security of her own people and territory, at the same time as the husband is discharging important obligations to her parents by hunting meat for them and forging close ties to his brothers-in-law. Whereas the girl will ultimately move to the band of her husband, her brothers remain in their father's group until they are seized as a preliminary to circumcision. For them, marriage will not be possible until 10 to 15 years after the beginning of their adolescence, when their initiation into full manhood is completed.

MALE INITIATION

Initiation for males involves a vital transition from the status of child, who undergoes symbolic death and transformation into a man. This is accomplished largely through the youth acting passively as the recipient and not the initiator of activities

[7] Among the southern neighbors of the Mardudjara, girls undergo a hymen-cutting operation, in a ritual called by the same term as male subincision, but this is not practiced by the Mardudjara.

that will accomplish the transition. What is required of the initiate is unquestioning acceptance, silent endurance of physical pain, and a strong commitment to obey his elders and guard the secrets of the men, and to hunt meat for the elders in exchange for the knowledge he is gaining.

Growing boys have mixed feelings about their coming initiation. They are frightened of the ordeals that undoubtedly lie ahead, yet others ahead of them have survived; so when their time approaches, they become anxious to be inducted into the secret world of the men, to attain adulthood, and eventually to earn the right to marry. Although the Aborigines keep no track of actual ages, they decide when a boy is ready by his physiological maturation. Precocious behavior or troublemaking may precipitate one of two decisions: a seizure and induction ahead of the planned time, to put a stop to his nonsense, or a deliberate delay of a year or two, leaving him to suffer the embarrassment of seeing his peers begin the road to manhood while he is left as *murdilya* ("uncircumcised boy"). Usually several boys are operated on at the same big meeting, so there is often an age difference of two or three years among them. The shared experience of being initiated in the same year sets up among the youths a ritual relationship, *yarlburu,* akin to an age-mate status; this bond of lifelong friendship and mutual support provides each youth with a network of reliable friends in several different territories.

Tooth Evulsion   This rite, called *yiraburda* ("tooth-hit"), is not practiced by the Mardudjara but is common among their southern neighbors, so some Mardudjara boys have it performed on them when their bands come into contact with southerners. They are aged between 10 and 12 when they are seized without warning and taken into the bush away from camp. There, to the accompaniment of songs concerning Marlu and Walbadju, two Dreamtime Kangaroo-men who first performed the rite on each other, several boys have a front incisor knocked out with stones used as hammers and sharpened sticks as chisels.

Nose Piercing   For most Mardudjara boys, their first initiation rite is *nyiirnga,* the piercing of the nasal septum, performed when they are young adolescents, called *mulyadjudu* ("nose-closed"). The ritual is timed so that there are distantly related people of the boy's "own side" generation level grouping available to perform it; there is a ritual division of labor between Activists and Mourners (see Figure 3–5, p. 59, for easy reference to these dual divisions).

Budjaga is about fourteen, tall for his age, with sandy-colored straight hair, a big smile, and several small cicatrices on his shoulders, put there by his "B" and friend Dabuni. His potbelly is gone, and he has the beginnings of a moustache. He is camped at Banrīgur rockhole (in the McKay Ranges, west of Lake Disappointment) with about forty people, currently traveling in three bands. He and four or five boys are at the rockhole, killing finches with stones and eating them, so he has not noticed that a group of his relatives (Mourners) have just placed a quantity of vegetable food (fresh quandong fruits, bush tomatoes, and seedcakes) on the ground not far from his family's camp. With a high-pitched, attention-getting cry followed by hand signs, the boys are called back to camp. Budjaga barely has a chance to notice the food before he is seized by two distantly related men, a "WB" Wibudjun and "grandfather" Libana. The Mourners, who sit by the food, bow their heads and wail softly as Budjaga is brought over and surrounded by members of the Activist group. The younger children have stopped playing and are watching from what they judge to be a safe distance.

Budjaga is held and comforted by Libana and another "grandfather" while Wibudjun pushes a sharpened spear point into his septum and another "WB" Giya braces a *mulyayidi* ("nose-bone") against the other side of his septum. The bone is from an eaglehawk's wing, chosen because Warlawuru, the Eaglehawk-man, is the

Dreamtime creator of this rite. Budjaga winces in obvious pain but makes no sound and holds still as the spear point is twirled to enlarge the hole and Giya pushes the nose-bone through. His "grandfathers" loudly announce to the Mourners that it is all over and there is no bleeding; still wailing, they return to their camps. Budjaga and the Activists then sit down and eat the feast. His "grandfather" Libana feeds him, because he is not permitted to talk or feed himself until some days later, after some Activist relatives have taken him hunting. They tell him to move the bone frequently so as to keep the hole open. Later he will not wear the nose-bone constantly, but will sometimes use the hole as a convenient place to carry a spare hook for his spearthrower, in case the other breaks or is lost (see Gould 1969).

Circumcision   Despite the fact that it occurs early in the long road to manhood, circumcision is the initiation stage surrounded by the greatest elaboration of activities, both public and secret-sacred. Because it ultimately concerns so many people and so much organization, this stage entails considerable planning and discussion on the part of a boy's male relatives, headed by his real and classificatory elder brothers, who must seek the permission of his father and other close patrikin before any action can be taken. A division into Activist and Mourner groups pervades all the activities, and both groups are indispensable to its proper performance. But the major burden of the care, comforting, and instruction of the youth lies with the smaller Activist group. His "grandfathers," in particular, stay close by at all times and are a great source of reassurance. His "EB" are members of the Activist group but are described as "a little bit *garngu*" so on certain occasions they side with the Mourners. Two other named groups are important: the *djilganggadja* ("travelers"), the Activist men who accompany the youth on his precircumcision travels after he had been seized, and the *manggalyi*, the distantly related "mother's brothers" and "wife's brothers" who are selected to perform the actual operation; of these, one of the two "MB" will bestow a wife upon the young novice.

Since this initiation stage embraces a time period of several months and a host of different activities, this account provides only highlights of the sequence of major events. No two sequences are ever exactly the same because particular circumstances favor the inclusion or deletion of minor details, and even when two or more youths are cut at the same meeting, there must be changes in the personnel involved since for each individual the membership of the two major groupings differs—not only because the groups are egocentrically based, but also because in each case some people decide for themselves whether their feelings for the novice are such that they must side with the *garngu* and play the more passive Mourner role.

(a) *Seizure.* From the moment he is seized until his circumcision, a novice is termed *marlurlu* (it was Marlu, the kangaroo-man, who first took a novice on a long precircumcision Dreamtime trip through the Western Desert). From this time until six to eight weeks after the operation, when he returns to the life of the band after seclusion, he will not speak, and no one will utter his name, exactly as if he were dead. This accords with the idea of circumcision as a symbolic preenactment of death; there are many parallels between the two kinds of transition, and the terminology surrounding this stage reflects them—for example, after circumcision, the novice is termed *bugurdi* (*bugu* = "dead"), and the act of return is called *yudirini* ("being born").

Waga, aged about sixteen, is a thick-set youth of quiet disposition. His band has met up with two others, one of which is Mandjildjara like his own, the other Warnman, at a soak called Nyanggabudadjara in limestone country (c. 22.5°S., 124°E.) northeast of Lake Disappointment. It is mid-afternoon and he is relaxing after a long but successful lizard hunt with his father. He is taken completely by surprise as two distantly related Warnman Activists approach quietly and grab him. One, Laldjan, his "S," places a thick hairbelt around his waist and thus becomes his *warluṅgga,* a kinlike ritual term that connotes a subsequent avoidance relationship between the pair. On seeing this, Mourners of both sexes burst into loud and prolonged wailing, and Waga's mother and several other women seize digging sticks and stones and gash their scalps as Activist women rush to restrain them.

Waga is taken from camp by a group of dancing Activists to a site about 400 yards downwind, safely out of earshot of camp. After dusk, they are joined by the Mourner men, for an all-night session of singing and dancing of the Nyurnguny ritual.[8] The Activists and Mourners sit in two circles, their faces lit eerily by small fires. They alternate slow sonorous rhythms with very rapid, exciting bursts of singing when the vigorous banging of wooden sticks on the ground sends up billowing clouds of choking red dust. The songs they sing highlight some of kangaroo's exploits with other Dreamtime beings. Waga lies just outside the Activist circle, head down, as Minudji, a "grandfather" lightly covers his ears during the singing, and spreads his fingers across the youth's eyes during dances, so that the dangerous powers of these secret-sacred sights and sounds will be lessened.

Nothing is explained to him, but the Activist men keep telling him that this is *yurlubidi,* "the Law," the truth, the real thing, what life is really all about, something powerful and dangerous, never to be divulged to the uninitiated. Whenever one of the short dances is performed, the men identify the ancestral being depicted. Waga, exhilarated but tired from the nervous tension, is prodded to keep him awake several times when he appears to doze. Just before dawn, the Mourner men leave the rest and return to camp to assemble the women. Waga is told to stand, and, led by the arm by one of his "grandfathers," he is taken back to camp surrounded by the dancing Activists. In the camp, the Mourner men and women lie facing away from Waga, wailing softly and watched by the Activist women who sit nearby, silent. Two strongly built Activist men seize Waga by his head and feet and tell him to hold himself rigid as they lay him at right angles across the backs of the Mourner men and the sides of the Mourner women, then the entire assembly wails as he is led away a short distance. Later, when the four or five Activist men who will accompnay him are ready, Djanu, an old "spouse," and Malyudina, an old "grandmother," walk over and present Waga with a firestick and a club. In kind but firm tones, they tell him to bring back many people from afar and say, "Don't you become homesick for your family or worry about them; they will be waiting when you come back." Waga's guardians anoint themselves and him with red ochre and fat, put on hair-string forehand and arm bands and thick hair-belts, so that they will be readily identified as *djilgaṅggadja* ("travelers").

(b) *The Trip.* The purpose of the trip is twofold: to contact as many distant groups as possible and issue them formal invitations, symbolized by bull-roarers and carved "message" sticks whose power is such that it impels people into acceptance;[9] and secondly, to acquaint the novice with the totemic geography of distant, hitherto unknown territories through instruction and the performance of rituals with bands encountered there.

Whenever the travelers see smokes, they send one or two messengers ahead to make contact and alert the band of the coming of the *marlurlu.* Waga is kept at a distance until the locals have had time to alert other nearby bands, gather at the one place, and ensure that the Mourners in the local bands have had time to amass some food for the

---

[8] Nyurnguny, the most widespread Western Desert ritual, is çlosely associated with both circumcision and subincision. Since it follows the path of Kangaroo and associated Dreamtime beings through thousands of miles of the desert, it comprises literally several hundred songs, so in one session only a segment of the total would be sung.

[9] Other messengers go in small groups to contact groups elsewhere in the area. They carry with them a special hair-belt, *gadjabuga,* which is a symbolic subsitute for the novice himself.

travelers. After the locals have assembled, the travelers chant and dance into the area around the wailing Mourners, then place Waga on the latter's backs and sides. The same night, after the travelers have been fed, all the men take Waga to a suitable spot for a long session of dancing and singing. The travelers may spend several days with the local people, performing the Kangaroo and other rituals day and night during their visit.

The travelers continue, heading southwest then south past Lake Disappointment until they locate the Giyadjara bands from which Waga's *mañggalyi* "operators" will be drawn. These Giyadjara people and other bands encountered during the return journey join the travelers and swell their ranks as they head north through Gardudjara country en route to Giridji rockhole (six or eight days' travel east of Nyañggabudad-jara) in his father's estate, where the big meeting is to be held. Messengers go ahead from the approaching bands to give the bands in the Giridji area time to assemble and make the necessary preparations, which include preparation of the *warluburgu* ("circumcision ground") by Activist men.

(c) *The Arrival and Circumcision Preliminaries.* The incoming group makes camp at Djunyba, a soak a short distance from Giridji, where it will await the arrival of groups from other areas, come to attend the big meeting. When smokes have ceased to appear on the horizon, and it is assumed that no more groups will be arriving, preparations for the actual welcome begin among both the local groups and the visitors. Seedcakes are sent to the visitors, who eat a meal about mid-afternoon before they begin putting on their body decorations.

Mourner women of both visitor and local groups put on red ochre, and Activist females of both groups don white ochre. All local men decorate with a charcoal and white Kangaroo design, and all visitors in this case have chosen a Nyanayi design (see Chapter 5). All men supplement the body design with arm, neck, and forehead bands of hair-twine or possum fur, feather-bundle headdresses, whittled wood "pompoms" stuck in their forehead bands, and pearlshell neck and pubic pendants. They carry boomerangs painted with white ochre stripes. The children are decorated by older siblings and their mothers with white ochre patterns, and they and the women carry leaf-bundles in their hands, which they shake in time with their stamping dance steps. Both groups, each hidden from the other by a stand of mulga thicket, practice their massed dances in readiness for the ceremonial welcome.

Figure 4–1 shows how the local people arrange themselves in readiness for the entry of the visitors. Led by the arm by two Activist young boys, Waga is completely surrounded by the dancing, chanting crowd of over a hundred men, women, and children as they approach the assembly at Giridji. In front of the visitors are the Activist men, who feint with their boomerangs as they approach the line of crouching local Activist men who are ready to "defend" their people against the "invaders." After completing a noisy circuit around the locals, the visitor Mourners lie on the shrubbery bed and join the local Mourners in wailing while the Activists and Waga continue to circle. Two "WB" visitors seize him and place him crosswise on top of the local Mourner men and women, and then on the visiting Mourners; then they seat him close to and facing each of the local and visitor Activists. This done, two Activists lead him to a spot close to the circumcision ground, well away from the camping area, and wait with him there. Meanwhile, both groups complete their welcome dances and spend the next two hours before dusk settling disputes so that the ritual activities can be carried through in an atmosphere of peace and goodwill, a condition that is essential to their success.

Before the women and children arrive at the ground, a group of visitor Activist men decide to perform the tossing rite on Waga. They toss him high into the air, while one of them hits him with two long leafy branches. They do this in emula-

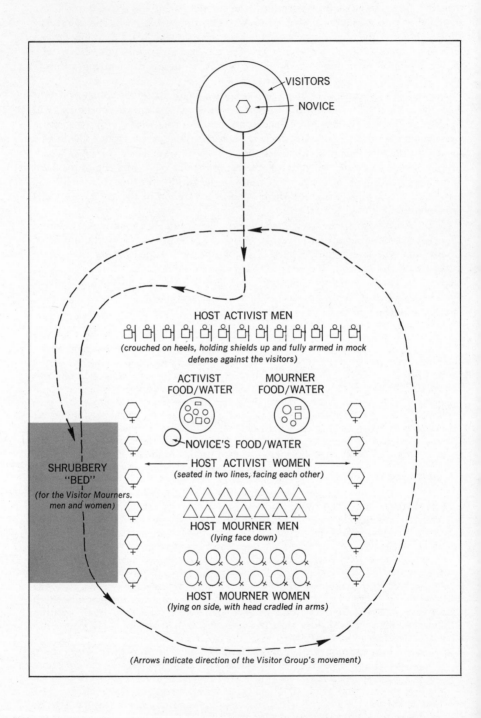

Figure 4–1. The arrival of the novice.

tion of Kangaroo, who tossed his Dreamtime *marlurlu* high into the sky to release his spirit and make his penis "light" so that it would not bleed or cause great pain during the subsequent cutting. With his spirit thus released, Waga will not die during the operation.

Everyone assembles close to the ground (a rectangle measuring some thirty by twenty yards), which has a large shrubbery windbreak at one end. Local Mourner men enter it first, light a large fire, then dance in rapid sidesteps up and down before they sit in a circle near the windbreak end. This activity is repeated by the following local Activist males, who then sit a short distance away in a separate circle. The women of both groups and "sides" enter and sit inside the windbreak; the visitor females are preceded by their Mourner males who enter and dance before joining their local counterparts. The visitor Activists are the last to enter and dance, then they and the local Activist men commence singing some Kangaroo ritual songs that can safely be heard by women and children, who are all by this stage present at the ground. Some of the Activist women stand and dance *nyambi*, a distinctive shuffling step, done with feet together, that leaves a double furrowed track as they propel themselves along with arms swinging in time with the singing and beating of sticks on the ground by the men. Meanwhile, the Mourners sit quietly, except for some gentle sobbing and wailing. Then, after quietly informing the local Mourner men that they have chosen suitable operators, and having received the Mourners' permission to proceed, four Activist males walk across and suddenly seize four *maŕggalyi* ("operators") from the ranks of the visitors: two "MB" will do the actual cutting, and two "WB" will assist.

Waga is now led onto the ground and told to lie down close to the circle of singing Activist men. The operators line up on one side of a small fire, and the local female Mourners file past the other side to identify them before they return to camp, followed by the rest of the women and children, who are loudly ordered from the ground by the Activist men. Then the local Mourner men view the operators and return to camp, because they are too "sorry" to remain for what follows. By now it is early evening; the wind has dropped and an almost full moon is helping light the scene.

(d) *The Operation.* Waga is led to the center of the ground by his visitor Activist "grandfathers," one of whom lights the main fire while the remaining Mourner men lie down facing away from the ground. Some of the Activists sit nearby, softly singing. Two visitor Activists leap to their feet and do a rapid dance up and down the ground, holding shields. They then crouch over the weapons near the big fire, to be joined by six more local and visitor Activists, who crawl beneath them from both sides and raise them on their backs to form a human platform for the operation. One of the assistants carries Waga and lays him on his back on the table, then sits on his chest, facing his penis and the large fire. He pulls up the foreskin and twists it, being careful to keep the head of Waga's penis under the thumb of his other hand. The other "WB" operator supports his head and gives him a boomerang to bite on during the cutting. Several "grandfathers" (both "MF" and "FF") circle the table to watch the cutting and comfort Waga, while the rest of the Activists quietly sing, and the Mourners softly wail.

The two "MB," each with his own newly sharpened and magically prepared stone knife, take turns at cutting the foreskin. Waga neither utters a sound nor struggles in any way, but his teeth have sunk into the hard mulga of the boomerang; he lies inert, as if self-anesthetized, betraying his suffering with an occasional grimace. Beneath him, the men forming the table joke with one another, complain of the discomfort and Waga's weight, and urge the operators to hurry up and get the job over with, while the "grandfathers" hover and keep up a chorus of reassurances, for the benefit of Waga and the Mourners, saying that the operators have almost finished.

Once the foreskin is finally severed, the "MB" who finishes the cutting pushes what remains down to reveal the head of Waga's penis. Then the operators retire to a small fire that has been set for them, and the "grandfathers" lead Waga to a small fire they have lit close to the two circles of men. He is told to kneel on a shield over the smoke, with an "EB" supporting him on each side. The "grandfathers" inspect his penis and report to the rest of the men present that the operation was a good one and that there is little bleeding. The Mourners sit up and view Waga from a distance, and the Activists recommence singing. The operators collect several hair-belts and weapons that they had left near the ground earlier, and then file past him.

Waga's supporting "EB" raises his arm in a gesture of acceptance of these gifts, and both they and the operators make the distinctive *mariggalyi* noise (a sort of whistling noise always made by two people so related; this identifies their relationship to others present). The "MB" holding the foreskin makes to present it to the boy, but one of the "EB" places his hand over Waga's and takes it in such a way that Waga does not see it. The operators leave the ground, are each given a lighted firestick by the Activists, then reenter the ground and dance in front of the main fire to show themselves for the last time before leaving. A short distance from the ground, they throw the firesticks high into the air and make a high-pitched "baubaubau" sound, thus alerting all those back in the camping areas that their work is done; this signals an outbreak of loud wailing by all those in the camping area. The operators retire to sleep a short distance apart from the rest of the camps.

Waga sits over the smoke fire, dazed and in pain, but silent. One of his "EB" tells him to open his mouth and swallow some "fat" or "good meat," but without chewing on it. The foreskin is dropped into his mouth and he swallows it, gulping at the effort. His "grandfather" Diludu now tells him that he has eaten "his own boy" and that his foreskin will grow inside him and make him strong, and will give him the ability to become a skilled cutter himself when the time comes.

Several Activists go and retrieve some bull-roarers which they hid in the wind-break earlier in the afternoon. They circle the ground, swinging them all the while to produce a loud, low-pitched throaty sound that carries back to camp. Two of these are presented to Waga, and his "grandfathers" instruct him to press them to his stomach. They rub them over his face and chin to promote growth of his body and beard. He now knows the truth about them, since all his life he has been told that the noise produced by them is the angry cry of *guṟubulbur*, small malevolent spirit-beings who are in the bush and are hungry to be fed. Waga is told that he must guard these sacred objects closely because they are from the Dreamtime, are dangerous and powerful, and are his true "mother" and "father." He must keep them stuck upright in the ground behind his head when he sleeps, and must never let them fall over, lest his parents die. Whenever he wants food, he must swing one of them. Everyone now returns to camp, except for several "EB" and "grandfathers" who will camp with him in men's country for the duration of his seclusion time.

(e) *The Seclusion.* Waga is joined within a few days by three other youths who are circumcized after him; they camp nearby and can communicate only by sign language since talking is forbidden among ritually dead people. The morning after Waga was cut, all the Mourner and Activist men, except for the operators, assemble near his camp. Several "EB" anoint his head and shoulders with blood drawn from their arm veins until his hair and face and upper body are drenched. He is not told why, but the Mardudjara say it is done to promote the growth of hair, which will eventually be cut for spinning into twine, after his subincision.

In the camping area, ceremonial gift exchanges take place between Waga's close Mourner relatives and the operators. This short rite is called *yulburu* ("dust," because it involves the sprinkling of dust on the ground by both groups), and appears to be a symbolic peacemaking between the "bereaved" and the "killers." This rite clears the way for the latter to reenter society, and for members of the two groups to come into physical proximity in everyday life, although direct interaction between the novice's family and the operators will henceforth be highly restrained and minimal. At the same time, *yulburu* is a manifestation of the profound bond that now exists between the families concerned.

Many nights during the seclusion period, the men organize rituals that can be performed in the camp area and attended by the entire assembly. Meanwhile, at secret dancing grounds out of sight of camp, the men hold periodic performances of the Nyurnguny ritual at which Waga and the other novices in attendance are permitted to see some of the dances through their "grandfathers' " fingers. The novices cannot yet see most of the sacred objects used in the dances, however, since they are too dangerous at this early stage of initiation. Later, Kangaroo ritual is supplanted by the Walawalañgu ritual, which centers on the creative exploits of Two Men (Wadi Gudjara), who traveled extensively within and beyond Mardudjara country.

Walawalañgu is always held at night, at a special ground in men's country, because its songs and dances are secret-sacred to initiated men. The men sit in two circles divided in most cases on a patrimoiety basis. Waga and the other novices lie on their backs in the center of the opposite moiety circle, with a "MB" supporting each novice's head and periodically hitting him lightly on his chest with a bull-roarer as the songs are sung to a hand-clapping accompaniment. (Later, the novices will learn that this is done to make them strong, and to magically protect their upper body against spear wounds). The men wear no decorations and there are few dances, but there is an important instructional element in that many of the well-known Dreamtime beings associated with this ritual turned into heavenly bodies (principally stars, constellations, and dark "holes"), which are pointed out to the novices as the appropriate song is sung. No detailed information is given, but the names and locations of the various beings are pronounced and pointed out, together with impassioned comments on the great power of this Law and the absolute necessity of upholding it.

(f) *The Return.* By the time that the novices' penises are considered well enough healed, the main business of the big meeting is over and many groups have already departed for the return journey to their home areas. But the families of the novices and some other groups have remained to help celebrate the return of the youths to society at large. After informing the camp that the novices are healed, Activist guardians take them hunting to get meat in order to pay for the ritual knowledge that is being revealed to them.

Waga and the others arrive back in men's country about dusk, carrying the lizards and small game they have hunted and cooked. They find all the men assembled at the Walawalangu ground in their two circles, with a simple charcoal V-pattern decorating their chests. The novices are given some seedcake to eat, having not eaten or drunk all day, while the men feast on the meat and other seedcakes prepared earlier by the women. It is clear moonless night, specially chosen so that the stars and other heavenly bodies will be clearly visible when they are pointed out during the singing, which will continue throughout the night. The two circles sing simultaneously much of the time, each following a different track of the Two Men, one covering areas to the north of Mardudjara country and the other to the south, until the tracks converge in the Durba Hills south of Lake Disappointment, where the Two Men finally departed from the earth (see Chapter 5). Several dances are featured during the night, but the climax of the ritual comes just before dawn. Waga and the other novices, who have been kept awake all night, are led by Activist men to a spot near a large fire that has just been lit close to the ground. Each novice sits crosslegged with one of his bull-roarers or a shield held horizontally against his stomach to prevent blood reaching his penis, while about ten Activists heavily anoint him with the arm blood and sing a song that tells of the Dreamtime anointing that the Two Men gave each other shortly before they left the earth.

As this occurs, one man goes back to the camping area and rouses all the women and children. The close relatives of Waga and the other youths don red ochre and sit together between the dancing ground and the camp, while all the young boys stand facing the direction of the (unseen) ground, holding a supply of bark boomerangs at the ready, to prevent the entry of the malevolent spirits which can be heard crying out angrily as the returning novices approach. The noise is, of course, that of the bull-roarers being swung by Activist men as they accompany the other men and the novices, whose "EB" run them from one small fire to the next en route. At each fire, the novices are made to kneel down with their heads in the smoke (to make them strong), while the dancing men circle the fire and swing bull-roarers. While still out of sight of the waiting women and children, "MB" put large hair-belts on the novices, and a possum-fur pubic tassel to cover the penis. The women cry loudly as they hear the increasingly loud noise of the bull-roarers, but this suddenly ceases just before the men appear in a headlong dash toward the camp. There is a momentary pause as the young boys fling their boomerangs over the heads of the novices and men. Waga and the others are each led into a group of their close female relatives, who clasp at him and wail very loudly for several minutes.

Several older uncircumcised boys come and take the novices to camps they have set up for them a short distance away from the main camping area. There they sit, covered in dry blood, heads down in embarrassment, looking much the worse for wear as the smaller boys crowd around to gaze at them and probably ponder their own future initiation. Waga eats; he is alive; but he is not the youth who left them several months before, and never again will he revert fully to the carefree behaviors of childhood. He has seen and heard new things, and in revelation came learning, and through trauma came irreversible change—dead is the boy, and newborn is the man-in-the-making.

Although the Mardudjara say that the anointing is to make the youth strong, the return to the life of the society by the blood-covered novice is clearly symbolic of birth. In some parts of Australia, the novice is said to die when swallowed by a giant rainbow python, which later regurgitates him, proof of which is his forlorn and blood-covered state. The return is not yet complete, however, for the novice must camp with the boys for a short time before he can move into the single-men's camp within the main area.

(g) *Betrothal*. In return for having ritually "killed" Waga, one of the two "MB" who removed his foreskin bestows a small daughter on him. This brief ceremony takes place shortly after his return to society, in public and as part of the *yulburu* rite (discussed above). The little girl is carried by one of her older brothers to where Waga sits, surrounded by his family and other close kin. He is given a spearthrower which he gently lays on her head or across her back while the spectators tell him that he must look after the girl from now on and hunt meat for her and her parents (who watch the ceremony from a short distance away).

Subincision Waga and the other novices remain in the status of *bugurdi*, wearing their hair in a bun, until sometime within the following year when another big meeting is held and some suitably distant relatives will be chosen as operators. Subincision, practiced by all Western Desert Aborigines, entails the slitting of the ventral surface of the penis, which is opened along most of its length to expose the urethra, which does not heal closed. Its physiological effects are to make urinating splashy and ejaculation less forceful, although it does not therefore adversely affect male fertility.

The sole reason offered by Mardudjara men as to why they practice subincinsion is that it is the Law, done in emulation of Dreamtime male beings who subincised one another as badges of full manhood and proof of their right to participate in the sacred life. Men point to the emu, in particular, as proof of the practice, because the emu

has a distinct penile groove not unlike that of a subincized man. Although, like circumcision, the ritual associated with subincision is the Kangaroo line, the songs and
dances that accompany subincision pertain to Garlaya, the Dreamtime emu-people,
while the dances that are performed in the days following the operation involve
Kangaroo and other ancestral beings. The operation itself is surrounded by less ritual
than circumcision and affects the community at large far less. Also, subincision is in
itself less significant than subsequent ritual use of the urethra as a source of blood, and
the symbolic significance of the subincized penis as the physical manifestation of
manhood.

About nine months after the big meeting at Giridji, Waga is at a similar assembly, taking place at Barabalgara, a rockhole in the Rudall River in Warnman
country (c. 22.5°S., 122.5°E.). He does not know that a decision to subincise him
has been made (though he fully expects it) until a group of "EB" come and seize
him in the camp area, then accompany him to tap the shoulders of all the men
present, a gesture that is commonly used to summon men to the bush for secret-
sacred activities. The assembled group, surrounding Waga, sets off toward the
small subincision ground in men's country, dancing and chanting. One man, playing the part of a Dreamtime emu that is injured, limps past the group toward the
ground. "Look! A wounded emu!" the men cry out to Waga as they set off in pur-
suit, leaving him with the older Activist men who bring up the rear. One of the
men who runs ahead expertly makes the tracks of an emu and sprinkles arm blood
on the ground to simulate bleeding from the injured ancestor's leg.

The men already at the ground hurriedly prepare for two dances: Muunuru, an
insect being who traveled with the emus and others, is the first dance. A line of
men stand with legs apart, forming a tunnel through which Waga and one or two
Activist men crawl. Waga and all the men then follow the blood trail to a spot in
the bushes just off the subincision ground, where the second dance, Two Emus, is
performed as Waga and the others draw close. One man lies on his back with legs
apart, and the other sits between pretending to eat either the penis blood or feces of
the first.

Waga is led to one side, and singing commences at the ground where the two
circles of men assemble. The "EB" hold a brief meeting to decide on the two operators, who will be distant "WB" and "MB" in most cases, preferably one who was
cut by Waga's father, as a reciprocal act to achieve a balance. As soon as this is
decided, the "EB" tell two of their number to seize the operators, who are taken to
one side and given a stone knife in readiness. Several "B" lay leafy bushes on the
ground, then three "MB" lie face down and form a table on which Waga lies on
his back. The Mourners lie on their sides, facing away from the ground and holding small leaf-bundles which they shake gently in time with the Activists' singing.

Several "grandfathers" stand nearby to comfort him, and one gives him a boomerang to bite on. One of the operators then sits on his chest and holds his penis
upright while the other carefully cuts it open, while the Activists sing and the
Mourners quietly wail. The operation takes about ten minutes, since great care
must be taken to center the incision, and cutting delayed while a small wooden rod
is inserted into the urethra to act as a backing for the knife as it cuts. As soon as
the operation is completed, Waga is led to a small fire that has been made nearby;
he sits astride it so that the heat and smoke will stop the bleeding.

The men leave the ground to prepare for the dances that will follow later that
day, leaving Waga with a guardian. In the late afternoon he sees for the first time
dances associated with both Kangaroo and Two Men that feature sacred thread-
cross-type objects that are constructed from spears and wooden crosspieces around
which hair-string is painstakingly wound. Following the dances, the Activist elders
tell Waga briefly about the significance of the dances and the thread-crosses. One of
the crosses is roughly rubbed back and forth across his chest as he lies on the

ground to give him strength through a transference of the power that is inherent in all sacred objects "of the Dreamtime."

Waga remains in seclusion for about a week, during which time the Nyurnguny ritual is continued daily. He is seated in his "own side" singing circle, taught how to beat time with the wooden stick, and encouraged to begin singing the songs. Another day he is "dressed"; that is, an Activist relative decorates him with a forehead band, thick hair-belt, and a *djininy,* a carved wooden ornament worn on the back of the head during dancing (it is similar in size and shape to a bull-roarer, but can be seen by women and children). Another day he dances for the first time, and another he has his arm vein pierced and anoints some of the dancers with blood. More and more dances and associated sacred objects are shown to him.

Food and gift exchanges have already taken place between Waga's family and the operators, but a further *yulburu* (see above) takes place between the two groups after his return to camp, as a gesture of conciliation and an acknowledgment of their new status vis-à-vis one another. Waga now is a *giridji* ("bachelor"), and he will remain so until he is considered qualified to marry. From now on, Waga's progression through further initiation stages depends in part on his reputation among the older men as a provider of meat, a willing participant in all activities, and a "quiet one" who does not cause trouble through excessive sexual activity. The following decade or so involves the gradual revelation of more and more secret-sacred elements and his assumption of greater responsibilities in ritual activities.

Intermediate Stages   The brief descriptions that follow cover the most important of these:

(a) *Buñgarna.* A year or two after subincision, the young man is presented with a small pearlshell pubic pendant, or *buñgarna,* which he will wear on appropriate ritual occasions thereafter. The presentation is made by "EB" in the camp area and elderly Activist women instruct him to look after the shell, obey the Law, and keep away from trouble over women.

(b) *Mirdayidi.* As noted in the previous chapter, Mirdayidi is the revelation of the storehouse of sacred objects and eating of a ritual feast, which is a very important stage in a young man's initiation.

All available initiated males assemble somewhere close to the camping area, then the novice is seized and the Mourner women wail for him. The men sit in a circle, into which the novice is led, then made to lie face down on the stomachs of all present. "Own side" relatives tie several hair-belts around his waist, then he is sent off, accompanied by several young men, to hunt a large quantity of meat in payment for all that he will soon be privileged to witness and learn. He and his companions will spend two or three days hunting; meanwhile the old men who are guardians of the storehouse go to the site to clean the sacred boards and prepare the nearby ceremonial ground. Some of the older men and women who hold the high ritual status of Mirdayidi food preparers work at a spot not far from the camping area; the women grind and mix the grass seeds into paste, while the men do the actual cooking of the large seedcakes.

When the hunters return, the novice, laden down with cooked game and weak with hunger and thirst (he has not been permitted to eat or drink while out hunting), must run the last quarter mile or so past men who leap out from hiding and pursue him, hitting him on the back with the small sacred boards they are carrying. The larger boards, all more than eight feet in length, are stood upright in two lines close to the storehouse, and the novice runs between them to throw the meat down and collapse at the feet of the singing men. They tell him to glance at the biggest boards before they are put away. He is again made to lie on top of all the men present—presumably to gain strength and power through contact with so many *nindibuga* ("knowledgeable ones")—and then he is formally shown the boards. Men sit on both sides of him to form a line, along which each board is passed. The smallest boards are sent through first, and in time to the singing, each is rubbed by each man against his stomach as it passes, to impart the spiritual power of the object into the bodies of the men. Excitement mounts as the bigger boards are passed along. Finally, the men perform a brief ritual to break the novice's silence: a piece of seedcake is rubbed along the board to pick up some of the red ochre and fat before being put into the novice's mouth. He and the hunters now eat the Mirdayidi amid more ritual. Each type of sacred board is named and identified for the novice, together with a brief explanation of the mythological and territorial associations of the designs carved on it. The men will make much of the boards that have been carved by the older brothers, father, father's brothers, and father's father of the novice, impressing upon him their labors on behalf of the Law, and the importance of continuity, for he must do likewise. Throughout the revelations and instruction, Activists hold center stage and exhort the novice to be a good Law carrier. If he has been making trouble with women, he will have been severely beaten with the boards as he approached the storehouse area, and during the passing of the boards he is loudly and severely chastised by his many "EB." Following this, the rest of the men eat the Mirdayidi seedcakes and meat before the boards are carefully put back in their hiding place and everyone returns to camp.

Having now completed this major step in his initiation, by being shown what are in a sense the sacred roots of his own being, a young man must embark on journeys to the estates of many other groups to be initiated into their storehouses and eat Mirdayidi with them. This vital step must be taken before marriage can be contemplated because it is only through these ritual activities that he gains rights of access to other territories. In sharing the secrets and the food of these other groups, he in effect shares their ancestral substance with them: he has eaten off the boards, thus ingesting their power in a shared sacrament. He is thus committing part of himself to these groups and their Dreamtime beings, becoming a kinsman in spirit as well as flesh. Later, he and his family will be free to hunt, gather, cut weapons, and camp in their territories, and he will know much of the totemic geography in those areas, including sites to avoid. The requirement that young men travel widely and thus broaden their geographical and religious horizons is of great pragmatic as well as spiritual significance in the life of the Mardudjara.

(c) *Board Carving.* After he has eaten Mirdayidi in several different areas, a young man's qualities are discussed by the men of his and closely allied bands, who decide that he is ready to progress to the next stage, which involves the carving of sacred boards.

The young man is seized and is taken to the storehouse of his estate-group, usually in the company of a few others of the same status, and at a time when several bands are camping together or during a big meeting. After being shown the remaining very large sacred boards, in a ritual similar to that of the Mirdayidi revelation, each novice is presented with a small wooden board that has been shaped and outlined with a geometric design but is uncarved. Several native doctors magically remove carving chisels from the bodies of older men whose carving is of high standard, and insert these into the young men's torsos, arms (to steady their hands), and heads (to allow them to see clearly while carving). Activist relatives then present the novices with *djimirliri* ("chisels") of sharp stone or animal teeth hafted with spinifex resin to a short wooden handle. The Activists instruct them in the use of the chisel, since the carving of the fine, parallel grooves is an exacting task requiring great skill and patience. The "EB" or "grandfather" who traced the design outline explains its mythological significance and territorial associations. The pattern will be a variant of the three of four commonly used by the Mardudjara. The novices remain in seclusion, fed and supervised by Activists, for about a month until they have finished carving their first board. They then hunt large quantities of meat to repay their elders before returning to their families. Later, a young man will be given more small boards to carve, but will outline them himself, advised by an older estate-group relative regarding the appropriate designs and themes for his estate and its Dreamtime beings.

(d) *Board Cutting*. Some time after he has successfully carved several sacred boards, the young man will be seized, along with others of the same status, by Activist men who send the novices out to hunt and bring back plenty of meat for the old people.

On their return, each is given an axe and after the food has been eaten, a large group of men accompanies the novices to a suitable stand of trees where they are instructed in the selection and cutting of wood that will be shaped into sacred boards. Each cuts and shapes a small sacred board and presents it to his Activist elders for one of them to carve. When this is done, the boards are presented to the novices in a ceremony at the estate-group's storehouse. The men exhort them to continue cutting and carving boards throughout their lives, since each will become a repository of life essence, identical to the boards carried by the Dreamtime beings wherever they traveled and deposited in storehouses throughout the land.

With the completion of this step, the young men are now termed *garndamari* and are eligible to claim their *bilyur* ("promised ones") in marriage.

MARRIAGE

A marriage takes place when the parents of a man's betrothed send her to his camp, and the couple then cohabits on a permanent basis. There is no marriage ceremony among the desert people.

A large number of marriages—of girls to much older men—take place as the result not of a circumcision betrothal, but of arrangements made between a suitor and the girl's parents. There may not be an outright request, lest a refusal cause embarrassment, but intermediaries take meat and other gifts to the girl's parents to initiate the relationship, and such gift giving continues over a period of years whenever circumstances permit it. The Mardudjara say that if a couple has a daughter not yet betrothed, they think about who has been generous to them and decide to promise her to a man who has supported them. A formal betrothal may then take place, or the girl will be encouraged by her parents to visit the suitor's camp and take gifts of vegetable foods to him. Since marriage is never solely the concern of the couple, but brings two family groups into closer alliance, the attendant reciprocity helps guarantee that every effort will be made to ensure that the girl will eventually cohabit with her suitor as promised. In many cases a girl is very much younger than her husband, and she enters marriage as a co-wife whose food-gathering skills may be of greater value to the family unit than her reproductive potential, especially in the first few years when she is unlikely to conceive.

On the other hand, a man's first wife may be a much older woman, a widow whose abilities as a provider are proven and who is usually considered much less likely than a young wife to pursue the kinds of adulterous liaisons that lead to conflicts or an elopement. People view marriages of this kind favorably because not only will the older woman be a reliable and steadying influence, she may also become a companion, co-worker, and chaperone of the young girls who may later become wives of her husband. Many men rely on their older wives to keep an eye on the others, which accords with the status difference that exists among them; the younger are expected to defer to the older.

Sexual jealousy may at times cause discord between co-wives, especially if the age difference between them is slight, since men tend to favor the younger woman as a sex partner. However, the prevailing state in most polygynous families is one of comparative harmony. If an older wife no longer has young children of her own, she shares fully in the rearing of her co-wife's children and is at least as much a mother to them as their genetrix. Because social parenthood is stressed, most children grow up with at least two "real" mothers with whom they have close emotional ties, as well as many other "M" toward whom they feel varying degrees of attachment. Most older women welcome the addition of a young strong girl to their family unit because she will contribute much to the daily labor of gathering and preparing food, and will hopefully bear children upon whom they can lavish much love and attention.

There are no rules restricting the number of wives a man can have, but practical considerations such as the availability of eligible women and a man's ability to control and retain them limit most to between one and three wives at any given time. Since the number of male and female births is about the same, and there is no evidence that infanticide is practiced differentially with regard to an infant's sex, there is no excess of females to males (male conflicts that result in death are likewise rare). Therefore polygyny is made possible by a cultural practice: delaying the age of marriage for men while ensuring that females are married very young.

This does not mean that young men are denied sexual access to women, apart from periodic demands for abstinence occasioned by ritual activities (some of which entail celibacy for married men as well as bachelors). People admit the inevitability and even the necessity of sexual activities, but premarital and extramarital affairs or liaisons are subject to certain norms. They should not be "incestuous," and they should be conducted as discreetly as possible; however, secrecy is virtually impossible to maintain for long, since even a small child can read tracks and draw the correct conclusions. Also, such affairs should not cause a woman to neglect her wifely or maternal responsibilities, and above all, they should not be such as to pose a threat to an existing marriage.

Any move by a pair of lovers which brings public attention to their relationship is seen as tantamount to a declaration of intention to elope. Elopement is strongly condemned because it threatens the continued functioning of at least one family unit and, equally seriously, it threatens affinal alliances whose rupture would badly affect relationships between at least two kin groups and many individuals. Little wonder that eloping couples, if and when eventually caught, are severely punished or even killed, if a wronged husband and his kin are sufficiently affronted and the couple stand in an "incestuous" kin relationship to each other.

Elopement certainly occurs from time to time among the Mardudjara, despite the risks of punishment entailed and the inevitable disturbance of the social status quo. The very few who suffer ostracism and severe punishment to remain together are still not considered married, however, until the woman's former husband or betrothed has publicly relinquished his claim to her. People acknowledge the possibility of personality clashes and incompatibility of temperament between spouses, but do not consider these to be grounds in themselves for divorce. The family is very rarely a socially isolated unit. The continual presence of close kin and the daily separation of the sexes mean that husbands and wives generally spend less time together than they do with others of their own sex. It is therefore probable that the marriage bond itself is subject to far fewer pressures and demands than, say, in contemporary Western society, and there is less chance that spouses will get on each other's nerves because their interaction so often includes other adult members of the band. In the life of the camp, other families are always within sight and earshot, and the level of interaction among them is high.

Men are more fortunate than women in having a socially acceptable reason to remove themselves from domestic annoyances or tensions. They can always claim a pressing need to engage in "men's business," then retreat with some of their fellows to men's country where women and children cannot follow. It is a moot point whether the considerable time they spend in such areas is taken up with idle chatter and siestas or more serious discussion, planning, and performance of ritual and other religious activities. Yet the men's preoccupation with religious matters is so great that their frequent absence from camp, other than when they are out hunting, is rarely a pretext. On the other hand, women's secret-sacred ritual activity is much less frequent, being confined usually to the time of big meetings; also, their child-care responsibilities are much greater than men's.

Most couples settle easily into the roles of spouse and parent. Although protestations of love and devotion are absent, and couples are not given to public demonstrativeness, it is nevertheless apparent that a great deal of mutual concern and regard exists between most spouses. The stability and durability of most marriages would seem to reflect this; divorce is uncommon among the Mardudjara. Given the volatility of many people, however, domestic tranquility can be quickly disturbed by real or alleged neglect, laziness, infidelity, dereliction of duty, and so on, resulting in conflict. In such cases, women may be more than a match for their husbands verbally, but in physical exchanges they usually fare less well (see Chapter 6).

People say that most men punish their wives only if they wantonly neglect their domestic responsibilities or are excessively active extramaritally; thus, men and women alike tend to be unsympathetic to wives who are beaten. Women have far fewer marital rights than men. A man who has committed some kind of serious offense may offer his wife or wives for intercourse with those he has wronged, as a gesture of atonement. His spouses should comply without complaint. Also, he may offer them as temporary partners to "B" who are visiting, as a demonstration of hospitality and friendship. Again, the women concerned should raise no objections, whether or not they are consulted prior to the "lending." However, neither wife offering nor wife lending is a frequent or long-lasting occurrence.

GROWING OLD

By middle age, Mardudjara men have very detailed knowledge of the secret-sacred life and assume increasing responsibility for the organization and performance of religious activities. Some will eventually attain the status of a leader for the rituals with which they are most closely associated. For married women, too, prestige and authority in matters connected with their own as well as certain male rituals increase with age. Provided they remain alert and responsive, the older people derive considerable stature from their accumulated wisdom. Becoming older, or being an elder, means less active participation in subsistence and ritual concerns, but greater responsibility for the caretaking and directing of the religious life.

In keeping with this changing role, elderly people can expect material assistance, in the form of foodstuffs, from younger relatives who respond willingly to the strongly expressed imperative that old people must be fed and looked after in return for having reared their children. The norms of classificatory kinship assure older, less active hunters and gatherers that there will always be relatives to support them. Also, a

number of choice foodstuffs are normally reserved for old people; for example, the por-
cupine-like echidna whose flesh is considered a delicacy. In the religious life, too,
hunting commitments by younger men assure their elders of meat.

The elderly are generally well treated and cared for, but should they become senile,
they are no longer venerated or sought after for advice, so their social importance
declines accordingly. They remain in, but not of, Mardudjara society in the sense of
making their presence felt in positive ways. They continue to be fed, but unlike infants with whom there are some parallels of helplessness, they become marginal, not
central, in the life of the band. The ability to remain mobile is essential; every effort
is made to spare the elderly and infirm too frequent or arduous movement, but hard
times inevitably demand this of them on occasion. Some may pronounce themselves
unequal to the task and ask to be left behind to die. If no alternatives exist and the
lives of others are endangered by a band's lessened mobility, this wish may be
granted.

It has been suggested that the willingness to feed and care for the elderly is a major
factor in the maintenance of bands, which allow a more even distribution of the burden of providing such support (Peterson 1972). One group of Western Desert people
are known to have carried a lame man for about two years until he could support himself with the aid of a crutch. Peterson, in the same paper, suggests that the territorial
anchoring of bands stems from the strong desire of old men to remain as close as possible to their natal estates and to die in or close to the area of their birth; they thus
become the nodal points around which bands form. As noted in Chapter 3, the men
are motivated by a strong sentimental attachment and by important ritual and guardianship responsibilities they develop for sacred sites and objects within the estate.

Old people who feel that their lives may be coming to an end prefer to die close to
their birthplace so that their spirit will thus be spared a long journey on its final return to its original home. I have never heard old Mardudjara talk about their own
death or express fears or uncertainties in this regard. They seem to accept its inevitability but not its finality, since the spirit is immortal.

DEATH AND ITS AFTERMATH

As in most other societies, a Mardudjara death is almost always a traumatic experience for the bereaved, because it evokes strong passions of grief, and sometimes anger
and resentment, and it disrupts the network of kin ties and social interaction, with
sometimes important consequences for the tenor of intergroup relations. Unless the
death is of a very small baby, many relatives become involved in the activities that
follow, and they adopt active or passive roles according to their emotional distance
from the deceased and their membership of either the Activist or Mourner group.

In terms of what transpires after a death, a distinction can be made between physical and metaphysical concerns, between substance and spirit, since the Mardudjara
themselves recognize such a dichotomy. Activities directed toward preparation of the
body, burial, bone cleaning, and reburial all deal with substance, but are in effect
subsidiary. The major concern is to cope with the immortality of the spirit, which is
thought to be distressed at its separation from the living and is intent on continuing
its close association with them. Thus all the efforts of the survivors have as their
utlimate goal the return of the spirit to its home in a permanent separation from the
living.

The intensity of emotion generated by a death depends considerably on the social
status and age of the person concerned. Neither the very old nor the very young are

mourned as long, loudly, or intensely as those older childdren and adults in the prime of life who are suddenly lost. The deaths of socially integral people leave large gashes in the social fabric, because by middle age they have built up a widely ramifying network of interpersonal ties. Regardless of their social status, however, the deaths of all but the very young are treated in much the same way in terms of the procedures followed.

Activist relatives must send messengers with news of death to as many other bands as can be located in the general vicinity, so that their members can assemble to pay their respects and assist with the proceedings. Since most members of a deceased person's band are closely related and therefore Mourners, more distantly related Activists from other bands assume responsibility for the tasks associated with the disposal of the body. For their efforts, they will eventually be recompensed by the Mourners, in the form of foodstuffs, hair-belts, and other gifts. If a person becomes seriously ill and death appears imminent, messengers may have already gone to summon others to the camp, and those who assemble cry and wail for the afflicted relative. This response might seem like a pessimistic prejudgment of the outcome, but to the Mardudjara it is a gesture of concern and a reflection of the social worth of the individual.

When death actually occurs, loud and emotional wailing breaks out and people of both sexes attempt to inflict bloody scalp wounds on themselves with whatever sharp object is near at hand. Despite their own grief, Activist relatives must intervene to prevent excessive bloodshed and keep a close watch on the Mourners. When more people arrive, there are renewed outbursts of grief and self-injury. Some of the newcomers will attempt also to punch some of the close relatives of the deceased as they sink to the ground and embrace them in loudly expressed grief. Older children take no active part and view the emotional and turbulent events with an air of seeming disinterest; small children and babies usually react with fright and loud crying. Dogs invariably set up a loud wailing, on the same high pitch as that of the humans, such that it is often impossible to distinguish one from the other.

When the wailing finally subsides, nonfamily male Activists carry the body well away from the camping area, which everyone abandons shortly after. It will not be occupied again for some years, initially because of the alleged presence of the spirit of the deceased and later because the site will arouse unhappy memories among the surviving relatives. The Activists dig a rectangular hole about three feet deep, line the bottom with leafy bushes and small logs, then place the body inside. Hair-string or bark is used to tie one arm, elbow bent, to the shoulder, and the legs are tucked against the buttocks. The arm that is left free allows the spirit to shoo away wild dingoes that may want to eat the body. To prevent this, the grave is left well covered with branches, logs, and heavy stones. If the deceased is male, his spears and thrower are broken and stuck upright in the ground close by; if a female, her digging stick is left. These objects warn others of the presence of a grave, which they will avoid. If they are deliberately broken, this is done to discourage the spirit from going off hunting or gathering.

Before leaving the grave, an old Activist relative who knew the deceased well, addresses the spirit, saying things like, "Don't look back again at your wife, and don't think about your children. Keep away from the camp and don't follow us. You have to go the other way, to your own waterhole." The burial party then returns to the camp, where the rest of the Mourners lie assembled, wailing. The Activists throw leafy branches over the "dead" Mourners, perhaps in a symbolic burial, for the latter remain still for several minutes until told that the deceased has been buried properly and that they must now leave. The Activists burn most of the remaining belongings of the deceased (lest they serve as reminders of the death, and perhaps also to avert the possibility that the spirit will come in search of its gear). A dead man's personal secret-sacred and other ritual paraphernalia will later be passed on to members of distant groups, as part of the gift exchanges that occur during big meetings. Since spirits of the dead (*gurdi*) are believed to be resentful and therefore malevolent or even quite dangerous, people stay well away from the place of death until the time comes for reburial to take place, some time between about six months and two or three years. Also, the name of the deceased is henceforth tabu, and in reference he or she is termed *bugura* ("the dead one"). Should some other person carry the same or a similar sounding name, it will no longer be called. Instead, they become *gurnmanu*, a term with a meaning akin to "what's-his-name." If the dead person's name was that of a waterhole or plant or animal species, that name is dropped and alternatives are adopted.[10]

The widow and other closely related females usually cut their hair and remain anointed with red ochre throughout the period of mourning. All close relatives become *dadji;* that is, they refrain from eating plains-kangaroo, echidna, native cat, possum, and dingo for a period of one or two years or even longer. This tabu is forcibly ended when Activist relatives seize them and force-feed some kangaroo fat, or at least rub it across their lips; I have seen Mardudjara of both sexes violently resist this, saying that they are still "too sorry" to cease being *dadji*. The only explanation for this tabu is that it comes from the Dreamtime. However, one man suggested that the deceased's spirit may decide to inhabit the body of one of these animals, so close relatives who are *dadji* avoid the risk of eating the dead person in animal form. The informant equated this act with cannibalism, a distasteful custom allegedly practiced by far-distant "stranger" peoples and by malevolent spirits.

When the time for reburial approaches, the widow is expected to gather a large group of distantly related kin to assist in the proceedings. (If the deceased is a woman, her husband will be the organizer; if a child, its parents have this responsibility.) En route back to the grave, the assembly sings songs from the Laga ritual nightly. This ritual is held only in connection with death and mourning, and centers on the activities of a group of Dreamtime emu-people who instituted it to mourn one of their dead. Within a mile or two of the grave, the party makes camp, and they sing and dance until dusk. Next morning, Mourners gather and prepare food for the burial party of 10 to 15 Activist men and women which heads for the grave, accompanied by the widow(s). As they draw near, the widow lights a small fire and everyone sings out to warn the spirit of their presence. The spirit, which should be somewhere in the vicinity, will answer in the form of a birdcall. The widow approaches with a native doctor, whose powers include the ability to see the skeletonlike *gurdi*. He catches it and puts it inside his body, so that it will not harm any of the nearby humans.

The men of the reburial party go to the grave, and after wailing briefly, they remove and clean the bones of the deceased. They rub them on their bodies and carry the skull to the widow, who does likewise against her body. If foul play was suspected in the death, the men examine the bones and gravesite for clues as to who killed the man. They look closely for wooden slivers and if any such foreign bodies are located, they scrutinize them for a *ñgamiri* ("signature mark") that will identify the attacker. They may also examine a lock of the deceased's hair, which the widow had cut and kept for the inquest. Should any clues be found, the native doctor will send out the deceased's spirit to locate the killers. The spirit may use a little bird, which will perch

[10] The flexibility and dynamism of Western Desert dialects is such that groups will even replace words that are basic to their language; for example, the Warburton Ranges people changed their first person pronoun for *ñgayu-* to *ñgangu-* after the death of a man called Ngayunya! (Douglas 1958).

on the shoulders of the man or men responsible. This identifies them to the watching spirit, which then informs the native doctor. Close male relatives of the dead man may later decide to mount a revenge expedition against the alleged killers, but if the latter are identified as malevolent spirit-beings, nothing can be done.

The bones are reburied in a small hole, their final resting place, and the main grave is filled in. The party returns to the main camp and a feast is eaten. A meeting is held to decide on the widow's new marriage partner, a "B" of the dead man. The widow has a say in the decision, although ideally she should abide by the wishes of her brothers and her late husband's patrikin.

The spirit, which has been trapped inside the native doctor, may remain with him for some time, acting as a spirit-familiar, or it may sometimes visit its living kin to warn them of some impending dangers. But inevitably it must return to its place of origin because the living have fulfilled their responsibilities toward it. It will then remain in its home, immortal but separated from the realm of the living, and visible to them only during dreams. It may or may not remain vindictive toward human beings, other than close kin whom it is believed incapable of harming. It watches over its home area and may cause illness among strangers who venture too close; in other words, as a spirit it continues its guardianship of certain sites and objects in a carry-over from its human state. The Mardudjara believe that most spirits of the dead soon "settle down," and it is not *gurdi* but the malevolent spirit-beings which have existed on earth since the beginning of the Dreamtime that cause most illness and misfortune. Fortunately, in most cases native doctors possess magic powerful enough to combat that of the *malbu* spirit-beings.

With the final return of the spirit comes an eventual balance. The *gurdi* that returns is not the same entity as the *djidjigargaly* ("spirit-child") that emerged to enter its mother and begin life as a human being, but the cycle is nevertheless completed, and the spirit lives on, as all spirits must.

5 / The religious life

It should be clear from Chapter 1 that the cosmic order of the Mardudjara is firmly grounded in the land and its features that are believed to be the creations of Dreamtime beings. It seems quite likely that the technology of subsistence and the development of social organizational forms would have preceded the elaboration of the complex cosmology of the Aborigines and its attachment to the physical world. Regardless of which elements were prior, in every human society the creations of mind and body can take on an objective reality and, paradoxically, a life and power of their own. This power acts back upon its creators, helping to shape and order human existence within an externally imposed framework we call "society" and "culture."

The religion of the Mardudjara, elaborated in times long ago by their human forebears but credited to the creative genius of Dreamtime beings, has become an all-powerful integrating force in their lives. It touches all parts of their existence and imbues it with strong motivations and meanings. Cultural and social elements that are logically prior are thus denied this status and instead become constituent parts of a comprehensive and grand religious design.

All significant happenings in the creative epoch are contained in one or more of the "vehicles" through which the Aborigines learn and transmit and diffuse their religion. These include mythology, songlines, rituals, sacred sites and objects, and living actors, which are diverse yet closely interrelated elements. This chapter focuses primarily on the nature of these elements and the parts played by them in Mardudjara religion.

THE SEXUAL DIVISION OF RITUAL LABOR

Initiated men are principally responsible for the maintenance of community well-being through religious activities. Regardless of the degree of community participation, all such activities can be viewed as contributing to this well-being. However, men say that the performance of secret-sacred, men-only rites is crucial, and women do not dispute this assertion. The Mardudjara do not rank rituals or particular religious activities according to importance or efficacy, since all derive ultimately from the Dreamtime. But secret-sacred rituals and any others that include secret elements are especially significant in that they entail the display and use of objects whose great power, danger, and sacredness derive from their intimate link to the Dreamtime. Most of these objects and associated songs, dances, and usages are under the exclusive control of initiated males. Although women are known to possess their own secret-sacred objects and rituals, these occupy very little of their time and energies compared to those of the men.

In the religious life, men control and direct women and leave them very little autonomy. Nevertheless, women are by no means unimportant to the successful functioning of Mardudjara religious activity. They are active participants in many rituals, and even when not involved, they play a major support role by gathering food and maintaining the life of the camp while men are ritually preoccupied. Many rituals are performed in the camp area where women and children can attend, and in some rituals everyone joins in the singing and dancing. Women also play valuable contributory roles in the execution of many men's secret rituals. Their main task is the grinding and preparation of seedcakes that are then cooked by male elders and served at special feasts which are a common and integral part of these rituals. Most female "cooks" are middle-aged and older, active in the leadership of women's rituals, and well regarded by the community. As with their male counterparts, selection as a food preparer enhances their status. However, food preparers of both sexes may include younger people who have been causing trouble of some kind and are selected as a punishment, to bring them into line by giving them much of the hardest work; the older women and men act more as supervisors. Here the imposition of ritual tasks and related specialized knowledge is used as a weapon of punishment (M. Tonkinson, personal communication). People are pressured to conform, and the assignment to them of a privileged role is a forceful reminder of their manifold responsibilities to the maintenance of the Law, as well as the imperative of proper behavior toward their fellows.

Women are involved in many activities associated with male initiation, and although their roles seem peripheral to those of men, their participation is essential. They and their children represent the life of the camp, the normal society from which a novice is removed and later returned to as a new social person. In their public displays of grief at the "death" of the novice and their celebration of his safe return, women actively reaffirm the worth and social importance of the novice to the community.

In a passive sense, too, women and children comprise a vital baseline for the men's dichotomizing of life into dangerous—exclusive and mundane—inclusive aspects. Young males are only temporarily excluded, until physical maturation entitles them to entry into the secret life, whereas the exclusion of women is permanent. This practice could be seen as a chauvinistic device of jealous males intent upon reinforcement of their sexual identity, solidarity, and superiority. Yet the facts of everyday life reveal little or no anxiety on the part of either sex concerning their status vis-à-vis the other. Men are convinced that there are spiritual forces too powerful and dangerous for anyone other than themselves to deal with. This conviction gives the men's religious life much of its excitement and tension, and it leads to a great many proscriptions and activities directed toward the proper insulation of the rest of society from these dangerous forces. Among the Mardudjara, the exclusion of females is manifested much less in expressions of male superiority or solidarity than in a genuine concern for the safety of their women and children, since contact with highly dangerous powers could well be fatal for them.

MYTH, RITUAL, AND SONGLINE

The media of myth, rite, and song are three of the many through which Aborigines gain an awareness and appreciation of the Dreamtime and its overwhelming significance to their past, present, and future existence. These interdependent media are clearly different modes of expressing basically the same profound truths about how the cosmos is constituted and how harmony among its major elements must be maintained.

The discussion that follows has a twofold aim: to delineate the major characteristics of each medium, using some illustrative examples, and to examine their interrelationship, highlighting the differing possibilities they present for individual and group manipulation and for the inclusion of new knowledge.

Mythology In volume and detail, Mardudjara mythology embodies more information about the Dreamtime than any other medium; much of what people come to know of the creative epoch derives from this source. From an early age children are told stories that recount Dreamtime happenings; such myths are most often brief accounts of how something came to be as it is now. Thus they learn why, for example, Manganya the echidna has spines (he was pincushioned full of spears in a fight with Gadabuda the lizard-man), why Gaarnga the crow is black, why Garlaya the emu cannot fly, and so on. In addition to these short "situational" myths which pay little attention to the physical setting, there are longer descriptive narrative myths that relate the wanderings of well-known creative beings (Tonkinson 1974). These detail the many exploits of the Dreamtime heroes: their encounters with others, their hunting and gathering, and their naming and creation of the many sites they visited. Many such creative acts are intentional, as when, for instance, they dig for water and thus create a major waterhole. But when Gunagalyu the snake-man leaves a winding creekbed in his wake, or when the depression left by the sleeping bodies of the Wayurda possum-people becomes a huge claypan, the creativity is unintentional, yet equally important. In both their mundane and ritual activities, the Dreamtime travelers were in reality preenacting much of what was to become the Law of their human descendants.

Because narrative myths tell of things secret and dangerous as well as mundane Dreamtime events, some of their detail is known only to initiated men. When women tell them, no sacred objects are mentioned, and at such times men delight in exchanging knowing looks, or in whispering asides to the anthropologist, such as: "That wasn't a spear the owl-man threw at the Ngayunangalgu cannibals; it was a sacred board and that's why the whole mob died instantly"; or "Those Minyiburu [ancestral women] left behind grinding stones at that waterhole, but they were really sacred stones; they're still here and that's why women and children can't go into that place."

By Western dramatic standards, these myths lack excitement and tension, dwelling as they do much of the time on the naming of places and the movements of ancestral beings from one spot to the next. Yet because many tell of journeys covering hundreds of miles of desert, through areas that Mardudjara in many cases have not seen, they broaden the cosmological and geographical outlook of the Aborigines and give them a strong feeling that they know those areas. In the same way, narratives bring alive and make immediate the landforms created by ancestral beings in areas that are familiar to the Mardudjara. More importantly, through the links of ancestral and conception totemism (see Chapter 4), every individual has a direct link to the activities of Dreamtime beings; these shared ancestral totems give everyone a feeling of spiritual kinship with others elsewhere who were left behind by the same beings. This awareness of a wider unity and shared identity, which is fostered by the multiplicity of Dreamtime beings and the spread of geographical areas traversed by them, contributes greatly to cordial intergroup relationships in the desert.

The excerpt that follows, taken from a long narrative myth, is included to convey some feeling for their content and structure. It is part of the exploits of Two Men, the cross-cousin "B" and close companions who as lizard-people traveled widely in the desert (see Chapter 4).[1] The major events detailed below occurred in the heart of Mardudjara territory. One of the elders who narrated this myth also made a crayon "map" of the area (at my request), shown in Figure 5–1. The setting is south of Lake Disappointment in and around the Durba Hills (Map 3).

Two Men traveled on and made camp at D̄ibil waterhole. Next morning, they got up and went hunting. They spotted some dingoes lying down in the shade. They crept close, then speared and killed them. They gutted them, threw away the guts, picked up the livers then threw them down and they turned to stone . . . you can still see the livers at that place. They then went and cooked and ate the dogs. They named that spot Buṅggulamangu then headed off in the direction of their home country. En route they camped at Birli rockhole, then went on to Djiluguru, their main camp. There they put down all the sacred things they had been carrying with them on their travels, and went hunting in the afternoon. They climbed a high sandhill to sit down and rest; as they sat they untied their beards [which they had bound with hairstring], which unrolled along the ground. The Milaṅgga brother's beard was shorter. Their beards turned to stone; you can see those two rocks there now. They returned to camp and lay down, but a large rock was blocking the sun so they split it open, and called it Mulyayidi. They carved three clubs and left them in the sand to dry out while they hunted for meat. When they got back they saw that the clubs had turned into snakes—"quiet ones" [probably rock pythons, which are harmless]. They fed some meat to the snakes, then left them and the sacred things and went on a hunting camp-out, to Binbi. Then they got up and went eastwards, towards another waterhole called Yiradjiwara, where they camped . . . I don't know, maybe three nights.

Guridji, the mother of one of them, had followed their tracks into Djiluguru. Seeing that they had left, she tracked them to Binbi and saw that they had camped there, then followed their tracks until she spotted them in the distance, lit up by lightning being carried on the head of Barmalgunda the Lightning Man, who happened to be close by at the time. She put down her seedcakes [the food she had been carrying for them], kept herself hidden as she crept closer, then in a crouching run, closed in and grabbed them, and wailed for them [because she had not seen them in such a long time]. And they in turn cried for her. Then she picked them up in both hands, sat them down, went back and picked up their food, then gave it to them. They ate all of it. Then they got up and she put them on her shoulders and headed off towards home. She carried them "half way" then stood them up at a claypan, called Bulyubulyunindja. She then picked them up, one under each arm, then carried them away to her own camp where she put them down—never to return. Guridji's husband, Gamuṙubul, who had been out hunting, had killed some meat for the Two Men, and was lying down in his bush camp when he saw the Lightning Man, whom he thought may have taken his children away. Next morning he got up before dawn, tied up the meat with some bark, then set off. Not far along, he came across some tracks and said, "They are surely Guridji's! Perhaps she's taken them and gone!" He tracked them to their home camp and saw that they had left their sacred things there. He followed their tracks. "Which way did they go?" he asked himself. He followed them to Binbi and beyond, until he finally saw that they really had been taken by their mother. He cried, saying, "Here is where their tracks end; she grabbed them and headed northwards." Then he left everything he had been carrying and began following in the tracks, forever.[2]

These great Dreamtime beings went up into the sky at the conclusion of their lives on earth and became heavenly bodies, which can still be seen.

[1] A different segment of the same myth is related in Tonkinson (1974:73).
[2] Details from this myth are beautifully depicted on a wooden figure carved by the same elder, and fully described in Mountford and Tonkinson (1969).

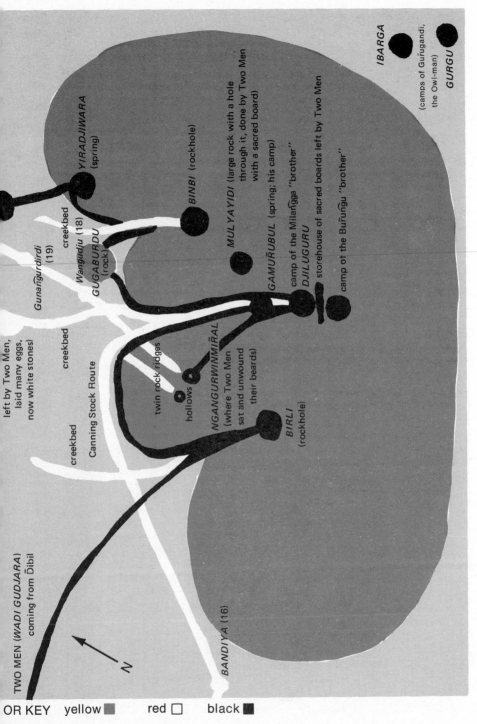

Figure 5–1. Crayon drawing of the travels of two men (Wadi Gudjara) in the Durba Hills area.

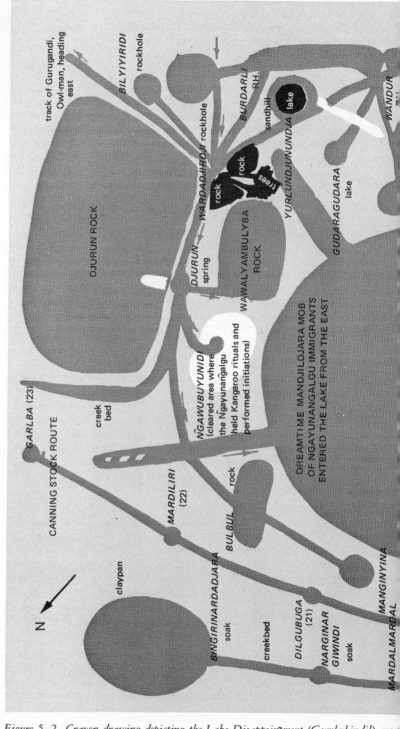

Figure 5–2. Crayon drawing depicting the Lake Disappointment (Gumbubindil) area

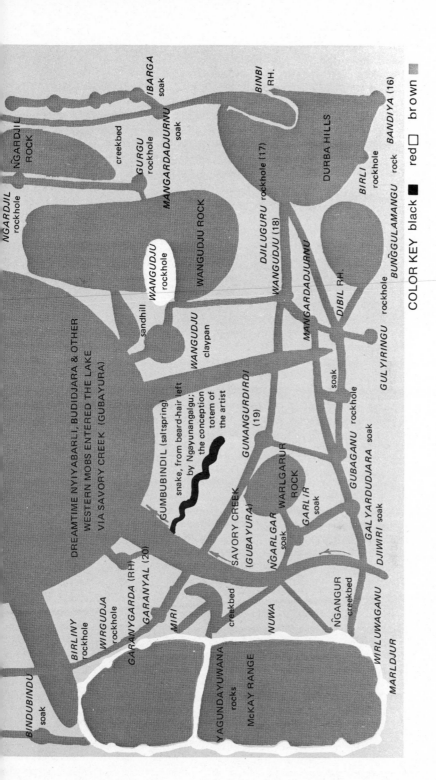

BINDUBINDU
soak

NGARDJIL
rockhole

NGARDJIL
ROCK

IBARGA
soak

GURGU
rockhole

creekbed

MANGARDADJURNU
soak

BINBI
R.H.

BIRLINY
rockhole

WIRGUDJA
rockhole

GARANYGARDA (R.H.)

GARANYAL (20)

DREAMTIME NYIYABARLI, BUDIDJARA & OTHER
WESTERN MOBS ENTERED THE LAKE
VIA SAVORY CREEK (GUBAYURA)

sandhill

WANGUDJU
rockhole

WANGUDJU ROCK

WANGUDJU
claypan

DJILUGURU rockhole (17)

WANGUDJU (18)

DURBA HILLS

BIRLI
rockhole

BUNGGULAMANGU rock

BANDIYA (16)

MIRI

creekbed

GUMBUBINDIL (saltspring)
snake, from beard-hair left
by Ngayunangalgu;
the conception
totem of
the artist

SAVORY CREEK
(GUBAYURA)

GUNANGURDIRDI
(19)

WARLGARUR
ROCK

GARLIR
soak

MANGARDADJURNU

DIBIL R.H.

soak

GULYIRINGU
rockhole

YAGUNDAYUWANA
rocks

McKAY RANGE

NUWA

NGARLGAR
soak

GUBAGANU rockhole

GALYARDUDJARA soak

NGANGUR
creekbed

DJIWIRI soak

WIRLUWAGANU

MARLDJUR

COLOR KEY black ■ red □ brown ▨

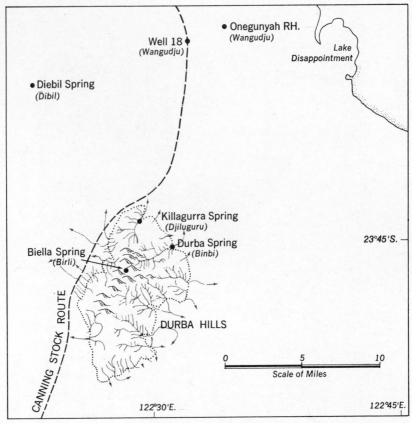

Map 3: The Durba Hills area.

Since there are literally hundreds of myths known to the Mardudjara, it is impossible to convey here the diversity of content that coexists with their striking uniformity of structure. But whether long or short, narrative or situational in general type, all myths bring people to a vivid awareness of the reality and relevance of the creative period. Just as there is no formal education among them, no formal inculcation of mythology occurs and the telling of myths is not given a special place by the Mardudjara in the framework of ritual life. But there are times and situations when it is felt appropriate to recount them; for example, when people are taken into territory previously unknown to them, or when newly found or imported objects, dances, rituals, and such are seen for the first time. Myths thus contextualize, incorporate, and connect isolated elements into the broader scheme of things.

Ritual   All religions are concerned with the maintenance of good relations between humans and spirits, because greater-than-human powers are believed to lie in the spiritual realm. The control or manipulation of these powers is an abiding concern of believers. Although withdrawn from direct contact with the physical world, the creative powers are immortal presences which have a strong interest in their human descendants as perpetuators of their original life design. As the Mardudjara understand their sacred contract, if they obey the Law and perform appropriate rituals, these acts will cause a reciprocal flow of life-giving power from the spiritual realm. By ritual

Two boys decorated with white-ochre rainmaking designs in readiness for a ceremonial welcome at a big meeting.

performance, people are also brought into close contact with those powers, and when correctly done, it releases power for the benefit of humans and other living things.

In the Mardudjara case, the elements of manipulation that are always present have more to do with individual acts than with major ritual activities, which are directed much more broadly toward a reciprocal flow of life force. The Aborigines do not see the Dreamtime beings as being involved directly in any of this reciprocity, but they presume that if their ritual activity and conformity to the Law were to cease, the spiritual powers would react by halting the transfer of power and the maintenance of life on earth. However, this view is expressed only in answer to the hypothetical question of the anthropologist; it is not a topic of speculation among the Mardudjara, who consider the possibility beyond comprehension.[3] When the Dreamtime powers wish to affect the living, they use spirit-beings as intermediaries, who are sometimes encountered by Aborigines during dreams or ritually induced states of altered consciousness.[4] The transfer of new knowledge, which is power, is effected through these spirit-beings whose impingement on human affairs is taken as proof of the existence and interest of the Dreamtime powers in the human world.

(a) *Individual Ritual.* Individual ritual acts can be performed virtually anywhere, at any time; most are socially approved and take place in public. They may be performed by anyone who knows the correct technique or invocation that aims to secure some desired result. The motivations for such acts are many and varied; some danger is perceived; a vexacious weather condition, often connected with spirit-beings of some kind, is warded off; or some desired weather (for example, rain) is being encouraged. In situations such as these, native doctors are favored as performers because of their allegedly greater magical powers, which include the ability to detect evil spirit-be-

[3] For the effects of culture contact on this concern, see Chapter 7.
[4] These beings are identified as *djidjigargaly* ("spirit-children"), but the stem *djidji* ("child") connotes their small size, not an ignorance of religious knowledge.

ings. They can use their magical objects to catch troublesome spirits, scare off human or spirit intruders, and so on. Their activity may include talking to or shouting at some spirit, singing songs, waving their arms, dancing, selecting certain objects or substances that will discourage or encourage continuance of some condition, and perhaps directing the behavior of others present. These ritual acts are usually spontaneous; for example, a native doctor leaps up and "slices" a strong wind that is disturbing a ritual, thus diverting it around the fringe of the assembled group. Or perhaps a large thundercloud on the horizon prompts several men and women to sing appropriate rainmaking songs as they beckon the cloud toward them, perhaps waving small bundles of bird feathers which attract the attention of the rain spirits that are believed to compose the cloud. Such acts, most often carried out with a minimum of formality or drama, are common occurrences in the lives of the Mardudjara.

The unseen or metaphysical is just as real as the visible and physical in their perception. The Aborigines make no clear distinction between natural and spiritual realms, in common with many other peoples in the world. They consider themselves and nonhuman entities and forces to be all equally real inhabitants of their cosmic order. All ritual acts reflect the confidence that the Mardudjara have in their ability to exert a measure of control over aspects of their world. If the strong wind persists or the thundercloud refuses to come closer, there are always reasonable explanations for such failures. But winds do die suddenly, and thunderclouds often approach, so there are always successes to reinforce and justify ritual acts.

(b) *Increase Rites.* One crucially important kind of ritual, which involves few actors yet indirectly affects the lives of all desert people, is the increase rite.[5] Scattered throughout the desert are *djabiya,* sites which the Aborigines believe are the spirit-homes of many different varieties of plants and animals, left there by the Dreamtime beings. At each site, which can be as unspectacular as a small flat stone or a hole in the ground, the spirits of that particular species are thought to reside.[6] This huge mass of spirits awaits only the summons of their human guardians (male estate-group elders in whose territory the site is located) each year to emerge and be plentiful. To the Mardudjara, fertility has nothing to do with insemination, pollination, and so forth. It results from human actions which evoke a reciprocal response by spiritual forces. Within the estate of every group there is at least one such site, so all groups have an important responsibility to perform properly the relevant rites each year. If a particular species seems to be in quite short supply in a given season, suspicion of inadequate performance is cast onto the group in whose estate the increase-center of that species is found. Distant groups may be prompted to send messengers with a small sacred board as a gift or reminder to the guardians and the spirits.[7]

Should there be no people in the area of a *djabiya* at the appropriate time, which is shortly before the expected appearance of large quantities of the species, this presents no problem. The local elders can always visit the site in dream-spirit form and "bring out" the spirits. In much the same way, men associated with rain-centers can bring it from there back to their territories or to wherever it is needed.

The rite itself is short and uncomplicated in most cases, consisting mainly of a

[5] This term is in common use to describe such rituals. It is true that the Aborigines commonly request large quantities of the species and urge it to be plentiful everywhere, but their main concern is with the maintenance of needed resources rather than any cumulative "increases."

[6] For some species there are more than one spirit-center, but these tend to be widely separated.

[7] This object is called a *yumbu,* which is also the name of sorcery objects associated with paid killings. This suggests that an element of threat is present, yet the Mardudjara stress that this kind of *yumbu* is "for food, not killing." (See p. 110 for a discussion of sorcery.)

cleaning of the site and perhaps bloodletting and singing in addition to spoken requests and exhortations by the visitors. As the following example shows, the association of site and species stems from a Dreamtime incident that resulted in the metamorphosis of that species into stone or a tree or some other physical form. A mythological validation always exists for both the association and some of the form that the ritual must take. Because increase rites are so localized, no two are identical, although in general structure and intent they are homogeneous throughout the desert.

> Badjirganya is an emu *djabiya* that consists of a clump of rounded stones with a large stone close by, said to be metamorphosed eggs and their emu mother. Wirdun, an ancestral eaglehawk-man of the Banaga section, who was left-handed, saw the mother on her nest one day while he was out hunting. He crept up to a gap between two long rocks, behind a tree, and threw a spear at her, but he missed. The Two Men, who were also out hunting, happened along at that moment, and scolded Wirdun, telling him that if he killed the emu there would be no more to lay eggs in the future. So Wirdun desisted, and at the end of the Dreamtime the eggs and emu mother turned to stone. The guardians, who may or may not include men with totemic links to Wirdun or emus, gather together whatever initiated men are available in the area at the time and go to the site before emu egg laying season every year. The men prefer to go in a large group because the spirits are thought to respond favorably to the presence of many people. One of the guardians stands exactly where Wirdun did and throws a spear in the direction of the "nest" with his left hand. Then the group approaches the site and the men clean all around it. Then one of the elders steps forward and addresses the emu spirits inside the *djabiya*, thus: "We want emu eggs. Make plenty. Give us lots. We want some for eating, some for emus—for meat! Keep them coming! You will do it because we all came to see you and to start you."

The implication of the essential verbal element of the increase rites is that the spirit-beings of the species concerned, as "kin," must automatically respond, and respond generously, to such requests from their human guardians and others who have come in good faith and carried out their part of the bargain.[8]

(c) *Group Ritual.* The high points of Mardudjara life are the big meetings, with their intensified sociality and the generation of great excitement and emotional and physical energy among performers and spectators alike. But there are many other times during their travels that the Mardudjara stage rituals that involve many or all members of a small assembly. Their repertoire consists of a large variety of rituals, many of which are performed also by other desert groups. Widely shared rituals usually center on the exploits of much traveled ancestral beings. This shared knowledge and performance of most of the major rituals is an inevitable result of the diffusion of religious lore that is continuous among Western Desert peoples. This does not mean, however, that every group therefore performs the same set of rituals, because just as each has a body of local mythology which is not widely known or shared beyond its estate, there may also be rituals (in addition to increase rites) which are associated with a particular local area and Dreamtime beings who did not travel widely and are little known by distant groups.

This kind of ritual may be owned collectively by the group in whose territory the associated Dreamtime events occurred and whose totemic connections with these particular beings are probably therefore strongest. Performance rights to these rituals

---

[8] All ancestral beings are considered to be kin of the living, but they are elderly and respected kin to whom a measure of deference and respect must be shown. In reference to them by kinship, Mardudjara use only terms for first and second ascending generation levels; for example, "F," "MB," "FF," "FM," and so on, which imply that respect is owed.

may not be given; instead, their restriction to a home area serves as a magnet to draw distant groups to be initiated into them at periodic big meetings held there. The senior men who are the acknowledged leaders for a ritual of this type decide as a group if and when they will allow the transfer of the necessary ritual paraphernalia and performance rights to others. The same is true of new rituals derived from dream-spirit revelations (see below). Performance rights for these remain restricted until those in control decide to release them, usually after a newer ritual is composed.

In addition to the sexual dichotomy discussed above, most rituals feature different male and female status divisions too, and the division of labor that takes place is based largely upon these. People of both sexes "rise through the ranks" by repeated ritual participation over a period of years and by the satisfactory performance of their allotted roles. Among initiated men there is a hierarchy of statuses which form the basis for a generalized division of labor that operates in the context of ritual. First are the "cooks," the older men who prepare the many different ceremonial feasts, act as advisors and directors of most rituals (and perform the most important "big" dances), and are guardians of the caches of sacred objects. Next are the active middle-aged men who are responsible for the mechanics of ritual activity. They transmit directives from the "cooks" to the statuses beneath theirs and perform specific tasks such as butchering game and dividing seedcakes for ritual feasts, greasing sacred boards in the storehouses, performing many important dances, and leading the hunts that are integral to all rituals.[9] The third status level is that of the "leg-men" who assist the second-level men in a variety of tasks and have major responsibilities as hunters and supervisors of novices, whom they discipline when necessary. The lowest level is that of the partly initiated young men who are novices. They must remain silent and do exactly as they are told during rituals. Men of the senior "cook" status together choose worthy candidates to join their ranks and in collaboration with those of the second status select new members for that level.

The most common stimulus for ritual is the encountering of neighboring bands, which temporarily increases the population sufficiently to allow for adequate performance of large-scale rituals that require more personnel of various statuses than are available in a single band. The decision as to which rituals to perform would depend on many factors, including: the presence of men with authority to direct a particular ritual; the locality and its totemic associations; the greater popularity of some rituals than others; the availability of paraphernalia needed for proper performance; and recent events, such as the death of a close relative which may prescribe the performance of an appropriate mourning ritual, or the arrival of novices being taken on pre- or post-initiation journeys of revelation. Whichever choice is made, the men usually include some rituals that can be staged in the camp area, at least in part, so that women and children can participate.

Many rituals are ideally suited to general performance, regardless of the number of people available. In many, women can also sing the songline and dance; also, a minimum of paraphernalia is needed. In some, only men sing the songs, and only women dance; in others, women and children dance, or perhaps women and girls, not boys. In most dream-spirit rituals (see below) men and women sing, men do most of the dancing, and in a concluding section, men dance with secret-sacred objects, unseen by the women and children.

[9] The sacred boards are kept heavily greased with fat and red ochre to protect them against termites. They are always kept carefully hidden, not only because they are extremely dangerous to women and children, but also because strangers may wish to steal them and channel their great power in order to kill someone, using sorcery.

At the other extreme are wholly secret-sacred rituals that exclude all opposite sex members and the uninitiated, apart from novices who are currently being inducted. Most such rituals are men's, which are held in men's country, well away from camping areas. More common than wholly secret-sacred rituals are those comprising both secret and nonsecret sets of activities; for example some of the rituals associated with circumcision (Chapter 4). In some of these composite rituals, men's secret rites are held in the bush while male and female "cooks" prepare a ritual feast and the rest of the community is secluded under male supervision some distance away. In the case of the Ngaawayil rainmaking ritual, when the secret bush rites are concluded for the day and the feast is ready, the rest of the community assembles at the ceremonial ground close to the camp to greet the men in ritual fashion upon their return from the bush. After the men have eaten and drunk (women do not eat at such feasts), the ground becomes the scene of much singing, dancing, and boisterous rainmaking activities that continue well into the night, with the entire community present (see Tonkinson 1972, 1974).

To illustrate a ritual that contains both secret and nonsecret elements in its structure, a brief description is given of an important Mardudjara ritual that has not traveled widely. The Nyanayi is based on the Dreamtime exploits of a kangaroo-man, Manggurdu, and his pursuers, who are in two groups: first, a large mob of bird-men, "featherfeet" killers (*djinagarbil,* "feet-tied," referring to the footwear used to disguise their tracks), who are of many different species, and second, a mob of cannibal-men called Wadjayidja. These creative beings are said to have traversed a wide area to the south of Lake Disappointment during a long and eventful chase after Manggurdu, their *gunga* ("intended victim"). The Nyanayi has over fifty associated dances and hundreds of songs, all dealing with the theme of ritual killers and their successes and failures. Men say that when a featherfeet expedition is organized to pursue and kill someone guilty of a grave offense, preparations must include songs and other elements from the Nyanayi.

There are two distinct locales for Nyanayi performances, the camp area and a secret bush ground. Activities alternate between them, with nonsecret performances at the camp ground every evening, and daily sessions at the secret ground, attended by initiated men and perhaps some novices. To begin the sequence, which may continue for a week or more, there is an evening session at the camp ground, lasting about two or three hours.

The men sit in a circle around a small fire, with another larger one a short distance away on the side opposite to where the women and children form a semicircle; the latter neither sing nor dance. The men, undecorated the first night, beat time on the ground with clubs or thick sticks. After the singing is under way, men leave the circle to dance, in ones, twos, or larger groups, using movements and gestures appropriate to the ancestor(s) being portrayed. These dances are brief, lasting rarely more than a couple of minutes. They elicit much laughter in the audience, which shows its approval of good dramatic performances with a characteristic tongue trill that indicates strong appreciation of some act well done. To conclude the session, the women and children are sent back to the camping area, with instructions not to look back, then in a secret-sacred dance, a man wearing a grass head-ring portrays owl-man's wife, who is calling out and looking fearfully around her as she travels in search of her mate.

In the evening sessions that follow, most of the men will be wearing body decorations from the day's performance. Some women will get up and dance around the circle of men in their typical *nyambi* style (Chapter 4) for some time prior to the men's dances. The variety of men's dances increases, and two secret dances usually conclude the session after the women and children have left. The duration of the evening performances may also lessen towards the end, as the men become progressively more tired from the daily singing and dancing activities.

The secret sections of the Nyanayi are structured very much like the Kangaroo ritual (Chapter 4). The men leave camp in a group sometime during the morning and disappear into men's country for the rest of the day. At the Nyanayi ground, they form a circle and begin singing. The several elders who are the acknowledged leaders for this ritual will have decided the previous evening which dances are to be performed. In consultation with other middle-aged and older men, some of whom intend to dance, they choose some younger dancers from among those still learning the ritual. Early in the afternoon the dancers leave the circle to decorate and prepare the objects that they will need. They work out of sight of the men who remain to form the audience and supply the musical accompaniment when the dances eventually take place. The task of constructing the various dancing paraphernalia may take several hours, although in dances featuring the younger men little is worn or carried besides body designs.

Late afternoon, when the dancers signal that all is ready, growing excitement manifests itself in the singing, which becomes loud and spirited as the dancing is due to begin. In the hour that follows, as many as twelve different dances, each with its appropriate song, may be performed. These range from solos, to pairs, to large groups. The dances differ widely in form: in some, the performers merely walk towards the audience, whereas others require the actors to crouch or lie down and their body movements in the dance are therefore quite restricted, and the stress is on subtle movements of chest and shoulders. Still other dances call for rapid arm and leg movements. In one memorable dance, two featherfeet emu-men advance on the audience, and as they get closer their faces are seen to be hideously distorted; they have been blackened with charcoal, divided into puffy segments by tightly drawn hairstring, and their everted lips are smeared with blood. Their hair is tied into many small topknots, thus adding to their bizarre and frightening appearance. They convey a most realistic impression of having just feasted on some victim. None of the young novices laugh at this performance and they recoil as the actors confront them menacingly.

Almost everyone laughs loudly, however, when an old man dances as Yanma, a Dreamtime woman whose anus and vagina are hot and sore from a sorcerer's attack. He appears in the distance, carrying a firestick in one hand as he laboriously advances, and with the other frantically fanning his rear end as he turns it toward the audience. [The Mardudjara have a keen sense of humor that pervades all their activities, including ritual. There are very few occasions so awe-inspiring or momentous in their religious significance that laughter and joking would be thought out of place.]

The "big" dances that come at the end of each day's performance may not be witnessed by the newest initiates, in keeping with the idea of initiation as a process of gradual revelation. As in most other rituals, the opening Nyanayi dances are considered of lesser import and are danced by the younger men who are in the early stages of learning the ritual. Anyone who makes trouble or who fails to hunt diligently risks the ignominy and shame of being held back or even excluded from such rituals. Normally, however, young men are eventually selected to perform more and more important dances.

The one or two dances each day that the initiates are forbidden to see will probably involve dangerous paraphernalia, such as large fencelike thread-cross arrangements; or they may involve no objects at all, but they depict a happening of major mythological importance.

The Nyanayi has a particular charcoal and ochre body decoration for each animal and bird being depicted, but it is notable for the variety and beauty of the thread-cross ornaments worn or carried by the performers. Made from grass, sharp sticks, or sacred boards into frames onto which hair-twine is threaded, these face-pieces,

Madimadi decorated ready to perform a Nyanayi dance.

headdresses, crosses, and such are all representations of what the Nyanayi beings themselves wore when they traveled.[10] In the mallee hen dance, for instance, each of the dozen or so performers carries a spear-based thread-cross, which he sticks upright in his "nest" (a circular depression lined with leaves), around which he then dances in a crouch step, making the mallee hen call. After this dance, which usually comes near the end of a Nyanayi sequence, the watching initiates are told to lie down on their backs, close together. The dancers then stand on two sides of them and rub the thread crosses violently back and forth across their chests and stomachs, and break the small wooden crosspieces against them. This brief but painful ordeal over, the young men stand and clutch the tattered objects to their chests. They are surrounded and harangued by the older men, who remind them of their obligation to reciprocate by hunting and to uphold the Law, amd scold them severely for their real and imagined shortcomings. Careful not to let the young men see their grins, and suppressing laughter at their own witticisms, they mount a ferocious verbal onslaught, trying to outdo one another with salvos such as: "Leave the women alone until your penises are long enough for the job!" or "Keep your minds on the Law, not what hangs between your legs!"

Although, typically, the initiates are not told why the sacred objects are rubbed across their bodies, the old men say that this helps protect them against human and supernatural attack—no doubt through a transference of the life force that is inherent in all such objects. During this initial exposure to the Nyanayi, they learn little

[10]This category of objects, called *wanigi* over most of the Western Desert area, is characterized by its impermanence, since a thread-cross can only be used once, and must later be dismantled. The hair-string with which it is threaded, however, is rolled into balls and may be reused indefinitely.

of the meanings of the ritual, except for its association with featherfeet bird-men and their search for victims. But through repeated attendance in later years they will learn the songs, dance the dances, and fill in for themselves the gaps in their knowledge of what it is all about.

(d) *Ritual Categorization.* The Mardudjara make a semantic distinction between two types of ritual: *mangunydjanu* ("from the creative period") and *bardundjaridjanu* ("from the dream-spirits").[11] Most rituals belong to the first category; that is, they are believed to have been instituted by ancestral beings and therefore are essentially Dreamtime products. But every few years one or more men will be "given" a new ritual during sleep, when a person's *bardundjari* ("dream-spirit") leaves the body and wanders. Sometimes it encounters spirit-beings who, as intermediaries between the withdrawn creative beings and the living, may reveal a new tune, song, dance, or sacred object. Because the Aborigines attach much significance to their dreams, a man will usually disclose his dream to others, but not usually until a half-dozen or more songs and other information have been "found," lest the spirit-beings become angry or jealous and decide against making further revelations. Excited, and perhaps rendered hypersuggestive by what they have been told, other men may soon dream about similar happenings or themes and wake up remembering songs or dances that they, too, have been given during their dream-spirit experiences. Women, too, may "find" songs and report these to the men for inclusion in the ritual. What happens in dreams, then, is the transfer of new knowledge between two kinds of spirit-beings which transcend time and space to link the eternal truths and powers of the Dreamtime with the here and now.

The ritual that is finally built up has a distinctive tune, body decorations, set of dances, and thread-cross designs; its songline may have a hundred or more verses.[12] Women and children learn the songlines by listening to the men, and these become popular, being sung day or night, regardless of whether the ritual is performed or not. Only a small number of the dances, and perhaps songs, are kept secret, and it is with these that the sacred objects are displayed. This occurs at the end of each evening's performance when one of the dancers throws a firestick as a signal to the women and children to face away from the ground and cover their eyes.

The great appeal of these rituals is that they require minimal preparation and no special grounds, and relatively small groups can stage them effectively. They remain the property of the man or men to whom they were revealed, until such time as their "owners" decide to hand them on to another group. With this transfer, their travels begin, and most significantly, the magic of time and space operates to transform them from *bardundjaridjanu* to *mangunydjanu.* To the groups hundreds of miles away on the opposite side of the desert they are attributed to the Dreamtime, stripped of all information regarding the circumstances of their relatively recent creation in the process of diffusion. They rapidly become timeless and imbued with all the power that a Dreamtime origin connotes. This process is almost certainly how most of the huge corpus of Aboriginal rituals originally came into being.

Among the group that originates it, a dream-spirit ritual is relatively short-lived in terms of full performances because in a year or two it will be supplanted by a newly "found" or borrowed dream-spirit ritual. But the songs are remembered indefinitely, especially if they have a popular and catchy tune. The Mardudjara, men and women,

---

[11] The dream-spirit is said to resemble an eaglehawk when in flight. But, when traveling in this form, a man's legs become wings, his testicles become eyes, and his anus his mouth, in a kind of back-to-front transformation that is said to protect the traveler in the event of likely encounters with malevolent spirit-beings.

[12] A detailed description of a dream-spirit ritual is given in Tonkinson (1970).

need very little excuse to break into song. Although favorite choices are often dream-spirit songs, men like to sing from their repertoire of several thousand secret-sacred songs when they are out of earshot of women and children.

Another aspect of Mardudjara ritual classification concerns the notion of function or purpose. With some kinds of ritual there is a clear-cut primary purpose, one that the Aboriginal actors readily identify; for example, to bring up a particular species at an increase-center, physical initiation, causing rain to fall, separating a deceased's spirit from the living, and so on. They may also mention more general functions that these and other rituals fulfil, such as engendering good feelings among the participants, bringing together different groups in ideally harmonious union, transmitting the Law to younger men, acquiring strength and protection against malevolent forces, and so on. If the many functions that are discernible to an outside observer are added to this list, it is obvious that any given ritual simultaneously contributes to or fulfils a diverse range of functions, most of which are complementary and mutually reinforcing in their effects.

One major function of ritual which must be considered is that of boundary mainte-nance, the reinforcement of ethnocentrism and promotion of in-group solidarity. It has been noted how effectively ritual can underline male exclusiveness and separate the initiated men from the rest of society. But to what extent does it serve to differentiate each linguistic unit from its neighbors or encourage an inward-looking "elitist" ethos in a given social group? Among the Mardudjara, ritual serves much more to unite each group with its neighbors than to separate them. Desert ecological conditions make it essential that social structures minimize rather than create boundaries of whatever kind, because for continued successful adaptation there must be a relatively unrestricted flow of people and ideas. Strehlow (1965:131), contrasting the compara-tive lack of cultural conservatism among the Western Desert peoples with the intense and jealous conservatism of the Aranda of central Australia, says:

. . . the Western Desert nomads, whose wanderings frequently took them into the lands of distant tribal groups, remained open to the suggestions of their neigh-bours, and even of other "tribes," in religious, social, and artistic matters. Unhin-dered by the rigidity of outlook that results from centuries of residence within safe hunting grounds, the Western Desert people borrowed religious concepts, social norms, and artistic practices freely. . . .

The very same totemic geography that binds a group to its estate and fosters pride and ethnocentrism also, through the many ancestral tracks, links them to all their neigh-bors and to other individuals and groups in distant areas. Likewise, the exclusive per-formance of each group's own dream-spirit rituals soon yields to an urge to share it proudly with neighbors and others.

In many other, more favored parts of the continent—where population densities are higher, ranges smaller, and boundaries more significant and where clearly defined, well developed clan structures exist—totemic groups assume considerable importance, and ritual prerogatives are generally jealously guarded. Under such conditions, the illegal appropriation by one group of another's totemic clan design or songs is cause for a major feud, with bloodshed and sometimes deaths resulting. Such exclu-siveness—a "luxury" that the Mardudjara and their desert neighbors cannot afford—may in part be why social totemism (the linking of a social group to a particular animal, plant, and so on) is unimportant and cult lodges are absent among them.

The overriding significance of totemic associations to the Mardudjara is their link-ing of *individuals* to the life-sustaining spiritual realm rather than the linking of par-ticular *groups* to the wider cosmic order, since the latter implies separation and exclusiveness, in that totemic associations are ascribed by birth, never achieved. Even members of the same estate-group may have different ancestral totems, as was noted earlier. Totemism, like ritual, dilutes rather than reinforces parochialist tendencies among Mardudjara groups.[13] Thus it is significant that role allocation in their rituals is based on seniority and specialized knowledge of the particular ritual rather than on totemic association in most cases; for example, in the Nyanayi, a man having Emu as his ancestral totem is as likely to be chosen to dance White Cockatoo as Emu, since his "descent" from emus is not thought to make him a better or more rightful performer of an Emu dance.

Songlines Singing is an essential element in most Mardudjara ritual performances because the songline follows in most cases the direction of travel of the beings concerned and highlights cryptically their notable as well as mundane activities. Most songs, then, have a geographical as well as mythical referent, so by learning the songlines men become familiar with literally thousands of sites even though they have never visited them; all become part of their cognitive map of the desert world. Because ancestral beings traveled from waterhole to waterhole much of the time, song sequences imprint knowledge that may have practical value should people ever travel in the area depicted. They may also provide vital clues as to what dangerous or sacred sites must be avoided in distant territories.

A song may contain anywhere from two to a dozen words, and when performed during a ritual is repeated many times over. This combination of few words and much repetition obviously aids in its quick memorization, but a much more difficult feat is that of keeping the songs in the correct sequence. At the same time, the singers have to remember to delete any that mention sites which are the birthplace, home base, or name of any recently dead person. The singing of such a song would bring a sudden and painful reminder of the death, and thus distress close relatives in the audience. These songs, in literal translation, reveal very little. They are, it seems, just words strung together, yet they are usually full of meaning to those who know. To illustrate from the Ngaawayil rainmaking ritual:

(a) *ii burnunya burnu ñgadjinya ñgadji yuwanya yuwa*
    lightning stones   to me?   give   give

Explanation: The two major rainmaking ancestors, Wirnba and Garbardi, met up and exchanged rainmaking stones (sacred) as a gesture of friendship.

(b) *ii warlurmaliny warlurmaliny garbuñgga garbuñgga Minganbula ñgarindja*
    rainclouds   daytime   [Place name]   lying
Explanation: Rainclouds, flat and long, are sacred wooden boards, seen in the daytime at Mingan waterhole, that lay across the ancestor Wirnba's chest as he traveled around creating waterholes and bringing rain to the land.

It should be noted that some of the major rituals performed by the Mardudjara (and the Ngaawayil is one) are sung in dialects of people in far distant areas, and the men are therefore unable to identify with certainty many of the words in the songs they sing. What matter are the main details and themes.

In their singing, the Mardudjara employ a great variety of tempos, and although each songline has its own distinctive tune, almost all require a very wide vocal range

---

[13]Maddock (1972) discusses the nature of economic and religious opposition throughout Aboriginal Australia between forces promoting parochialism and those that reinforce an outward-looking "universalism." He shows how the widespread "owner–manager" distinction operates to deny descent groups autonomy in the performance of their own rituals, since members of both categories are needed for the ritual to be staged. (See also Meggitt 1962 and 1966 for the ritual significance of this division among the Walbiri Aborigines.)

for both men and women. The often guttural and nasalized singing of Aboriginal men, who frequently punctuate it with screams, whoops, grunts, and falsetto ululation, is quite distinctive and impressive; it has been described by an ethnomusicologist as ". . . completely different from most other vocal qualities of the world" (T. Jones 1965:367). The sung word is so different from the spoken as to be almost unrecognizable, and the effect of a large group singing is often quite exciting, especially in loud songs that have strong percussive accompaniments. Purely instrumental music is absent, and virtually all dancing is accompanied by singing. It takes young men many years to build their repertoires to the level of their elders. The Mardudjara also have a category of songs known as *nyirbu,* composed by members of either sex from everyday happenings of many different kinds; for example, a flood, a lost lover, a hunting incident, a fight, and so on. Because many of these nonsacred songs have a locational referent, they help vivify the physical as well as social environments in contemporary, human terms, thus adding another dimension to that of the mythical in uniting an event with a place.

The Interrelationship of Myth, Ritual, and Songline   Myths speak of the wonders of the creative epoch; songlines trace ancestral tracks and illustrate Dreamtime happenings in abbreviated, rhythmic, and exciting fashion; and rituals bring some of these happenings to life in a dramatic setting while binding people and the spiritual realm into close association. All three elements share an explicit connection to the Dreamtime, but the nature of their interrelationship is far from a simple one-to-one arrangement, and in fact there is considerable autonomy among them.

Most myths have no related ritual or songline, although the reverse is not true. In any given ritual, the associated myth and songline may share clear thematic similarities, but the songline is no mnemonic for the myth, such that the latter could be reconstructed from the former. Shared themes, however, may make the association between songlines and myths closer than the association of either with concrete ritual elements, such as dances. The words of a song generally offer no clue as to how the dance it accompanies is to be interpreted; in most cases it does not even identify the ancestral being(s) concerned. Yet in an important sense songlines and dances are alike in being very much more circumscribed and controlled in their performance than are myths. In the narration of myths, there is much greater latitude for individual elaboration and character development than could ever be tolerated in publicly transmitted songs and dances, which must be performed accurately and in conformity to the Law for the ritual's success. The unity and integration of these elements are achieved through their relationship to the Dreamtime concept rather than by any tightness of fit to one another.

SITES AND PARAPHERNALIA

The landforms that stand as the creations of the Dreamtime beings and the paraphernalia associated with the religious life are here considered together because both are physical referents—the one fixed, the other portable—of spiritual presence, power, and potential. A timeless quality is accorded the multitude of landscape features which are imbued with mythological significance and are thus brought to life. These features include in some cases large trees, rock carvings, and paintings and other manmade constructions such as stone cairns and large ground arrangements of stones, all attributed to the actions of Dreamtime beings. These are the fixed referents, the anchors that hold particular individuals and groups to them through close bonds of sentiment.

The great variety of portable referents derive sacredness and power from their intimate association, through "actual" contact or structural similarity, with some Dreamtime event or being. Many, such as thread-crosses, body decorations, and carved boards, are produced in emulation of those worn or possessed by ancestral heroes. Such boards are hidden in caches where certain Dreamtime beings are said to have placed their boards. Red, white, brown, and yellow ochres are all attributed to Dreamtime events; red ochre, the metamorphosed blood of those beings, is the most important. High-quality red ochre from a few well-known quarries diffuses widely through the desert via gift exchanges at big meetings as well as through personal networks. Because the ancestral beings frequently used it in similar ways, initiated men make much use of blood, drawn from their arm veins and penis, in secret rituals.

The objects considered to be the most highly sacred and dangerous are stones, varying in size and shape, some natural formations and others obviously at one time shaped and smoothed and perhaps incised with designs. These stones are held to be metamorphosed parts of the bodies of ancestral beings, or else of objects owned and carried by them. These group-owned objects, like sacred boards, are believed to be replete with power and are kept well hidden. Although most of them play no prominent role in group ritual performances, they are often displayed, to be gazed at, stroked, touched against the body, and discussed in awed tones by those fully initiated men privileged to be exposed to them. Certain of them may be passed from group to group, together with an account of their origin and totemic association, perhaps in company with a ritual that centers on the being(s) from which they derive. As gifts, they are the ultimate in generosity, and the donors can expect an eventual reciprocal gift of stones of similar significance.

In addition to the boards and stones that are always the property of groups of men, every initiated man has his personal paraphernalia, which he usually carries with him from one camping place to the next, carefully wrapped in a small bark, fur, or hair-twine bundle. Its contents will be an assortment of objects, by no means all of which are secret: hair-string bands, pearlshell pendants, bird-feather bundles, eaglehawk down-feathers, ochre, spinifex gum, and small stone knives used in ritual operations. There may also be a few objects useful for magic, such as polished stones, small bull-roarers, and possibly love-magic charms. The number and variety of such items vary from individual to individual, and those having a specific ritual use may be left hidden at a particular spot and retrieved only when they are likely to be needed. As with all portable artifacts, personal bundles are kept to a minimum size and weight so as not to impede mobility, and they are left near camp whenever men go out hunting from there.

Since men frequently discover new items and receive others through exchange, one of their favorite activities whenever bands meet is to display, contemplate, and discuss the objects that each possesses. Since all natural and many man-made objects are held to be of Dreamtime origin, they trigger animated discussions of relevant mythology among the men which are aimed at fitting all such items into the grand scheme of things.

MAGIC AND SORCERY

Although it is impossible to separate convincingly "magical" from "religious" elements in any society, the above heading is meant to focus attention on the characteristics and actions of individuals who claim to use extrahuman and human powers to protect, cure, or harm others.

Mabarn   Men who most often use their special powers for socially approved ends are termed Mabarn throughout the Western Desert; the same term refers to the magical stone or shell objects they are said to carry in their stomachs.[14] Since neither "native doctor" nor "medicine man" is a satisfactory gloss, the vernacular is used in the discussion that follows. Most Mabarn inherit their special powers from their fathers, but *mabarn* objects can be obtained from others. Almost all are men, and perhaps 10 or 15 percent of Mardudjara males are Mabarn. They are not required to go through the elaborate special initiations, modeled on death and rebirth, that have been reported for the Eastern Desert regions (Roheim 1945, R. and C. Berndt 1977, Elkin 1977). Nothing in their appearance or demeanor distinguishes Mabarn from their fellows, and as specialists they practice part-time only, since all their other activities are the same as those of other men. Their distinctiveness lies in their possession of special skills, knowledge, and psychic powers that give them greater and more effective access to the spiritual realm. In their communications with the spiritual world they are aided by spirit-familiars, usually small birds or animals, that assist them in all sorts of ways but are most useful as messengers between themselves and the spirit-beings that possess limitless magical powers from which the Mabarn draw.

The Mardudjara rely heavily on their Mabarn for the treatment of persistent or worrisome illness. If no Mabarn happens to be present and the patient is too sick to walk, someone will go to neighboring bands to find one. Although individual techniques vary a little, all Mabarn adopt a similar approach in their treatment of illness. A Mabarn first uses his magical powers to "see inside" the patient and thus locate the source of the problem, which is most often a foreign object lodged deep in the body. The treatment consists of massage, pounding, slapping, manipulation, and applying pressure with hands (and sometimes feet) to the body, as well as biting and sucking; its purpose is to remove the lodged object. If a patient is feverish, "bad" or "hot" blood is removed by sucking and then put into a shady spot to cool down, thus cooling the patient.

After the initial "X-ray" examination, the Mabarn walks a short distance away to manipulate his own stomach and withdraw his *mabarn* (or one of them since he may have many) which he blows onto in order to charge it with extra power. Approaching with his fist firmly clenched around his *mabarn,* he then inserts it into the body and directs it to its target by massage or other means so that it will drive out the foreign body, which he withdraws using similar manipulation. He again walks away to examine his catch; he may then cast it away, but more often he returns to show it to the patient.[15] The fact that, to an outside observer, the object is produced from inside the patient by the Mabarn's sleight of hand should not be grounds for impugning his sincerity. He believes in the efficacy of his powers, as does the patient, who inevitably feels much better when he or she sees, for example, a one- or two-inch sliver of stone or wood that allegedly caused the trouble.[16] Such tricks of the trade are never a topic of conversation among Mabarn or others.

Nonphysical treatment also plays an important role in a Mabarn's curative activi-

[14] For this reason, Mabarn is capitalized in reference to the practitioner, and uncapitalized when referring to the magical objects possessed by them.

[15] Mabarn "throw" and "retrieve" their own magical *mabarn* as well as other objects in a variety of situations; they look for signs on the returned object that will provide information. For instance, a circumcision knife is "thrown" just prior to its use; if it returns "bloodied" then it cannot be used, lest the novice bleed to death. Mabarn also throw their *mabarn* to scout ahead and to detect the presence of evil spirits or featherfeet in the vicinity.

[16] It is interesting that the name given to objects "fired" by sorcerers and evil spirits is the same as the generic term for sacred boards, whose great power can be used for either good or evil.

ties. For example, Wagadjirar, who is considered one of the most powerful and effective of the Mardudjara Mabarn, sometimes cures serious illness with the help of his *bibiruwar* (butcher bird) spirit-familiar.

Nyalbun, an old man, had been unwell for about two weeks, and sent for Wagadjirar to treat him for the pains in his chest that were bothering him. Wagadjirar examined him and diagnosed that his heart had a hole in it and was crumbling into ashes—too big a defect for Wagadjirar alone to fix. Waiting until Nyalbun had fallen asleep, the Mabarn magically removed his heart and gave it to his bird-spirit to take to Lake Disappointment and leave for the Ngayunangalgu cannibal-beings to repair (see Chapter 2). Since in the Dreamtime *bibiruwar* were traditional friends and allies of the Ngayunangalgu, they are safe from attack. The Ngayunangalgu Mabarn took the heart, cleaned it by washing it with a special hot water, then covered it with eaglehawk down-feathers and replaced it on the surface of the lakebed, where it was retrieved by the bird-spirit. On receipt of the repaired heart, Wagadjirar pushed it magically down through Nyalbun's head while he was still asleep. He subsequently made a rapid recovery, after the Mabarn gave him a full account of the problem and his treatment of it.

Mabarn are also called upon to recover missing objects, predict future events, explain unusual phenomena, and protect people against nonphysical attack. Their ability to detect the presence or influence of malevolent spirits or featherfeet killers makes them invaluable in a variety of ritual and mundane situations. Mabarn are believed to travel inside whirlwinds or as dream-spirits on raftlike arrangements of sacred boards. Sometimes they travel at the head of a group of people in dream-spirit form, riding on the back of a magical hair-string that becomes a snake in flight. The leadership of Mabarn on such trips is said to be highly desirable because on visits to distant areas the likelihood of encountering evil spirits is high. Without Mabarn to help them avoid such meetings and protect them from attack, dream-spirits may be weakened or even captured, in which case the body that they have left will weaken and eventually die. During performance of the Ngaawayil rainmaking ritual, for example, it is essential that male participants be taken in dream-spirit form to visit the many waterholes where the dangerous rainmaking ancestral snakes still live, to bring up the rain; it will follow the travelers back to the area where the ritual is taking place. Mabarn and people who have the rainmakers as their ancestral totem and will therefore be recognized by their spirit-kin ride at the front of the hair-string "snakes," thus assuring the travelers of a safe journey in and out of the waterholes, because the snake ancestors are quieted by the presence of the Mabarn.

Mabarn most often work alone, but in some cases they join forces with others—on difficult cases or where the community at large is thought to be threatened in some way:

Five weeks after his circumcision, Mani seems weak and his penis is not drying out as rapidly as it should. One of his guardian "grandfathers" claims to have seen Mani whispering to someone, yet there was no one anywhere near his camp at the time. Two Mabarn have treated him, yet he still seems listless, as if his spirit has been stolen. Two more Mabarn are called in (it is big meeting time and a large group is assembled) and the four experts go to work, using their *mabarn* to scrutinize the novice and his camping area. They are agreed: a malevolent spirit (male but with breasts) is hiding underground and has indeed captured the youth's spirit. The Mabarn first move some distance away, in different directions (but not in one another's firing line), using leafy branches to dust a clear path from the camp to where they stand to withdraw and "fire" their mabarn into it (the novice has been moved to one side). I am amazed to see a small whirlwind appear a yard in front of one of the Mabarn, as he stands pointing his *mabarn* between clenched hands, and then move unerringly (uncharacteristic of willywillys) down the path he has cleared and straight through the middle of the camp. (When I later comment enthusiastically on this phenomenon, my listeners shrug their shoulders: naturally—he's a Mabarn, isn't he!). When all four have fired their *mabarn,* they assemble at the camp and confer; they agree that they have hit the evil being and it fled, leaving the novice's spirit. He recovers quickly.

If a person is gravely ill, several Mabarn may mount a combined offensive against the forces deemed to be responsible for the problem. A Mabarn's task at such times is to convince the patient that his power is greater than that of the people or spirits being held responsible; if he cannot do so, death may soon follow. I have witnessed the death within a few days of apparently healthy Mardudjara who have announced that they are "finished" and have succumbed despite repeated efforts by Mabarn (and trained medical staff, in the contact situation) to cure them.

When Mabarn work together, there appears to be no sign of jealousy or rivalry among them. They operate with no clear expectation of recompense, but grateful patients may give them food or some other gift in return for their treatment. Other people are somewhat in awe of the powers of Mabarn, but this role does not place them apart from or above others; that is, they are not accorded any privileges or higher status in the community because they are Mabarn.

For all Mabarn, dreams and dream-spirit travels play a major role in their diagnosis and treatment of individuals and in many of the activities carried out by them for the common good. But dreams are important in everyone's life, and people who seek treatment from Mabarn often do so after self-diagnosis. A recurrent theme in Mardudjara dreams involves an attack by one or more evil spirits throwing missiles, some of which they are unable to dodge. Any adult who has a disturbing dream may take it as a bad omen, just as good dreams about great successes in hunting or gathering activities will come true soon. Dreams and a variety of other signs act as motivators or inhibitors of action. For example, seeing or hearing certain birds at certain times indicates some impending danger, such as featherfeet lurking somewhere nearby. The occurrence of nerve twinges or throbbing in different parts of the body is taken as a sign that someone in a particular kin category is ill, or dead, or is coming soon. For instance, *milyga,* a twinge in the groin, indicates that an "EB" or "spouse" is thinking of you; *wimalwimal,* a heart twinge, means that a "MB" not seen for a long time will be encountered soon; *dagarldagarl,* an itching in the nose, is a premonition of a serious fight or a death. Taken together, these many signs constitute a kind of psychic "sixth sense," commented on by many observers of the Aborigines, who have noted their sometimes uncanny ability to know when deaths have occurred among distant kin and to foretell other happenings.

Love-Magic   The practice of love-magic is not common among the Mardudjara, who claim that the techniques, objects, and rituals they possess were all obtained from other areas. Members of either sex may use it to attract a lover or rekindle strong desire between marriage partners. In secret activities carried out by one or two people, special songs are sung and the name of a desired one is spoken, usually over something belonging to that person. If the practitioners are men, they may swing small bull-roarers at a secluded spot, for the sound will penetrate the head of the desired one and make her weak with desire for the performer of the magic. All such techniques are thought to cause the person who is the object of them to become so obsessed with longing for the practitioner that they will be impelled to gratify their desires.

There are also several large-scale rituals that have strong love-magical connotations. These may or may not involve both sexes in the same place at the same time. Their aim is a more generalized arousal of all participants, brought about by the sexually explicit and erotic dances and songs that are performed. Although the pairs of dancers are of the same sex—and in many performances they simulate intercourse, much to the delight of the audience—there is no intent to rouse homosexual desires.[17]

Sorcery   Mabarn are said not to practice sorcery against close kin and associates, but they are sometimes allegedly involved in its practice against people in distant groups. Because the community image of its Mabarn is decidedly positive, their periodic resort to sorcery is presumed to be warranted and to be directed against some wrong-doing outsider. Any man (but never a woman) who possesses the necessary objects and techniques is capable of working sorcery, but since the practice is usually condemned, Mardudjara men always deny that they have ever engaged in it. Since sorcerers usually work alone and in secret, the practice is detected most often by its effects (sickness or death) rather than its performance. Except for the very young and very old, whose deaths may not be suspect, other deaths are considered unnatural, the work of malevolent forces, either human or spiritual.

The Mardudjara believe that malevolent spirits, called by the generic term *malbu*, were probably already on earth when the creative beings arrived, and although most were later killed off by them, some remained and have given people trouble ever since. Variously described as hairy, long-toothed, cannibalistic, and ill-disposed toward humans, the most dangerous *malbu* live in areas far distant from Mardudjara country. The more local spirit-beings, who inhabit several known and avoided sites within the area, are thought to be much less inclined to harm grievously their living "countrymen," unless of course someone inadvertently comes too close to their home. As noted earlier, some Mardudjara claim such beings as their ancestral totem, having been left behind by them. Groups of evil spirits that are associated with certain kinds of illness are mostly located in distant places, so when, for example, an influenza epidemic hits a band, the local Mabarn will soon know which group of beings is responsible.[18]

Proof of the activities of either *malbu* or human sorcerers is the removal of a foreign body from a sick person. Should countermagic fail and the victim dies, the inquest that eventually takes place can have minimal social consequences (as when spirit-beings are identified as the killers). Alternatively, it can lead to accusations and counteraccusations, physical violence, dire threats, and sometimes the organization of a group composed of the victim's close male relatives to search out and execute the alleged killer. Significantly, the Mardudjara claim that resort to countersorcery is rare among them; instead they prefer an open confrontation with the accused killers at a big meeting session devoted to dispute settlement. However, they tell of featherfeet expeditions sometimes being mounted. These involve elaborate ritual preparation of the members, including the dislocation of the little toe of each foot upward so that it will act as an "eye" which prevents them stepping on dry sticks that would break and thus alert the victim. Also, the travelers wear small sacred boards strapped to the back of each leg to "lighten" it and thus enable them to move fast and far without fatigue.

Disputes within the band or local group should be settled openly, face-to-face, not by sorcery. But, as the Mardudjara point out, a few people of bad disposition probably harbor great resentment after conflict and may therefore resort to *yumbu* sorcery, a

---

[17] Apart from some mutual masturbation among adolescent males, there is no homosexuality among the Mardudjara, but a great deal of homosociality in that members of the same sex, whose kin relationships allow a lack of restraint, often touch, hug, and engage in considerable body contact.

[18] People whose senility involves sometimes erratic and disturbing behavior may be thought to have become *malbu*. A few others, usually characterized by some behavioral inconsistencies, are said to be true *malbu* who were substituted for a human child in infancy.

"hired killer" variety named for the small length of hair-string that the hirer spins from his own beard and hair, then attaches to a small bull-roarer or wooden "killing stick" with a piece of spinifex resin. Wrapped securely in a feather-bundle, the *yumbu* is delivered to a distant Mabarn ally by a trusted messenger of the hirer, together with the intended victim's name. If the Mabarn keeps the *yumbu,* he is accepting the contract. Here is one informant's account of what would probably transpire:

> The Mabarn gets two or three close friends to help. Once the victim is in the area, perhaps at big meeting time, the killers either grab him from his camp at night (after the Mabarn has magically sedated everyone, dogs and all) or they ambush him when he goes to relieve himself. They dislocate his neck and he stops breathing, then they lay him on his back. Using a sharp stone knife they put a small slit in his abdomen and remove one kidney, some fat and a piece of his liver (to be later eaten by the Mabarn). They stuff green leaves into his body and seal the incision with *nyimil,* the white substance obtained by squeezing their noses, which is rubbed in with a heated stone. To revive the victim, the Mabarn removes a large whirlwind from his stomach and, standing some distance off, he sends it at the victim. He usually needs a second, smaller but stronger, whirlwind before the victim revives. The latter then sits up, sees his murderers, and abuses them thus: "You bloody shits! You've killed me! I'll tell the camp who you are!" He sets off back to camp, but the Mabarn has "shut up his ears" and by the time he reaches camp he has completely forgotten the entire episode. The next morning, he will awake feeling very angry, and will soon pick a violent fight with someone. If he receives the slightest injury in the fight, he dies. If not, he will die anyway within a few days.

This account gives a very common kind of explanation for sorcery. It neatly explains why there are no external signs of injury and why the victim often dies before naming his attackers. Its practice is thus not open to disproof. Although techniques differ (for example, *dalygu,* long wooden needles are inserted into the body from near the neck, and no internal organs are removed), the general principles of this kind of attack are the same.

Much alleged individual sorcery is of the "firing at a distance" variety. The sorcerer creeps to within sight of his victim, but remains hidden. He points a specially "charged" wooden object, most commonly a cigar-shaped pointed stick with snakelike markings burned onto it, from which *miyu,* a force akin to a ray of light in appearance, travels underground and up into the body of the victim. Sacred boards are also effective as sorcery weapons because of their great power. The preparation of such objects includes anointing them with certain substances, singing certain songs, and chanting the victim's name over them. Because the risk of backfire is great, users must be careful not to hold them with one end pointing to any part of their own body, lest they themselves sicken and die. Various forms of exuvial sorcery (worked on urine, feces, and such) are also alleged to be practiced.

I have seen objects identified as *yumbu* and many killing sticks in the possession of Mardudjara men, who invariably claim to have obtained them from some distant area and never to have used them themselves. The very existence of such objects gives the Aborigines good reasons (in addition to unexpected deaths) to believe in sorcery. Whether or not such activities actually take place or are attempted, leaving aside the magical operations that no "rational" outsider would believe possible, is an essentially irrelevant question. What matters, of course, is that Aborigines *believe* they happen, and such beliefs can have important consequences in their lives. Objective assessment of such beliefs is difficult because wherever sorcery is said to occur, it has a strong social control aspect. People must often contemplate antisocial behavior of some kind or other, but do not then engage in it because they fear that sorcery may be used against them as a result. There is certainly no constant fear of sorcery among the Mardudjara—but if serious conflict disrupts normal social relationships, the possibility of someone resorting to sorcery must enter people's minds; and after a sudden death, its prominence in ex post facto rationalizations is marked. By accounting for such tragedy it satisfies a strongly felt need. As a theory of causation it fills a large and disquieting gap, left open because their mythology supplies only a general explanation for human mortality, but neglects (wisely) to dabble in the specifics of why *this* person, why *now*. It is part of a universal human condition to attempt to fill these conceptual spaces in striving to impose cultural order on a chaotic world. Attempts to control, manipulate, and systematize spiritual powers so as to eliminate their arbitrary intervention are part of all peoples' attempts to render chaos unthinkable, or at least manageable, through religion (Burridge 1969a).

DYNAMIC ELEMENTS IN THE RELIGIOUS LIFE

The Dreamtime is of fundamental importance because it set for all time the parameters of a way of life which in its essence is held to be unchanging. In the Aboriginal view, none of these essential elements changes because the Law is followed and the founding patterns are thus perpetuated. Nowhere does their ideology admit structural change as a possibility. On the contrary, the emphasis throughout Australia is on continuity of present and future with past, and the notion of progress does not exist.

A few observers of Aboriginal culture appear to have accepted as fact its static nature and to have attributed the changes that do occur to contact with whites. They depict the Aborigines as incapable of independent thought and innovation (Strehlow 1947; Lommel 1970). They have taken ideology at face value and confused its heavy emphasis on fixed and immutable patterns with the realities of a life that is characterized by elements which make change inevitable: a high level of interaction between mobile groups and, in the absence of writing, heavy reliance on oral cultural transmission for its continuance. In precontact Aboriginal society, such changes were rarely radical and always occurred within an existing religious framework for action, so that the Aborigines did not find their adaptive abilities severely strained. As Stanner (1966:168) has so aptly noted, ". . . they welcomed change insofar as it would fit the forms of permanence"—that is, it was congruent with their preordained life design.

How is this congruence guaranteed? Detailed examination of Mardudjara religious life suggests that there is nothing essentially new under the sun. A newly revealed or imported ritual, when analyzed into its many constituent elements, will have a distinctive tune, body pattern, song wording, and arrangement of some of the associated thread-crosses. But virtually all other components—seating arrangements, dance steps, spatial configurations, raw materials in use, and so on—will be familiar from their appearance in various other rituals already known to the Aborigines. In other words, there are a number of basic ritual components common throughout and beyond the Western Desert, and each "new" ritual is a unique recombination of these preexisting elements. Since the possible permutations are virtually limitless, the Aborigines can continue to develop new variants. Stanner's "forms of permanence" are these basic elements. So while a tune will be new, it is never *greatly* different in its pitch and rhythms from all the others. The body patterns are distinctive but only slightly so. The song words are unique, yet the way they are sung, in what contexts, and with what accompaniments, these characteristics are shared with other rituals. In a study of rituals in northern Australia, Maddock (1969) reaches a similar conclusion:

a unique sequence is derived from a new combination of preexisting elements. Stanner (1966), who posits for the Murinbata Aborigines a fundamental characteristic of change within stability in both myth and ritual, has also presented convincing evidence to refute the notion of a static traditional religion.

To conclude this overview of Mardudjara religious life, four related aspects of its internal dynamism are discussed below: (a) the diffusion of new rituals, songlines, and objects between groups within the desert; (b) ritual innovation at the local level; (c) discoveries of sacred objects; and (d) the exploitation of myth's inherent flexibility.

Diffusion   The clearest evidence of a dynamic religion is provided by the central role of diffusion and continuous exchange of lore with the Mardudjara's neighbors. The focus for diffusion is the big meeting, held in emulation of the Dreamtime beings who instituted and exchanged rituals and objects on many occasions when their paths crossed. People look forward to them for many reasons in addition to the excitement of ritual participation and reunions with distant friends and kin. There are novices to be inducted, marriages to be arranged, new objects to be seen, stories to hear or tell about long journeys that a few people have taken to a distant area, and so on.

At big meetings it is not only through the acquisition of new rituals and sacred objects that religious knowledge is increased. Additionally, the benefits of mobility and of a curiosity that impels men of adventurous spirit to embark on journeys of enlightenment into "new" areas are passed on to their fellows at such gatherings. There, an atmosphere of heightened awareness guarantees them a rapt audience which shares vicariously the drama. The new knowledge thus obtained will in time be relayed to others in a never-ending process of diffusion. Not only physical journeys, but the equally valid metaphysics of the dream-spirit's travels form part of the information exchange. People dream about places known through myths and from the descriptions of others, as well as those sites that are known physically. The many songs that comprise dream-spirit rituals are examples of innovation resulting from an expanded individual consciousness.

Innovation   Local innovation refers to the composing of new rituals through dream-spirit journeys. These rituals, revealed to humans by spirit-being intermediaries of the spiritual powers, invigorate the life of the band because of the great enjoyment derived from them by its members of all ages. Although individual dream-spirit rituals wax and wane in popularity, their existence suggests a profound truth to the Mardudjara: the great creative powers continue to exist and are concerned and interested in human life. More important still, they approve, which is why they regularly reveal these rituals to the Aborigines.

Although individuals are denied an innovatory function in ritual creativity, they nevertheless have the vital task of translating piecemeal information into highly structured and integrated ritual wholes. The bones of "divinely" inspired elements are fleshed out into the ritual body only through the cooperative endeavors of human actors. This deemphasis on the individual as innovator effectively removes a potential source of status differentiation among men who are for the most part considered about equal in Aboriginal society. Instead, enabling powers are kept concentrated in the spiritual realm, and the grand life design embodied in the Dreamtime concept is thus protected from egotistical and potentially subversive impulses of individual humans.

Discoveries   The discovery of sacred objects is likewise not hailed as an individual accomplishment, since it too is revealed or hinted at through signs that prompt an individual to respond. Men tell of encountering spirit-beings during dreams, who tell them to go and look in some spot where they will find something important left by Dreamtime beings. Again, the resulting revelation of the find to other men, with a description of where and under what circumstances it was found, transfers the matter from individual to group level. There, consensus is sought and the "true" religious meaning of the find is assessed, on the basis of available mythological knowledge of the discovery's location and the characteristics of the object—shape, size, color, and so forth. For example, any natural or incised concentric circle motif strongly suggests its connection with Dingari beings (see Chapter 3).

The great significance of such discoveries is that they suggest to the Mardudjara an incompleteness of their knowledge of all that went on during the Dreamtime. For some reason, 'ancestral beings did not always leave clear evidence of their passage through certain areas; therefore some of their movements are unknown. In the case of most newly found sacred objects, their shape may be sufficiently general to allow identification with ancestral beings already known to have traveled or lived in the same area as the spot where they were found. For instance, an egg-shaped stone is easily linked with any of the vast numbers of different egg-laying beings. But some objects have characteristics so distinctive that they could have been left *only* by one particular being or group. This means that their association with the location of discovery of associated objects is now established and important new knowledge is thus gained. This must prompt men to anticipate some later revelation of further corroborative proofs.

The practical and political implications of this kind of incorporation are considerable. To take one example, the Ngaawayil ritual is "owned" and controlled by groups living in the Percival Lakes area (Map 2), many of whom claim descent from the major rainmaking beings. People wanting to participate in the ritual had to make the journey to one of the sites in that area because the Ngaawayil had not been passed on to groups in other areas. Eventually, when enough Mardudjara men had attained the highest Ngaawayil status, they were given permission by its leaders to construct the special grounds and perform the Ngaawayil in their home area. They were given the rainmaking stones and other sacred paraphernalia needed for its proper performance, since the rainmaking ancestors were not known to have traveled in Mardudjara country and thus to have left objects behind there.

Not long after the new ritual was established among the Mardudjara, very large cylindrical stones were discovered in several different places. These were positively identified as varieties of highly sacred rainmaking stones, proving that the rainmaking beings had not only been in this area, but had left for the Mardudjara peoples valuable repositories of their power. Because of these discoveries, the Mardudjara men are convinced of their fitness to hold the Ngaawayil successfully, since its associated beings can now be counted confidently among their own. Also, they have reinterpreted some of the more obscure Ngaawayil songs, which identify neither the location of what is being sung about nor the characters concerned. These songs are now cited in support of contentions that the event depicted took place in Mardudjara country, and when character interaction occurs, they are interpreted to refer to an encounter between a rainmaking ancestor and one closely associated with the Mardudjara area.[19]

Mythology and Incorporation   How does this kind of new knowledge find its way from the periphery into the actual structures of the religious life? In view of the highly proscribed nature of ritual and songline and the pervasiveness of an ideology of nonchange and a static cosmic order, this question must be posed. The answer lies in the final dynamic element to be discussed here: mythology, which is an ideal vehicle of incorporation because of its inherent flexibility. This characteristic openness has long been recognized by writers on religion. As R. Berndt (1952:52) has observed:

[19] These aspects of the Ngaawayil are discussed in detail elsewhere (Tonkinson 1972).

Mythology presented verbally . . . no matter how conventional the structure of the society, shows a certain amount of flexibility, since the only means of presenting, and thus of preserving it, must be the individual members of that society.

Stanner (1966:84–85) suggests that myths have inspirations and a logic of their own and, more importantly, considerable dramatic potential: "Every myth deals with persons, events and situations that, being less than fully described, are variably open to development by men of force, intellect or insight." This idea would explain why protagonists in myths are so often vague and ambiguous characters. Because of this variability in myths, there is no such thing as a single correct version, although a concern for consensus certainly exists with respect to the most important details of plot in major narratives. Those present at a telling would take into account the narrator's sex, approximate age, totemic associations with, and knowledge of the stretch of country where the action being described is set (R. and C. Berndt 1970).

The flexibility of myth allows for more than the embellishment of details of character and plot. Myths are capable of extension and expansion to permit the inclusion of new information that comes to light as the result of revelations by spirit intermediaries, and also from the finding of new objects and the subsequent deduction of new links between sites and creative beings. In this respect, Burridge (1969b:417) notes, with respect to the myths of the Tangu people of New Guinea: "Not only do the Tangu use their narratives to think with, and think from, but in their narratives new thoughts are deposited." The Mardudjara know best and in greatest detail the myths and parts of longer narrative myths that deal with happenings in their home territory among ancestral beings to whom they have the closest connections of "descent." But they know less of those of distant areas, and their grasp of the mythology associated with imported rituals is more sketchy. In learning the ritual's songline they usually gain a good idea of the sequence of major mythological events, but individual knowledge is more variable as to detail.

To return to the Ngaawayil example, the brevity and imprecise nature of the mythology of the rainmaking beings, added to its lack of close correlation with either songs or dances in the ritual, allowed Mardudjara men to exploit it. They have amplified the myth to incorporate the appearance of the rainmakers in Mardudjara country and to add details as to some of their activities there, including meetings with local beings. Through the discovered rainmaking stones and the reinterpretation of certain songs, they have enlarged the myth of the rainmakers and have made some of it their own.

Knowledge is not finite, since there is always something more to be revealed to the Aborigines, and there are gaps in totemic geography that allow new proofs of ancestral activities to be accommodated. It is perhaps therefore incorrect to describe the cosmic order of the Mardudjara as unified—if that word connotes a finished completeness. There must always be gaps, and the dynamism that enlivens their religious life is a result of continuous effort toward closure. It is an impossible goal because its attainment would really mean stagnation. Yet from the point of view of the Aborigines, and theirs is what counts, there is no talk of gaps or incompleteness. One only hears confident assertions of harmony and fit among the elements comprising their cosmic order. For them, no contradictions of any consequence exist. The human, plant, animal, and spiritual inhabitants of their cosmos are perceived as coexisting as one, within the all-embracing canopy provided by the founding design of the Dreamtime.

6 / Living the dream

It is perhaps appropriate to conclude this account of the Mardudjara with an overview of society as it should be and the realities of everyday life—and an assessment of the extent to which ideal and real approximate or diverge. The focus here must necessarily be on norms and values, conformity and conflict. These topics are examined at both individual and group levels, which are analytically separable but interdependent.

In considering the fit between ideal and actual, the consequences of desert ecological conditions should be kept in mind: small, separated but highly mobile bands, very low population density, and behaviors that maintain this kind of spacing as the status quo. The lack of crowding, the relatively low level of sustained interaction among different groups, and the ease of withdrawal by individuals and families from a band in anticipation of, or in response to, conflict, all make for lessened tensions beyond the level of the family unit.

THE IDEAL AT THE LEVEL OF GROUP AND SOCIETY

All the ideal Mardudjara social attributes are embodied in their Law. Put simply, the Dreamtime's legacy guarantees continuing fertility, security, and social stability in return for obedience to the Law, which fortunately allows sufficient variation for people to conform without feeling stifled or overly constrained by its dictates. At all levels of society, great emphasis is given to cooperation, the sharing through exchange of religious and mundane elements. Such exchange is promoted through conventions of hospitality, to be freely given as long as visitors are peaceful in their intentions and observe the correct etiquette. People who come upon a group as *ñgadjari* ("strangers") should never enter the camping area. Instead, they sit within sight of it and wait until local men go to greet them. Once the nature of their visit is known, they are taken into the camp for a *milyañggul* ("formal introduction"). Only after the various kinship links are known can interaction occur between members of the two groups. They will be given food and perhaps a ritual will be organized in their honor. If the visitors include men traveling without wives, and there are local women of the appropriate kinship category available, such women may be lent to them. The visitors may reciprocate with gifts of food or other objects immediately, but this is not necessary or expected. According to the ideal of generalized reciprocity, the same hospitality would be expected of them at some future time when they assume the role of host.

The many conventions surrounding the statuses of host and visitor reflect the importance both of proper behaviors when in some other group's territory and of generous hospitality as hosts. The ideal big meeting features an early, equitable, rapid, and relatively bloodless settling of outstanding disputes between individuals or groups seeking to air grievances or seek redress for real or alleged wrongs. Thereafter the em-

116

phasis should be on everyone's enjoyment of the proceedings and the exchange of valued goods, ideas, and rituals among participating individuals and groups. Through initiatory activities and exchanges, new alliances will be forged, and existing ones reinforced, with the promising and giving of females in marriage as a central element. When the meeting disperses, people should leave it with satisfied feelings about what has transpired.

With respect to the organization of such meetings and the coordination of the many different ritual activities that take place, authority and control rest with the collectivity of fully initiated men present, following an initial division of responsibility based on the host–visitor statuses. The men know that the women and uninitiated will comply with their expectations and that women will play a major role in the provision of food and water and the supervision of children during ritual proceedings. Should the women wish to engage in separate ritual activity, they must schedule it to fit in with what the men have organized, since male pursuits take precedence. Women should defer to men, and younger men to their elders. The assumption of leadership roles will be situationally defined and ritual-specific, changing as one ritual ends and a different one is organized. Within such specific contexts, orders can be given and will be carried out, but unless novices are involved there will be a complete absence of authoritarianism, for the essence of relationships among men in Aboriginal society is an unstated equality. As Maddock (1972:184) notes, "Egalitarian mutuality is the governing principle." However, the norms of kinship are virtually never overriden, regardless of context, and it remains the mediating principle for all social interaction. Thus a headman for a particular ritual could not ask a kinsman to whom he owes deference and respect to do something; instead, he may vaguely express a need for something to be done, and the person concerned will take it upon himself to fulfil it, or alternatively, an intermediary whose kinship link permits it will convey the request. In general, men playing the role of director will be somewhat diffident and reliant on suggestion rather than command, and will in fact be as nondirective as it is possible to be and still get the activity organized.

When dealing with young men whose initiation is not yet complete, their elders take advantage of ritual contexts to be stern and demanding in their demeanor.[1] They will play the role of taskmaster and tutor, expecting absolute obedience as they forcefully remind the young men of how much remains to be known and how all of it must be paid for with meat. Ideally, the only possible response on the part of the young men is dutiful obedience and willingness to reciprocate for the knowledge and power that is being acquired. The young men will acquiesce because this route is the only one to full adult status and because they are already playing important roles in ritual and as supervisors of younger novices. Females will have already been promised to them, and their bachelor status is not one of celibacy. They therefore know that it is just a matter of time and conformity until marriage, the eventual attainment of *nindibuga* ("wise one") status, and an influential place in the society.

THE REALITIES OF GROUP AND SOCIETY

Mardudjara society consists of somewhat isolated small groups of closely related people, closely attached to certain localities. This condition fosters a measure of soli-

---

[1] Their harsh attitude to young novices contrasts markedly with that toward fully initiated men who do not yet know the ritual in question. There is enthusiasm and excitement when objects are shown, but much less theater and no harshness or air of superiority; also, the initiators convey much more information and detail concerning the ritual to their fellows.

darity that finds expression in some ethnocentric attitudes and a rather inward-looking, parochial ethos. They are distrustful of the motives of strangers, and are prone to attribute negative, even nonhuman behaviors to those peoples about whom very little is definitely known but of whom much is certainly suspected.

At a superficial level, this local ethnocentrism surfaces in humorous comments and asides about differences in dialect and custom; the homogeneity of Western Desert culture cannot mask these variations. More seriously, when things go wrong, the dichotomy between "we of one country" and "they who are different" creates boundaries and exaggerates differences. The breach may be caused by actual events; for example, a member of one group elopes with the wife of a member of the other, or a serious quarrel results in bloodshed. Or it could be the result of an alleged offense, such as a sorcery attack, the theft of a sacred object, an attempted featherfeet attack or ambush, neglect of an increase center, failure to reciprocate adequately for something, and so on. The attribution of most deaths to sorcery, plus the belief that close relatives cannot resort to this practice, means that scapegoats are sought among outsider groups, probably those with whom there has been some prior trouble.

If the guilt of an individual is beyond doubt, as in the case of most elopements, resolution of the problem can be attempted with the consent of members of both groups concerned. The threat to social order that is posed by such offenses is conceded by all, and few would stand in the way if the wronged man and his close relatives invoke self-help to punish the pair. However, many offenses are regarded as difficult to prove, and are therefore not easily resolved in a stateless society; that is, one that lacks chiefs, judiciary, or other formal institutions to deal with litigation and render judgments binding on all parties. The men of both groups may not be able to agree on a course of action that will be acceptable to both parties. The only solution then is to separate and wait until the next big meeting. There the dispute can be aired, with both sides being free to put their cases to the assembled men (and women, if the dispute involves them). But should illness or death strike someone during the interim period, suspicion of sorcery is then almost certain to be directed at people with whom there is already a difference awaiting settlement.

There is no ethnographic evidence to suggest the existence of long-standing intergroup animosity akin to feud. There is no word for either feud or warfare in the language of the desert people. Their accounts of conflicts are phrased in kinship terms and on an interpersonal or interfamily rather than intergroup level. Instead of feud-inducing behaviors, the arena of intergroup conflicts is dominated by measures aimed at achieving a rapid, peaceful, and binding settlement.

One of the most important of these expiatory measures is for people to defuse the tension by physically punishing a guilty member of their own group; or if the offender is a man, to induce him to face the wronged group unarmed except for a shield. He will be showered with spears and boomerangs, or else they may close in and wound him with clubs and jabbing spears, until he is injured to their satisfaction.

Djadu, a bachelor in his late twenties, was repeatedly warned to stop pursuing and copulating with two young "wrong" ("ZD") women from a neighboring band. After several meetings between the groups concerned, where he tried unsuccessfully to justify his actions, his three older brothers ordered him to *ganduladjanamba,* to stand in the open and face his punishers. He did so, and successfully parried almost a dozen spears thrown by five of his "EB," mostly one at a time. As his "EB" closed in, only his older sister Wanda and two other "EZ" attempted to intervene to protect him. Even they could not prevent him receiving two spear wounds in the thigh and several very severe blows from clubs.

If members of two groups stand off and begin trading missiles as well as verbal insults, women of the two groups, aided sometimes by men who act as pacifiers, intervene actively. They dislodge spears from throwers and doggedly restrain the combatants until calm is restored and weapons are replaced by discussion. The venue may shift to men's country, because physical violence is forbidden in sacred areas. Much such conflict is highly ritualized in any case, with gradations of escalation and the certainty of intervention by others should a spear fight eventuate. Uncontrolled exchanges are usually short-lived, but quite fierce and frightening—to spectators at least. The combatants display an outward composure in deflecting and sidestepping missiles that defies adequate description.

Short of bloodshed—or following it if cool heads have not prevailed—there are other measures useful in effecting binding settlements. The most powerful, usually resorted to after a serious intergroup rift, is an exchange of sacred boards.

> The normally rather orderly dispute-settlement session at one big meeting erupted into chaos when a heated verbal exchange of accusations and counteraccusations of sorcery, leveled between a Gardudjara and a Mandjildjara group, suddenly became physical and escalated into a spear fight between all the Gardudjara and Mandjildjara present. Many boomerangs were thrown and several men on both sides were badly cut, as were several women who had intervened. When calm returned, a meeting of all the men decided to settle the dispute for good by means of the cutting and exchange of sacred boards by men of the two groups. The following morning, men of the two groups went out together and spent two days cutting and shaping two huge wooden boards from a rivergum tree; each measured about sixteen feet long by eighteen inches wide. Once properly shaped and smoothed, they ceremonially exchanged them, then set to work to carve them, a task that was to take teams of men weeks to complete. They worked in separate locations in men's country. Once both sides had completed this mammoth task, they reassembled for a communal feast, as each group ate seedcakes and meat provided by the other, and drank the coagulated armblood of the other from holes dug in the ground. Having eaten they then exchanged the two carved boards in a gesture that put a mark of finality on the conflict that had upset them. Any attempt to revive the conflict is henceforth unthinkable, because the Dreamtime beings who used this method of settling their disputes never again fought each other.

Barlgalu, the penis-holding rite, is another important method that men adopt to prevent or atone for conflict. It is also used by travelers to "pay for" their entry into the territory of a distant host group and into their ritual activities. At the same time it is an affirmation of peaceful intentions and the right of the visitors, by virtue of having been subincised, to be present at secret-sacred business.[2] In this simple rite, one group's members sit with heads bowed while men of the other group walk among them and grasp each by the hand, pressing their penis into the palm so that the urethral incision can be felt. If a man stands in the Mourner relationship (see Chapter 3) to the one who is offering his penis, he cannot comply and so will not allow his arm to be raised; instead, he will be tapped on the shoulder or head. Should all men in the seated group refuse to allow their hands to be raised, this signifies rejection of the conciliatory gesture, and physical violence will therefore follow. This would be a rare reaction, since *barlgalu* is a very serious gesture. The Mardudjara say that its acceptance, signified by a reciprocal act on the part of the receiving group, is virtually always assured.

[2] If the penis-holding rite takes place in the camp area, men will first signal women and children to lie down and cover their faces, since they are not permitted to witness the rite.

Nyubamarda, described by the Aborigines as a female equivalent to *barlgalu,* and a ritual that sometimes occurs in association with it, entails the women of one group being sent by their men to lie face down on top of every man (face up) related as "spouse" to them (*nyuba,* "spouse") for several seconds. Later the men concerned must reciprocate with gifts to the women. The *nyubamarda* of this kind that I witnessed all took place just prior to the start of rituals at big meetings. In this context, both *nyubamarda* and *barlgalu* are assurances of trust and goodwill that "open up" the proceedings and make for a successful meeting. But when they occur as atonement for some conceded wrong, it is likely that the women are sent to have sexual intercourse with men of the offended group.

The existence of so many measures directed toward the effective settlement of intergroup disputes suggests that strains toward the kind of ethnocentrism that exacerbates differences do indeed exist in desert societies. But they indicate, too, that people are at pains to prevent the resulting conflicts from escalating or enduring. The Mardudjara are aided by the fact that at least as many forces minimize boundaries as differentiate local groups or bands. Most potent are the norms of classificatory kinship, friendship, and affinal alliance, and the enormous unifying pressures of a shared Law. Added to these are the survival functions inherent in mutual hospitality and access to natural resources in both lean and bountiful times.

THE IDEAL AT THE LEVEL OF THE INDIVIDUAL

When the Dreamtime beings laid down the life design to be followed by their human descendants, they specifically excluded their many antisocial behaviors and included only those that now constitute the most highly valued behaviors in Mardudjara life. The worthy person is someone who shares unselfishly and without hesitation, who is generous without making an issue of it or asking for return, who fulfils ritual and kinship obligations without question. The ideal person is an active provider as parent, child of aged parents, and in-law, shows compassion for others, retains a close attachment to family and to homeland, and in behavior is unassuming and not aggressive, egotistical, or boastful to excess. Status in Mardudjara society is very much a matter of the fulfilment of kinship obligations in the style suggested by these valued behaviors.

With the exception of the native doctor, each adult shares with all others of the same sex knowledge and performance of the same range of skills. Individuals who excel at certain skills may be admired and respected for this ability, but such differences in individual performance are not made the basis for status differentiation. Likewise, individual status has nothing to do with the acquisition or accumulation of material possessions. The pressing demands of mobility discourage this, and besides, no one has a monopoly on any of the means of production. The older vigorous man who successfully manages four wives is admired, but this kind of achieved status is transitory and is part of the generalized status difference between old and young, and men and women.

In subduing egotism to the cause of society and imbuing its members with valued attributes of personality and behavior, the Mardudjara rely on the development of individual self-regulation, which is achieved through socialization, enculturation, and the internalization of conformity and of the emotions that facilitate it. Before it can walk or talk, a small child should learn about sharing with others. Throughout its childhood it should be constantly told of its kinship relationships to others and of behavior that is appropriate for each kin category. Through entreaty, ridicule, threat,

withdrawal of support, peer-group pressure, and so on, the child will learn to conform. From the models that surround it in the immediate family and band, it will
learn about sex roles and the division of labor. But the keys to self-regulation lie in a
child's development of a strong sense of compassion (*nyaru*), which will impel it to be
generous and to look after others; in shame and embarrassment (*gurnda*), which will
inhibit it from many antisocial or immoral behaviors; and in a yearning for family and
home estate (*gudjil*), which will act to draw the wanderer back throughout his or her
lifetime. After childhood, the protracted period of initiation will serve to induce in
the male an acceptance of, and commitment to, the religious life. This should occur
in such a way that a young man having the enormity of the secret life revealed to him
will experience neither skepticism nor rebellious notions.

It is a rapidly developing sense of shame–embarrassment that will induce boys and
girls to begin conforming in early adolescence to the norms of appropriate kinship behaviors without over-coercion from adults. The telltale signs are an awkwardness and
self-consciousness in certain social situations where interaction with adults is involved.
The more rapidly maturing girl will have made this transition at a younger age. Ideally, she will enter marriage well equipped with the necessary work skills and ready to
obey the wishes of her husband and any older co-wives. She should be hardworking,
dutiful, and willing to accept the primacy of his sexual rights over her. She should
have internalized these marital values so well that their periodic reinforcement by
means of verbal or physical abuse at the hands of co-wives or husband is rarely needed.

In sum, the effectively socialized Mardudjara man and woman should need little in
the way of external sanctions of compulsion to maintain their conformity to the Law.
The kinship system provides them with a blueprint for the parameters of most antici-
pated social interaction, and religious precepts provide additional coverage for the ritual activity in which they frequently engage.

THE REALITIES OF INDIVIDUAL BEHAVIOR

Most Mardudjara adults are normally agreeable people of pleasant disposition. But
both sexes have a capacity for rapid and passionate arousal of emotions to a violent
pitch, seen most often in either anger or sorrow. At such times they may attempt to
harm themselves; for example, when grieving over the sickness or death of a relative,
or they may vent their anger on others in conflicts. Great anger can flare over seemingly minor matters, resulting in quite intense confrontations between individuals. At
such times, the outsider observer has cause to wonder about the patronizing nonsense
that has been written about Aborigines as perennially meek, docile, and noble in their
"savagery." But lest an equally false impression be conveyed of a highly aggressive,
wilful, and conflict-oriented people, it is important to note that among the Mardudjara these quickly aroused passions usually abate almost as rapidly, and once calm is
restored, the incidents that caused them seem quickly forgotten.

Antisocial and excessive behaviors certainly occur among the desert people, for a variety of possible underlying reasons: imperfect socialization, excessive egotism,
ñgagumba ("madness, loss of control"), quirks of personality, poorly controlled temper,
and so on. In some cases the person who provokes the angry response may be held
responsible. In others some nonhuman force is deemed to be at work, as when a pregnant woman is "pushed" by the spirit-child within; in still others, the person is commonly acknowledged to be "mad" and therefore unable to help his or her behavior. In
most cases, however, a person who breaks the Law is held fully responsible for such
acts. Certain emotions are considered likely to lead people into trouble if not kept

under control: strong dislike (hatred seems too severe to describe it), *migu* ("jealousy, covetousness, envy"), promiscuity and unbridled sexuality, malicious gossip (and its mate, tale-carrying), and *yurndiṟi,* which I translate as "aggressive sulking."

These emotions can be very upsetting to people, who refer to this state of disturbed well-being as *wirla ṅgarnda* ("sick stomach"), a reflection of the importance of the stomach as the locus of Mardudjara emotions. Being upset connotes a dissatisfaction that demands some kind of action, from either the upset person or those held to be the cause of it. Becoming *yurndiṟi* is one of the most interesting of the many ways possible to make other people aware of one's upset state. A few people who tend to be disagreeable much of the time are said to be permanently *yurndiṟi,* and among them this condition is generally ignored. It is a natural condition among children and, as aggressive sulking, is more common among men than women, especially in contexts of informal meetings and matters arising from ritual activities.

It is midsummer, and a big meeting is just ending. A full series of Ṅgaawayil rainmaking rituals has just finished, and some thirty men are gathered for the distribution of various items of rainmaking paraphernalia to members of different ritual status levels. Among these objects are some fifteen large pearlshells, presented to the Mardudjara Ṅgaawayil leaders by some northerner visitors in return for hairbelts and spears that had been given to their group at an earlier big meeting. The distribution is being carried out by men of the highest Ṅgaawayil status level, and these eight elders discuss each shell and the likely recipients before making a final decision, whereupon the shell is formally presented.

Didiwagada was given a smallish shell; he sits slightly apart from the rest of the assembly, fingering the shell and seemingly muttering under his breath. Only two shells, large ones, remain to be presented, and it is clear that neither is meant for him. He suddenly stands up, noisily grabs his several spears and boomerangs, and stalks off as rapidly as the soft sand of the large creekbed will allow him.. A few men nudge one another and a couple call out, "Didi! Come back! What's the matter?" But he pretends not to hear.

About eighty yards away he turns, drops everything but his thrower and a single spear, which he loads and makes as if to throw in the direction of the men. He grabs a boomerang and feints with that, as a chorus of men shouts, "Leave it, leave it! Come back here and sit down!" Didi addresses them: "What about me? I've been a good man for this rainmaking; I worked hard; every time; you don't see me lying around in camp; I hunt, I sing, I keep the ritual going! No one thinks about me. I'm nothing, that's all. You're on your own next time around, you lot!" Having said his piece, Didi gathers up his gear and turns to go on. The men shout back, "Old man! [a term of respect, since Didi is in fact middle-aged]. Don't be that way; come back here. You're a good man for this ritual . . . everyone knows that! Don't be worried; come and sit down." Didi pauses, then slowly returns, to sit silently some twenty yards away, nervously pushing sand away from where he is sitting. There is a rapid, whispered consultation among the Ṅgaawayil leaders; one of them, Labayan, gets up and goes off to where his bundle of personal belongings is stored, in a tree fork on the creekbank. He takes one of his large shells, walks back and presents it to Didi, who appears quite satisfied and says nothing more.

The resort to *yurndiṟi* behavior signals that someone has a grievance which is upsetting them, and it focuses attention on them so that they can react by making their problem public. This action saves a person the great embarrassment of broaching the matter first. The Mardudjara, men and women, are extremely reluctant to address gatherings face to face, and most find it a painful ordeal at times. I once watched a man speak to a gathering of men with his head down, voice lowered, and his back to the circle for the entire 15 minutes of his speech. Some of the more outgoing and influential middle-aged and older men have less difficulty at such times, but public oratory is not highly valued. Most such gatherings typically begin with short speeches by two or three men proclaiming their complete ignorance of the matter about to be discussed! Appropriate verbal style in such situations is a quiet, self-effacing, and rather apologetic delivery, such that others will utter reassurances and words of encouragement: "No! Don't hold back; you're alright; that's a straight word you're giving us; we know you; you're a good man; go on; we need that good talk; keep on talking!" People are always heard out, and every effort is made to obtain consensus when decisions are being made at these ad hoc gatherings (but "consensus" really means that those few who have been arguing against the majority cease raising objections).

The marked reluctance of Mardudjara to deliver speeches to assemblies probably explains why so much airing of disputes among band members takes place at night. Each participant shouts from his or her camp, under the secure cover of darkness, and these exchanges can go on for hours. In the dark, people's level of confidence increases immensely, and the chances that weapons will be thrown if tempers are lost is minimal. It is a memorable experience to sit in camp in the middle of one of these sessions, surrounded by disembodied voices, wailing and yelping dogs, trying to identify the speakers and anticipate the drift of the conversations on a pitch black night lit only by stars and the glow of small campfires. In a society whose members are scattered in small groups most of the time, most public "oratory" is confined to such night sessions.

Violent conflict would be extremely disruptive in these normally closely knit bands, so there are strong pressures for upset people to keep the airing of grievances at a verbal level. But within domestic groups, particularly, a quick-tempered outburst may lead to blows being struck, and sometimes women are severely beaten by their husbands. Sometimes verbal exchanges prompt physical abuse when a woman swears at her husband and thus embarrasses him in front of other nearby families, who are certain to be watching and listening with intense interest. There is no such thing as a private altercation, but when a husband beats his wife, others are most reluctant to intervene, regardless of their assessment of whether such action is justified. Close kin intercede to restrain a man only if he appears to be seriously injuring his wife. The superior rights of men in marriage are undisputed, but women can and do arm themselves and fight back.

Bumana wanted to take Galidu, a young widow, as a second wife. Buli, Bumana's first and hitherto only wife, widely reputed to be a jealous woman, was incensed and threatened to leave him if he did so. She claimed that he had no right to the widow, since her elder brothers had not yet authorized her remarriage. One night during a big meeting, Bumana went and seized Galidu (who was agreeable to the idea) from her camp and took her back to his own. Buli delivered a withering verbal blast at them both, then stalked out of the camp. Bumana, angered by her jealous outburst, followed her and began beating her with a club. Although badly bruised on her neck and back, Buli managed to grab a club, with which she slammed Bumana across the shins, felling him like a stone. By the time he had hobbled back to his camp, Buli had sent Galidu on her way with several uncontested blows of the club. Bumana later abandoned his "project polygyny."

A bad-tempered man who habitually mistreats his wife without good reason may prompt her to leave him and return to her own people, who are not then likely to force her to return to him. They may strongly suggest that she go back to him, but can offer no guarantee that she will not run away again. For women to initiate physical attacks on their husbands is considered bad form. Such action earns them little in the way of community sympathy, regardless of their motives.

The Mardudjara say that fights between co-wives are uncommon because the older wife is "in charge of" the younger. But when co-wives are close in age and when, as is often the case, a man favors one over the other as a sexual partner, jealousy may inflame passions and a fight erupts. Women fight each other with great violence at times, wielding clubs or digging sticks to inflict bloody scalp wounds, or else using hands and teeth as weapons. Although women's fights within or between families are usually regarded by the local community as less serious than men's, and are viewed in many cases as light entertainment by men, their ferocity may cause other women to intervene. If prolonged, men may shout at the combatants and order them to desist, only to be ignored by the women until physical intervention occurs. Perhaps even more than their menfolk, the women show a remarkable capacity to drop the matter once the air is cleared. On several occasions I have seen women relaxed and chatting amiably together who still bore bloodstains from wounds inflicted on each other a day or two before.

There are many fewer conventions covering female than male conflicts. The most notable is the requirement that a woman who is clearly at fault must bow her head and accept the first blow uncontested. She thus admits guilt and offers "satisfaction" to her opponent, regardless of who actually fares better in the club fight that ensues. The only men's weapons that women are permitted to use in fights are clubs. A young woman who commits the serious offense of having sexual intercourse with a young bachelor whose kin relationship to her is incestuous in the classificatory sense must bear almost the entire burden of blame. She stands alone and faces the savage attack of the young man's "M" and "Z."

> Linya, a young woman in her late teens, took the opportunity of a big meeting assembly to renew an affair of a few years earlier with Djimin, a bachelor in his early twenties, and her distant "S," an incestuous relationship in Mardudjara terms. Caught once, the couple was loudly berated by both sets of close kin, but they persisted and were discovered a second time within a week. They ran away into the bush but finally returned to the camping area just before dusk of the same day. Djimin's MZ, seeing Linya's approach, picked up a large stone and ran at her, hitting her on the head with such force that she sank to her knees. She got up, blood streaming down her face, but made no effort to resist as five or six of Djimin's "M" and "EZ" surrounded and beat her. She again fell, whereupon two of the older women thrust their genitals in her face and attempted to urinate on her, to show their contempt and induce in her the shame that she so clearly lacked. Blows with clubs and fists rained on her, and intense verbal abuse: "You rotten little bitch; you're an animal, you copulate with your own son; you're hungry for penis, any penis, even your own family's; you have no shame; we'll kill you for this; you're mad!" Only after she had been severely beaten and deeply shamed did her mother and "Z" go and drag her away from the frenzied, screaming attackers. This incident ended the affair for good.

The incredible ferocity of such attacks is understandable when the seriousness of such affronts to social stability and the Law is considered. Regardless of genealogical distance, a "mother" and her "son" simply must not behave like this; they threaten the entire structure of kinship and social categories, and such cannot be tolerated.

When men fight each other, the unstated aim of the many conventions surrounding their conflicts is to allow maximum opportunity for the dispute to be aired verbally. This takes place in an atmosphere of great public drama and menace, so that honor is seen to be satisfied, but with a minimum of physical violence. The pronounced ritualization of such conflicts is evidenced by the ability of both observer and actors to predict the sequence of events in many cases. Yet imponderables often loom large.

> Old Binggulyara had for some time barely tolerated the obvious interest that Magun, a distant bachelor "B" was showing in Binggu's favorite wife, Dabudji.

One day when Magun refused to move away from Binggu's camp, the old man flew into a rage and called him all the insulting names he could think of. Humiliated, Magun immediately called Binggu out for a fight, and both men armed themselves. Magun chose only to rattle his spears and shout, since he knew his case, as an outsider who had joined the band to spend time hunting for his future in-laws (his betrothed was still a child), was a weak one. The old man threw two spears at him, and he easily dodged them both. Djadadjada, the father of Magun's betrothed, threw one spear in his direction, but only as a token gesture calling for an end to the conflict.

Meanwhile, Dabudji, the wife who had been having an affair with Magun, was attacked by Madjal, her "FZ," for allegedly causing the trouble. The two women, both large, exchanged several hard blows. Then Gidu, Madjal's brother, threw two boomerangs in the direction of old Binggu, because Binggu's wife had just injured his sister.

Virtually all the events to this stage were predictable in some measure. However. . . .

Gidu's second boomerang, thrown short so as to bounce high and clear Binggu by a wide margin, did so and was caught by the wind. It whizzed back into a fleeing group of spectators and sliced into the scalp of Babagada, a tough old woman with an iron constitution and an incredibly sharp tongue.

Outraged, Babagada snatched up a club and ran headlong at her "YB" Gidu, cursing him en route then belaboring him about the shoulders and back with the club while he stood, very shame-faced, and accepted the blows. The original conflict was by now forgotten, as Babagada's daughter's husband Wilyan suddenly entered the arena in support of his WM who by this time had been pushed to the ground by Gidu, who had decided that she had punished him enough. Wilyan sank his jabbing spear deep into Gidu's thigh. No further heavy blows were struck after this because of the many men and women who milled around and separated all the combatants.

Another kind of occurrence that frequently changes the course of a hitherto controlled encounter is when some man who has been quietly watching suddenly becomes enraged by something that is said, or by what he considers to be an unwarranted intrusion of someone who is supporting one combatant against the other. He snatches up his weapons, dashes into the open area (where most fights take place, away from campsites a little), and launches a couple of boomerangs and a spear before the surprised onlookers can run and hold him back. His supportive stance, called *burndurini* ("taking the place of"), can lead to a rapid escalation of a fight—especially if other men consider his intervention unwarranted, perhaps a mere excuse to air some personal grievance against one of the original combatants or one of their active supporters.

Whatever prompts violence, many spectators intercede to separate the fighters and prevent them from launching weapons, so as to bring the conflict back to a verbal level. Women play a crucial role in physically restraining men. They dislodge spears from throwers with sticks or hands, snatch boomerangs and clubs and throw them away, and cling firmly onto the men. It is a common sight during fights to see a man vainly trying to shake off two or three women, dragging them along the ground, kicking and hitting at them but quite unable to free himself from their determined embrace. Perhaps one important reason why men are forbidden to fight during secret-sacred activities is the absence of women (fear of upsetting spiritual powers notwithstanding). Without the most often restraining and calming influence of women, men might have to put their weapons where their mouths are, so to speak, with doubtless bloodier and more dangerous consequences. Do not imagine, however, that women are not capable of inciting men to violence in certain disputes. Older women, especially, sometimes break into a side-skipping dance and accompanying shouting that are highly inflammatory—an emotional and fervent encouragement to violent conflict. Women's primary roles, though, are to restore calm so that more reasoned resolution of disputes can be achieved.

Given the closeness of the kinship links involved, there are usually interested third parties among the men, and they too direct their efforts toward bringing conflict to a quick end. They help ensure that both parties obtain a measure of "satisfaction" from it, signaled by a mutual willingness to say so, or at least to engage in a ritualized exchange as final settlement. This exchange can take the form of a penis-holding rite, gifts, or temporary bestowal of sexual rights to their women, or after a serious dispute (for example, a spear fight between two full brothers), the cutting, carving, and exchange of sacred boards. If one man is clearly in the wrong, he must carve the board or boards cut and shaped by the offended party.

When a dispute arises from an obvious or admitted offense, the wronged person obtains satisfaction from the exposure of the offense to public notice and the punishment and group censure of the offender. In fact, very few transgressions can remain private in this society, where the ground can be read like a book, and gossip is a common and acceptable practice. A Law-breaker has the option of removing himself from the band for a time, but this act may not resolve the problem; instead it may only prolong dissatisfaction until an inevitable confrontation some time later. A prudent withdrawal may, however, increase the chances that the ultimate clash will be less physical than it would otherwise have been. Perhaps the fear of sorcery or of revenge expeditions prompts most Mardudjara to stay and confront the problem. The worst an offender can expect under normal circumstances will be a clubbing and some spear thrusts in his thighs. The multiple spear wound scars that every mature Mardudjara man and woman carry (and dismiss as of no account) attest to the popularity of this form of punishment. This method is favored because the jabbing spear can be guided accurately to its target, whereas thrown missiles are far less accurately delivered. Throwing spears are rarely aimed at the upper body, since their use is directed to wounding, not killing.

When there is no clear offense or admission of guilt by either party to a dispute, both are likely to derive satisfaction from a conviction that they got the better of the other, or that community sentiment favored them rather than the other. A rapid and relatively bloodless clearing of the air defuses tensions while providing an exciting and diverting interlude in the people's lives. The seeming disinclination of the Mardudjara to bear grudges or harbor smoldering resentment rests in large part on their many conflict-management conventions. These operate to bring about a "good feeling" in the stomachs of the principals, a sense of satisfaction, vindication, or finality that endures long past the immediate aftermath and survives the test of later calm reflection.

In all conflicts, regardless of scale, circumstances, and particular idiosyncrasies, the various roles played by those present, and the extent of their involvement or avoidance, have much to do with kinship, as was noted in Chapter 3. Depending upon their kinship relationship to the combatants, there are those who should chastise, who restrain, who substitute for and defend, who inflame, who appeal to reason and calm, and so on. For example, if a person is so enraged that he persists in attempting violence and refuses to calm down, drastic action may be called for. A man who is *manggalyi* ("operator"), or an *umari* ("wife's mother")—if either is present at the time—may enter the fray to confront and even touch him. This action, unthinkable in normal life because the relationships concerned are of strong avoidance, should so shame the man that he comes to his senses and calms down immediately.

For the outsider, a knowledge of the kin relationships of those involved in a fight generally proves to be a reliable guide. But in the heat of the moment people may forget or ignore kinship norms. In this case, prediction of their likely behavior is based less on kinship than on a knowledge of their personalities and of how they react under aggravation and stress. This knowledge is gained from having witnessed them in action many times before, or from having heard stories of their behavior in similar circumstances. Information of this kind is stored in each person's biographical "file" of all others with whom they interact at some stage in the normal course of life. The Mardudjara are great storytellers and love to talk about happenings seen and those unseen but heard about through the desert "grapevine."

In other words, the kinship system is indeed a fairly reliable guide to expected behavior, but it is no straitjacket. Nevertheless, if the gulf between Aboriginal kinship norms and actual behavior is compared crossculturally, it will be seen to be narrower than in most other human societies. The notable closeness of fit is attributable to the small scale of Aboriginal society, its marked stability, and the undisputed primacy of kinship statuses. These and many other factors suggest that kinship is a more pervasive and powerful force in Aboriginal Australia than elsewhere.

In terms of the ideal values outlined above, it is abundantly clear that in everyday life the vast majority of Mardudjara display them in abundance: unselfishness, an unquestioning willingness to provide and care for relatives, affection for children, an unspoken commitment to the Law, strong desires for cooperation and friendship rather than competition or antagonism, and a quiet unassuming manner devoid of public boastfulness or egotism that intrudes upon others. Also characteristic are a gregariousness, a love of animated discussion and repartee, and a keen interest in what transpires in all dimensions—social, natural, and metaphysical—of their cosmic order. Bonds of genuine and deep affection are felt within families and among close kin and friends. Above all, most Mardudjara face the world with a sense of humor which is rarely suppressed, and a readiness to laugh uproariously at themselves and others alike.

Circumspection and restraint are of course present in dealings with certain categories of kin, but there are plenty of other kin with whom humor can be generated and enjoyed. The superb powers of mimicry that facilitate their hunting activities are put to humorous theatrical use in parodying the mannerisms and characteristics of their fellows. The more extrovert comics sometimes reduce their audience to laughing helplessness with devastatingly accurate, but cunningly exaggerated, renditions of someone's peculiar gait or voice. Or they may suddenly jump up and act out the parts in a story they are telling which involves people known to their listeners. Should a target of this humor happen to be present, he or she takes it in good fun and shares in the enjoyment of the occasion. Personal afflictions—a limp, deafness, blindness, erratic behavior—are also parodied, in what might be branded sick humor in some other cultures. Among the desert people, however, such afflictions are facts of life that are often used as labels, both as terms of address and reference; a crippled person may be addressed as *mugundu* ("lame, cripple"), a blind person as *bambuřu,* and so on, with no insult intended or taken. Certainly no attempt is made to pretend that such conditions do not exist, or to shun people because of them.

It is difficult to do justice to the range and pervasiveness of humor in Mardudjara society. But the fact that people can maintain such a spirited and positive outlook in an environment as tough and mercurial as the desert speaks volumes for their strength of character and their great confidence in the Law, which answers life's biggest questions and attests that the human spirit is invincible. If it should be true that jollity, warmth, and ready laughter are but masks hiding some inner pain, insecurity, or angst, then this distress has remained remarkably impervious to the scrutiny of outside observers of the desert people.

There is no concept of suicide among the Mardudjara, nor any evidence of warfare, rape, sexual perversions (bestiality, child molestations, and such), vandalism, cannibalism, or theft (apart from occasional allegations concerning the theft of sacred objects), and murder is a rare occurrence. As noted above, there is anger, spite, jealousy, violence, and cruelty at times, to name some of the negative aspects of life. Yet the magnitude of the absent evils seems to be far greater than that of the problems that are sometimes present. Above all, the Mardudjara respect the individual, and their society allows ample recognition of the uniqueness of each person.

As Burridge (1973) notes, the self-same elements in kinship, totemism, social groupings, and social categories that unify and incorporate the individual with others operate simultaneously to differentiate, separate out, individualize, and make unique that person. The individual thus represents an amalgam of statuses that is like no others in its entirety yet shares every constituent element with some others.

For males, there is also the profound experience of individuality when during initiation they are made the focus of attention and the *raison-d'etre* of the entire big meeting assembly. True, they are traumatized and at times made to feel that as novices they are as yet nothing. Yet they surely cannot help realizing that all this is for them, and that for a time they are the center of the local universe.

It is a fact that individuals are denied authorship of their own creativity in favor of spirit-beings as the fount of all power and knowledge. This restriction would seem to be an affront to individualism and a major blow to the ego. But given the nature of Mardudjara worldview, great advantages can be gained by having man submit to a greater spiritual purpose and design. As individuals or members of groups, people are not passive receptors of the Dreamtime legacy, but must actively fulfil their part of the bargain if the design for life is to be carried forward in perpetuity. Passive obedience is not enough. Through ritual activity the men who hold the key to communication with the spiritual realm share a great responsibility. It is they who control fertility in the human and natural worlds and thereby guarantee the survival of those worlds.

Mardudjara men have greater ritual responsibility, higher status, more *de jure* power, and more rights than women. It is a male chauvinist society, certainly, but as in many other human societies, there is a discrepancy between ideology and reality, between *de jure* power and *de facto* influence. Thus no unbiased observer could fail to see the important roles that women play in the affairs of the family and the group, despite their exclusion from the secret rituals of the men. They, as a group, accept the status quo, for they know that their contributions as child-bearers, providers, and partners are vital, and that men accept this. They too are unique, and their place in the life design is also secured and validated by the Dreamtime.

7 / The Mardudjara today

It is now almost a century since the first appearance of European explorers in Mardudjara country. The later spread of the pastoral frontier took it to within 50 miles of the desert proper and the homelands of the Mardudjara people. Since the coming of whites, the Aborigines have been inexorably attracted to outposts of white settlement and have eventually abandoned the desert, at least physically. The last bands to leave the Lake Disappointment area did so in the mid-1960s, and this area is now uninhabited.[1]

Some Mardudjara left their homeland via a southerly route that ended for them in the small town of Wiluna. A few headed north and emerged at Balgo mission. Some who settled on pastoral spreads to the northwest later moved on to Nullagine and Marble Bar which, like Wiluna, were once thriving mining centers. But the majority headed west and eventually settled at the outpost of Jigalong (see Maps 1 and 2). This settlement is a community of about 400 Marjudjara and a dozen or so whites. Once quite remote and isolated, but now only a hundred miles from the massive iron-ore mining operation and town of Newman, Jigalong provides the focus for this summary of contemporary Mardudjara life. The pattern of Aboriginal emigration and the nature of frontier contacts have been detailed elsewhere (Tonkinson 1974). This brief account summarizes only the major features of cultural persistence and change in the postcontact era and some of the recent developments of significance in the lives of the Mardudjara at Jigalong.

ABORIGINAL EMIGRATION AND THE FRONTIER

Safely ensconced in their forbidding land, the Western Desert Aborigines were never overrun by whites. They were thus spared the terrible fate that overtook those living in the more fertile and accessible regions, where white settlement quickly took its toll through disease, mistreatment, and a shattering of spirit. A century or more after many Aboriginal groups had all but vanished, the desert people were thriving untouched. Most contacts between Mardudjara groups and explorers were brief and peaceful. The only aliens who had lasting effect were parties of men who between 1906 and 1909 surveyed and built the Canning Stock Route (Map 2). This thousand-

[1] Perhaps the last two Western Desert Aboriginal nomads were rescued from a soak in drought-stricken Mandjildjara country east of Lake Disappointment at the end of September 1977. Wari and his "wife" Yaduṅgga had remained in the homeland long after their relatives left, because they were wrongly married and feared punishment, according to the Mardudjara from Wiluna who successfully tracked them down. Their discovery was reported in all Australian newspapers, carrying headlines such as "Last of the Desert Men" and "The End of a Way of Life" (*West Australian*, October 4, 1977).

mile chain of wells connected northern pastoral areas to the railhead at Wiluna. Its subsequent use by drovers was rare, but the wells—many of them dug in established native waters—were used by the Aborigines. The route itself later became a kind of funnel for their north–south movement and eventual migration to the settled fringe areas.

The fact that all such white intrusions were transitory indicates that the desert Aborigines were not displaced; they remained free to choose whether or not they wished to initiate or maintain contact with white settlers. Although it appears that curiosity rather than need impelled them, in hard times the attraction of the whites' food and water must have been strong. Among some of the more recent immigrants, fear of Aboriginal revenge expeditions was cited as a motivating factor.

On the outlying pastoral properties where most Mardudjara saw their first whites, a pattern of periodic brief sojourns, followed by resumption of the old mobile life in the homeland, eventually led to a more settled existence punctuated by brief returns to the estate and range. Important factors that prompted this major transition were the Aborigines' rapidly acquired taste for tea, flour, strong tobacco, and sugar. Iron and steel tools, flints, and other useful and portable material items were also eagerly sought. In exchange for such objects and foodstuffs, the Mardudjara had little more than their labor potential and the sexual favors of their women to offer the frontiersmen. Most of the latter were bachelors and often alone, so they had strong needs for both.[1]

The frontier in the pastoral areas west of Mardudjara country along the desert edge was a predominantly peaceful one, promoted by the symbiotic nature of black–white relationships. In later years the swelling number of immigrant groups exceeded labor needs on pastoral properties and small mining settlements (where the demand for sex had probably always been greater than for labor). This situation prompted the state government to institute a system of "rations," regular issues of the now-staple tea, sugar, tobacco, and flour to "indigents." The Aborigines continued in most cases to supplement European foods with meat, and to a lesser extent vegetable foods, obtained from the bush. The wearing of clothing, usually old cast-offs, was adopted, and ration issues sometimes included blankets and clothing. Men learned the skills of stock work and of menial tasks such as woodchopping. Many young women became domestics, whose sexual relations with their white bosses were sanctioned by their menfolk as long as reciprocal benefits in food and other goods accrued from the arrangement.

At Jigalong, the great contrast between typical European frontier values and behaviors and those of fundamentalist missionaries who were much later arrivals in the area caused the Aborigines a little confusion and the missionaries much pain. Jigalong was a mission station between 1946 and 1969, but failed to become a viable concern evangelically or economically. The conflicts that plagued the mission and brought about its final demise are detailed elsewhere (Tonkinson 1974). As with the pastoralists, there was a symbiosis sustained by mutual exploitation; and the Aborigines managed to perpetuate a traditional strategy of maximizing returns for a minimal expenditure of effort. In the altered milieu of the contact situation, at least two factors favored the whites: their superior political power, sanctioned by government laws and manifest in the seemingly almighty police; and the fact that by this time the Aborigines were hooked on the "exotic" foods and other attractions of white technology. They were

[1] Some pastoralists traded food, tools, and so on for dingo scalps, on which the state government paid bounties. Dingoes were declared vermin because they were suspected of attacking sheep and cattle.

now either unable or disinclined to return to an arduous desert subsistence. Also, a younger generation was emerging for whom Jigalong, not the desert proper, was home.

CHANGE AND CONTINUITY

For the desert Aborigines, the most obvious change has been the disappearance of the bands that characterized their former local organization. The remnants of these groups, together with their descendants, now live in communities of a size once, if ever, attained only during big meetings and for brief periods. Shared links of kinship, marriage, religion, and residence have forged a new kind of solidarity among them. Based on their new location and expressed in their use of the term *mob* to distinguish themselves as a community from Aborigines elsewhere, this solidarity has increased over time. The new identity has been strengthened by an increasing incidence of marriage within the community and of an ethnocentricism that contrasts them favorably against other mobs. When such a contrast is made, it is usually with reference to continuing conformity to the Law and the correct and enthusiastic performance of ritual.

Despite the establishment of a new basis for local parochialism, the powerful bonds of a shared culture continue to link each community with the many others that are scattered along the desert periphery. Everyone has close kin, many allies, and friends in all neighboring communities. Informal visiting is frequent, and formal visits for big meetings and the diffusion of the Law take place every summer. These meetings are timed to coincide with the slack season on pastoral properties, since these remain the largest employers of Aboriginal labor in most areas. Considerable mobility is thus maintained in the contact situation, but by vehicles, now enabling large groups to cover long distances in relatively short times, despite frequent breakdowns and refreshment stops at bars en route. Big meetings now sometimes include visitors from several hundred miles away, from groups which never would have met up in precontact times. The interpersonal network is therefore very much larger than in the traditional culture.

In their adaptation to the contact situation, the Aborigines have had to adjust continually and change their lives in various and significant ways. They wear clothes, work for wages, subsist largely on bought foods, put their children in schools, gamble on cards as a major leisure activity, use clinic and hospital facilities, hunt with rifles, make increasing use of motor vehicles, and so on. None of these changes is denied by the Mardudjara, but in their perception little of importance has altered in their lives. The major transition from a mobile desert life to a sedentarized contact environment has been much more a matter of continuity as they see it. Their most highly valued norms and behaviors have been maintained in the contact milieu: the kinship system and associated patterned interaction and the religious life, exemplified in ritual, initiatory activities, and intercommunity cultural diffusion. In these most important aspects of living, the Mardudjara have successfully retained a strongly tradition-oriented outlook. They are still proud people, determined to follow the Law as closely as altered circumstances will permit.

Life in large, well-established communities has, on the one hand, led to an inevitable increase in interpersonal conflicts and in tensions between different linguistic groups. Offsetting these pressures, however, are strong stabilizing forces provided by the Aborigines' conformity to what is substantially the same Law. Fortunately, there has been very little direct intervention by agents of the wider society to outlaw or suppress aspects of this Law that run counter to their own. In this frontier region, the greatly outnumbered whites lacked the will and the strategies to impose and police reforms. Missionaries were certainly the most committed opponents of much of the Law. Yet they never succeeded in their attempts to turn the young against their elders, or in abolishing polygyny or replacing Aboriginal with Christian beliefs and rituals. Instead, through mandatory issues of rations (and from 1960, payment of social security benefits) and provisions of food and clothing, the Jigalong missionaries inadvertently promoted the Law. Their actions encouraged the stability of a large community, whose males, especially, devoted most of their leisure time to religious matters—traditional, not Christian, which they totally rejected. Many young and middle-aged men who had developed the necessary skills were involved in employment on pastoral spreads in surrounding areas. They were absent from the community for several months a year (seldom continuously, however), but their commitment to their wives, children, and the Law remained strong. The older men who lived permanently at the settlement were the caretakers and organizers of ritual activity, which was carried on periodically throughout the year. Every summer, most of the community's energies were directed toward the staging of a big meeting and to the organization of trips to attend similar functions in neighboring centers, which were normally attended by large numbers of men, women, and children.

The Mardudjara succeeded very well in keeping the whites at arm's length while continuing to socialize their young into the dominant values and behaviors of the Law. Because of this, their kinship system has undergone little modification, and, traditional marriage rules are still observed. However, in some kin behaviors there are signs of a lessening of restraint, and the number of infant bethrothals culminating in marriage is now probably much smaller than before contact with whites. The age of marriage for males is apparently decreasing, and the period of initiation following subincision has been somewhat truncated. This change is partly a response to competing demands for the labor of young men that stem from pastoralist employers. Well into the 1970s, the young men have demonstrated a strong enthusiasm for the religious life. There is no doubt that their commitment to the Law is shared with strong interests in some of the trappings of "civilization," such as motor cars, Western clothes and music, heavy drinking and associated "macho" behavior. The "cowboy culture" is strong among the young.

PROBLEMS IN ADAPTATION

The aspects of contemporary life that worry the older Mardudjara are alike in that most are not the result of any direct or wilful imposition of change by agents of white society. Rather, they arise from more subtle and indirect influences that operate insidiously on a society that has forsaken mobility and autonomy for a more physically secure but increasingly dependent existence. As a disadvantaged minority, the desert people have nothing to sell but the uniqueness of their culture—which is regarded as an inferior product in a land whose white inhabitants have been notoriously harsh on nonconformity of any kind, especially when allied with dark skin, a reputation for "primitiveness," and an alleged inability to adapt to fit the white middle-class mold.

Most of the problems that the Mardudjara see as threatening their Law have to do with social control and conformity, both within their community and in their dealings with other communities.

Conflicts and disruption within the Jigalong community are sometimes caused by people who are drunk or who use drinking as an excuse to act on real or imagined

Jigalong today: a group of young men, some of whom are not yet initiated.

grievances against others. Drinking periodically engenders problems that were absent in the desert where the use of alcohol was unknown. There are no traditional strategies for dealing effectively with dangerous drunks. The application of the many conflict-management techniques used before does not occur, because it is generally agreed that drunks are not fully responsible for their actions. There are no alcoholics, and some people never drink liquor, but the Aborigines see drinking as a difficult problem to overcome. Because liquor is not available at Jigalong, it must be fetched from 100–150 miles away; thus, drinking is a periodic activity there, whereas in towns where Mardudjara visit or live, frequent drinking is probably *the* major social problem.

Another difficulty is the refusal of some troublemakers to accept the judgments of the community as to their guilt and their obligation to make appropriate compensatory gestures. When the adult community as a whole, or the men only, meet to discuss issues and hear both sides of a dispute, they talk at length in an effort to reach consensus. Once it is obtained, an offender should accept the decision and act accordingly; that is, to take his or her punishment with good grace. Instead, some now defy the community to act against them, knowing that a dislike of police intervention is lessening the chance that traditional punishment, such as thigh spearing, will be carried out by the appropriate kin.

Here the clash between two different systems of law is most noticeably having an adverse effect on internal social control. When the police are reluctantly called in from the nearest town to investigate fights, they may well arrest the Lawful punishers instead of the offender. Attempts by initiated men to take as wives the young girls to whom they are betrothed also involve them in problems with the other law if these girls are under the legal age of consent. Also, an increasing reluctance of young women to marry old men to whom they have been promised is causing concern. Young women who are unmarried mothers receive a special allowance from the government, which enables them to be economically self-sufficient and independent, a condition that they value highly. Many young mothers are remaining defiantly single and are successfully resisting strong community pressures to end this status, which in the traditional society existed only during brief periods of widowhood. The uncontrolled sexual activities of these young women is being blamed for what people say is a greater number of conflicts in the community. Furthermore, these young women use the "free choice" of marriage partners in white society as an argument against betrothal. Another trend is for many old women to remain widows. They receive government pensions and are happy in the solidarity of like women, free of the demands that marriage would impose upon them. Nonetheless, they remain firmly embedded in the kinship system and retain close ties of interdependence with their married and unmarried children.

A fuller awareness of the whites' kinship system (or seeming lack of it) now exists among the young, who are exposed to comics, movies, and a white-oriented education system. Some are beginning to question the relevance of traditional marriage rules, and a few are persisting in affairs and relationships that are wrong in traditional terms; that is, those which are either "irregular" (the "MB"–"ZD" nyagadji union, mentioned in Chapter 3) or "incestuous" (see Piddington 1970). Despite fierce community resentment, abuse, and physical sanctions, two or three young couples are following the lead of some of their town-dwelling friends and relatives by cohabiting wrongly. The Jigalong elders claim that such arrangements are brief and transitory preambles to a "settling down" with Lawful spouses. So far they have been borne out by events, but there is no doubt that as contact pressures increase, traditional marriage rules will become more vulnerable to change. Repeated transgressions would ultimately undermine them, and by extension would adversely affect the kinship and section systems, thus altering the entire cultural fabric.

What the Mardudjara of Jigalong view as most serious is the continuing difficulty in relationships at the intercommunity level, particularly between themselves and their neighbors some distance to the north. The rift stems initially from the late 1940s when diverse groups of desert and coastal Aborigines joined forces in a successful strike action. They walked off pastoral properties and later embarked on cooperative mining operations, to which they unsuccessfully attempted to attract people from Jigalong. The people there were wary of a further emigration, especially to hilly "foreign" country, and the Jigalong elders were strongly opposed to the changes being made in the Law by the northerners. The latter, called the Pindan or "company" mob, were led by sophisticated coastal part-Aborigines who had lost much of their traditional culture in their long period of contact with whites. The few Jigalong families who moved north did not stay there for long. More recently the northerners have affirmed the strength of the desert Law and its rituals. But they have attempted to displace Jigalong from its hitherto undisputed status as the major stronghold of traditional Law. The northerners now claim that distinction for their community, which for some years has been located on a pastoral property not far from the town of Port Hedland (Map 1).

The northerners have been successful in exploiting old antagonisms and distrust between the two dominant linguistic groups at Jigalong. They managed to persuade most of the Mandjildjara speakers, who had been the last arrivals from the desert, to shift themselves and their community allegiance to the northerners. They have also attacked the integrity of the Jigalong people as upholders of the Law, which has caused a great deal of distress in the community. The response of the Jigalong leaders has been to avoid open conflict and a complete breakdown in relations at all costs. Their hope is that the breach can be healed and their missing kinfolk will again return home. Interarea tensions of this kind remain *the* primary worry of the Jigalong mob, because the departure of most of the Mandjildjara has divided a once solidary community; this is something that almost twenty-five years of missionary endeavor was unable to accomplish (see Tonkinson 1974; 1977a; 1977b).

RECENT DEVELOPMENTS

The tempo of change besetting Aboriginal Australia has greatly increased in the 1970s. It has entailed an awakening sense of ethnic identity and pride among acculturated part-Aborigines, and a general arousal of white consciousness about Aboriginal culture and the legacies of almost two centuries of mistreatment, neglect, and racial prejudice. The Mardudjara are far removed from the mainstream of this altered consciousness, secure in their relative isolation and never in doubt as to the basic superiority of their Law as the only proper blueprint for Aboriginal life. But the indirect effects of altered government policies and large increases in spending on Aboriginal welfare are being felt and are demanding creative responses from them.[2] Implicitly racist policies of assimilation or cultural absorption have given way to more enlightened attempts to promote Aboriginal community autonomy and local leadership. Government officials have given repeated assurances that groups will have greater opportunity to decide for themselves the rate and degree of integration they desire with the wider society. A more informed appreciation of Aboriginal cultural strengths is slowly beginning to replace the paternalistic attitudes of the whites, although at the level of the average white Australian, a great deal of prejudice remains. And in small remote communities like Jigalong, the gulf between the idealism inherent in policy and life's harsh economic realities remains considerable.

Community Autonomy   Following the departure of the missionaries at the end of 1969, little developmental activity took place at Jigalong until 1973. In that year, the community became an incorporated Aboriginal company, with an eight-member elected Aboriginal council assisted by white advisors. The company had to rely on government grants for its capital and operating expenses, with the hope that a substantial income could be derived in later years from expansion of its cattle-raising activities. (By 1975, such projects contributed the equivalent of one fifth of the community's total expenditure on maintenance and development.)

The local Aborigines, who had always asserted their autonomy in matters of major concern to them (kinship, marriage, and religion), were now given a measure of *de jure* control over some of their official dealings with the wider society. Most of the councilors were men of very little if any formal education, and their understanding of the complexities of white society was at best quite limited. For these reasons they relied heavily on the integrity and judgment of their white advisors, who therefore had considerable *de facto* power. Also, bureaucratic decisions concerning fund allocations and spending priorities, taken at government level, made a mockery of the concept of local autonomy and Aboriginal self-regulation. Yet for the first time since

---

[2] But the total amount spent by the Australian government on Aborigines is a pitifully small proportion of the Gross Domestic Product; for example in 1976–1977, the Department of Aboriginal Affairs spent about $A162 million ($US182 million) or only 0.2 percent of the GDP! Even if health, education, and welfare benefits are included, it is doubtful whether total expenditure would reach 0.4 percent of annual GDP. This budgeting is in part a reflection of the economic and political powerlessness of Australia's Aborigines. Although their population is growing at a much faster rate than that of white Australians, the present population of approximately 80,000 mixed-blood and 60,000 full-blood Aborigines represent only about one percent of the total Australian population.

coming into contact with whites, the Aborigines were being consulted as to *their* priorities and wishes. Furthermore, they now had the power to dismiss unpopular white staff members, an action that would have been impossible in the colonial situation of the past.

Ambitious plans for the provision of an adequate water supply and for decent housing were made. There was a flurry of survey and specialist activity, but very little progress was made, and funding levels were greatly reduced after a changeover in the leadership of the federal government. Very little of the considerable sums allocated to the community were of direct material benefit to the Mardudjara inhabitants. In terms of physical environment and living standards, little has changed since mission times. The Mardudjara still live in makeshift shelters of iron, canvas, and bushes, in generally unhygienic conditions. Although it is community policy to refuse unemployment benefits or any form of ration handout, the Mardudjara remain heavily dependent on social service income (old age, widows', and invalids' pensions). According to my estimate, per capita income at Jigalong in 1974 was about one dollar per day.

Fortunately, the Aborigines have retained their healthy skepticism of the promises and intentions of whites, and continue to be more concerned and preoccupied with their own internal problems. But there is increasing awareness of the injustice of their situation, evidenced by the speed with which white staff are accommodated in new houses, for instance. This is causing some of the younger, better educated people to become more vocal and critical in their attitudes to the government; and for the first time they are seeing the wider implications in the differential treatment that is accorded them as Aborigines.

Legal Representation   Throughout Australia, Aborigines are overrepresented in jails and in their involvement with the law in general, a condition owing partly to discrimination in the application of law (and also to their ignorance of their rights) and an often justifiable fear of police prejudice and brutality (Eggleston 1975). In the past the Mardudjara have been at times greatly disadvantaged in their dealings with policemen because of their conviction that the police are a law unto themselves.

In recent years, the influence of the Aboriginal Legal Service (ALS), a government-funded body set up to supply vital legal aid to them, has spread rapidly. Its effects are now being felt in communities as isolated as Jigalong. Through the operation of ALS, the Mardudjara have become very much more aware of the limitations of a policeman's power. They are learning that they have some basic rights before the law, rights that were never before explained to them in language that they could comprehend. Having once witnessed an ALS counsel refute a piece of evidence submitted by a police witness in a court of law, and then score a dismissal of the case, Mardudjara defendants never forget this lesson in hierarchy and power relations among the whites. As a result of the presence and activism of the ALS, police in this area appear to have become very much less cavalier in their dealings with Aborigines. The jail cell bashings which young Mardudjara men allege were once frequent after their arrest in a drunk and aggressive mood seem to have become less common.

Land Claims   The abandoned homelands of the Mardudjara remain uninhabited, and very few Aborigines have been back there in person. However, many people say that they visit their old haunts in dream-spirit form from time to time, and sometimes men go back to enter increase sites and bring up the species concerned (Tonkinson 1970). Emotional attachments to the desert remain strong. People are still moved to tears at the mention of a familiar waterhole or site in story or song, and they often tell of the abundance of meat and vegetable foods they used to harvest there. Except for an occasional party of travelers following the Canning Stock Route, their homelands remain unvisited and and undisturbed by mining activities.

In Australia the Aborigines were until recently denied ownership of their lands. When it came to power in 1972, the federal Labor government promised to work toward the recognition of Aboriginal land claims. Vast tracts of land had long been occupied by white pastoralists, and huge multinational mining companies were taking massive profits, with little or no compensation paid to the Aboriginal owners of the land concerned. Aborigines in northern Australia soon realized that foreign alienation of their homelands would be made more difficult, and would arouse the ire of liberal whites and Aboriginal activists, if they were actually living on that land. This belief—and an earnest desire to escape from the pressures of life in large white-controlled settlements—has prompted a decentralization movement involving a return to the ancestral homelands where small groups again hunt and gather. A resumption of full autonomy is not possible, so the provision of needed services and material goods is an essential part of the scheme.

In Western Australia, 49 million acres of Aboriginal reserve lands have been transferred from government to Aboriginal ownership under a Lands Trust. In the case of Jigalong, this provision covers the settlement and surrounding reserve area (a total of about a million acres), but not as yet the traditional homelands, which remain unalienated government land. In 1977 the Jigalong community took the first steps to rectify this situation by initiating claims to their home territories near Lake Disappointment. This claim is motivated in part by a squabble among several different government agencies over a proposed nature reserve in the area, including some sites of major importance to the Budidjara and Gardudjara speakers. Since the present Jigalong reserve is on land originally owned by the Nyiyabarli people, now almost defunct, the incorporation of the desert homelands will give the Mardudjara the satisfaction of title to the land that once succored them and is still a major focus of their multiple ties to the spiritual realm.

Widespread decentralization movements, to small outstation camps, have taken place along the southeastern and eastern fringes of the Western Desert. The Mardudjara now know something of these. A limited decentralization was budgeted for by the community after its recent acquisition of two nearby pastoral properties, but as yet this move has not eventuated. If a passable road is constructed between Jigalong and the Durba Hills area (Map 2), pressures may mount among some people for the establishment of an outstation near the Stock Route. To be successful, this community would need strong commitment from younger men as well as old. The advantages of a strategic withdrawal from alcohol and a strengthening of traditional norms would not be lost on the proponents of such a move (which would be over a distance of about 100 miles). Initiation into the totemic geography of the homelands would do much to make immediate and meaningful the associated rituals and myths for younger settlement-reared men. Then perhaps men would again begin to "find" dream-spirit rituals, which have not been composed in the past 10 years or more.

It is, however, quite possible that few people will want to move that far from their adopted home at Jigalong. Young men and women may well opt instead for migration further west, to large population centers with their many attractions. As yet, there has been no such trend, and the people who visit towns stay only briefly before homesickness for Jigalong compels them to go back. It is not difficult to appreciate why the Mardudjara prefer the familiarity and security of settlement life to the alienating and less secure atmosphere in the white town environment. Despite their better education and greater awareness of the nature of the outside world, younger Mardudjara seem not yet prepared to forsake their kin and the familiar surroundings of Jigalong for the decidedly dubious advantages of life among the whites.

CONCLUSION

The Mardudjara have shown good sense in refusing to let their dealings with the outside world take precedence over their concern for maintaining their traditions and upholding the Law. The people of Jigalong have remained conservative, ethnocentric, and somewhat parochial. They concentrate their energies on preserving the basic integrity of their kinship and ritual behaviors. The elders rely on their elected councilors to deal with the whites and "whitefella business" and keep them out of their hair. Their concern is with the pressing problems outlined above. The Mardudjara rightly perceive these unresolved issues as posing a very real danger to the continued functioning of the Law, which is still the foundation of their sense of pride and distinctiveness.

Basic economic problems remain. The desert and its periphery offer very little in the way of a resource base from which the Mardudjara and other Western Desert groups can develop their productive potential. Northwestern Australia is incredibly rich in minerals, and perhaps major finds will be made close to Jigalong. But as Rowley (1972:10) notes, such large-scale developments ". . . will pass by the Aborigines on the spot, using their services more sparsely, and with even more limited sharing of the product than has been the case with the pastoral enterprise." The huge operation at Newman, a scant 100 miles from Jigalong, is a major employer, but little effort has been made to employ or train Aboriginal labor, and the presence of Aborigines in the company town is definitely not encouraged. The bleak economic outlook means that the chances of Mardudjara Aborigines reaching a socioeconomic level anywhere near that of the very affluent white society remain slender.

On the positive side, the presence of several thousand whites at Newman has presented the Aborigines with a good market for the sale of artifacts. Jigalong is the site of the first full-time training center (developed by an adult education government body in collaboration with the local council), opened in 1975. About seventy local Aborigines are being trained in woodworking, jewelry making, pottery, leatherwork, and so on, as well as attending literacy and community administration classes. A large potential market exists for the products of these labor-intensive, cottage-craft activities in the town of Newman. The active involvement of many of the younger adults in these training programs may help ease some of the social control problems that have troubled community elders in recent years.

With extremely able and dedicated advisors and a much more responsive officialdom than currently exists, the Mardudjara could conceivably overcome some of their internal problems. Whatever their local successes in maintaining traditional strengths as they continue to adapt to changing circumstances, questions of economic viability will loom large. Equally important in the long term is the willingness of the dominant white society not only to accept, but actively promote ethnic pride and true cultural pluralism. In this period of constant adjustment, the Mardudjara Aborigines will be well served by their strong sense of identity, continuing commitment to the Law as the ultimate truth, and great pride in their traditions. They also have their great sense of humor and resilience of body and spirit that speak volumes for their determination to survive the change and uncertainty of the contact situation as ably as they did in their desert homeland.

Glossary

Activists-Mourners (*djindjanuṅgu-garngu*): a dual division of considerable importance in certain Mardudjara activities, particularly male initiation, death, and burial; Mourners, who include all a person's close kin and most members of the first ascending and first descending generation, play a passive role in the proceedings.

Affinal Kin: relatives by marriage; usually contrasted with Consanguineal Kin, who are relatives by birth, although it is possible for affinal kin to also be consanguines.

Ancestral Totem (*djugur*): the ancestral Dreamtime being (s) from whom a person is "descended" by virtue of having been left behind by them in life-essence form.

Band (also known as the Horde): the land-occupying group, consisting of one or more families, whose male heads are more often than not related patrilineally. It is a labile social group; i.e. varies in size and composition, and is the basic exploitative unit in Aboriginal society.

Bardundjari (Dream-Spirit): the spirit that assumes a bird-like form and sometimes leaves the body during sleep.

Barlgalu (Penis-holding Rite): a rite that identifies men as subincized and therefore eligible to participate in men's secret rituals; also used as a right of entry into other groups' territories, and in dispute settlements.

Big Meeting (*djabal*): the large assembly of Aboriginal groups from widely separated areas that takes place once or twice a year; a time of great ritual and social intensification, and the high point of the Aboriginal year.

Conception Totem (*djarin/nyuga*): the plant, animal, or mineral form that a spirit-child (which derives from the life essence left by Dreamtime beings) assumes before entering its human mother.

Cosmic Order: the totality of a people's conceived universe, including the physical environment, flora and fauna, human society, spiritual or extrahuman presences, and any other true or conceived realms that are assumed to exist.

Cross-Cousins: the children of a woman and her brother are cross-cousins to one another; Parallel Cousins are the children of a woman and her sister and of a man and his brother (among the Mardudjara, they are classed as siblings).

Djabiya (see Increase Rites)

Djidjigargaly (see Spirit-Children)

Djindjanuṅgu (see Activists)

Dream-Spirit (see *Bardundjari*)

Dreamtime (*manguny/djugur*): a complex concept of fundamental importance to Aboriginal culture, embracing the creative era long past (when ancestral beings roamed and instituted Aboriginal society) as well as the present and the future.

Estate: the heartland of a local group and the locus of their attachment to territory; its sites are of considerable mythological and totemic significance to group members, and it includes at least one storehouse of sacred boards.

Featherfeet (*djinagarbil*): groups of men who wear special moccasins to disguise their footprints while en route to kill somebody; their alleged presence in an area causes desert Aborigines great concern.

139

Garngu (Mourners): see Activists-Mourners.

Increase rite: a ritual that is performed each year at an increase center (*djabiya*) with the intention of causing the spirits of the animal or plant species associated with that spot to emerge and be plentiful.

Law (*Yurlubidi*): the Dreamtime legacy of social institutions, norms and behaviors that provide a blueprint or life-design for the Aborigines to follow.

Linguistic Unit: comprises all those groups which speak the same dialect; the people termed "Mardudjara" in this study are in fact members of several different but neighboring linguistic units.

Mabarn: this term refers both to the "native doctor" or "medicine man" and to the magical objects that are essential to his proper functioning.

Manggalyi: the two, three, or four men who are chosen to perform the initiatory operations of circumcision or subincision.

Manguny (see Dreamtime)

Men's Country: areas that are temporarily or permanently tabu to women and children; the venue of men's secret-sacred ritual and locations of storehouses of sacred objects, or mythologically validated sacred sites.

Merged Alternate Generation Levels: egocentrically defined dual division of considerable ritual importance; an Ego's "own side" is his or her own generation level plus those of grandparents and grandchildren, and "opposite side" is members of first ascending and first descending levels (e.g., parents, children).

Penis-holding Rite (see *Barlgalu*)

Range: the normal, habitual hunting and gathering territory exploited by a number of related land-occupying bands; it normally includes the estate.

Sections: division of a society into four named categories, which indicate intermarrying divisions (but do not regulate marriage) and are useful mainly as labeling devices.

Siblings: one's brothers and sisters.

Sociocentric Terms: objectively applied labels, usable by all members of a society; contrasts with Egocentric Terms, which are defined only from the viewpoint of the individual; i.e., "my group" and "other group."

Spirit-Child: a very small, humanoid being that magically enters a woman and is later born as a human. They are called *djidjigargaly,* a term which is also used for spirit-beings that act as intermediaries between the spiritual and human realms.

Subincision: the slitting open of the underside of the penis, which exposes the urethra; a ritual operation that is performed some time following circumcision and is an essential stage in Western Desert male initiation.

Thread-Cross: a class of sacred objects, secret to men, consisting of a wooden base (spears or sacred carved wooden boards) and crosspieces on which is threaded twine; must be dismantled after a single use; are used in dancing; some are very similar to the "gods-eye" type crosses of the Huichol Indians of Mexico.

Yurlubidi (see Law)

References cited

ALLEN, J., J. GOLSON and R. JONES (ed.), 1977, *Sunda and Sahul: Prehistoric Studies in Southeast Asia, Melanesia and Australia*. New York: Academic Press.

BARKER, GRAHAM, 1976, "The Ritual Estate and Aboriginal Polity," *Mankind* 10(4):225–239.

BERNDT, R. M., 1952, *Djanggawul*. London: Routledge.

————, 1959, "The Concept of 'The Tribe' in the Western Desert of Australia," *Oceania* 30(2):81–107.

————, 1970, "Traditional Morality as Expressed Through the Medium of an Australian Aboriginal Religion." In *Australian Aboriginal Anthropology* (ed. R. Berndt). Perth: University of Western Australia Press, pp. 216–247.

————, 1974, "Australian Aboriginal Religion." In *Iconography of Religions* V(4):1–37. Leiden: Brill.

———— and C. H. BERNDT, 1945, "A Preliminary Account of Field Work in the Ooldea Region, Western South Australia," *Oceania Bound Offprint*. Sydney.

———— and ————, 1977, *The World of the First Australians*. Sydney: Ure Smith.

BIRDSELL, J. H., 1967, "Preliminary Data on the Trihybrid Origin of the Australian Aborigines," *Archaeology and Physical Anthropology in Oceania* 2:100–155.

————, 1970, "Local Group Composition among the Australian Aborigines: A Critique of the Evidence from Fieldwork Conducted since 1930," *Current Anthropology* 11(2):115–131.

————, 1977, "The Recalibration of a Paradigm for the First Peopling of Greater Australia." In *Sunda and Sahul* (ed. J. Allen, J. Golson, and R. Jones). New York: Academic Press, pp. 113–167.

BOWDLER, SANDRA, 1977, "The Coastal Colonisation of Australia." In *Sunda and Sahul* (ed. J. Allen, J. Golson, and R. Jones). New York: Academic Press, pp. 205–246.

BURRIDGE, K. O. L., 1969a, *New Heaven, New Earth*. Oxford: Blackwell.

————, 1969b, *Tangu Traditions*. Oxford: Clarendon.

————, 1973, *Encountering Aborigines*. New York: Pergamon.

CARNEGIE, David, 1973, *Spinifex and Sand*. London: Penguin. (Colonial Facsimile of the 1898 ed.)

DIXON, R. M. W., 1972, *The Dyirbal Language of North Queensland*. London: Cambridge University Press.

DOUGLAS, W. H., 1958, "An Introduction to the Western Desert Language of Australia," *Oceania Linguistic Monographs*, 4. Sydney.

DURKHEIM, E., 1915, *The Elementary Forms of the Religious Life*. London: G. Allen.

EGGLESTON, E., 1975, *Fear, Favour or Affection: Aborigines and the Criminal Law in Victoria, South Australia and Western Australia*. Canberra: Australian National University Press.

ELKIN, A. P., 1954, *The Australian Aborigines: How to Understand Them*. Sydney: Angus and Robertson.

141

————————, 1977, *Aboriginal Men of High Degree*. Brisbane: University of Queensland Press.

ELPHINSTONE, J. J., 1971, "The Health of Australian Aborigines with no Previous Association with Europeans," *Medical Journal of Australia* 2:293–301.

FORREST, JOHN, 1875, *Explorations in Australia*. London: Low, Marston, Low and Searle.

GILES, ERNEST, 1889, *Australia Twice Traversed*. 2 vols. London: Low, Marston, Searle and Rivington.

GLASS, A., and D. HACKETT, 1970, "Pitjantjatjara Grammar: A Tagmemic View of the Ngaayatjara (Warburton Ranges) Dialect," *Australian Aboriginal Studies, 34*. Canberra: Australian Institute of Aboriginal Studies.

GOODALE, JANE C., 1971, *Tiwi Wives: A Study of the Women of Melville Island, North Australia*. Seattle: University of Washington Press.

GOULDE, R. A., 1968, "Living Archaeology: The Ngatatjara of Western Australia," *Southwestern Journal of Anthropology* 24(2):101–122.

————————, 1969a, *Yiwara: Foragers of the Australian Desert*. New York: Scribner.

————————, 1969b, "Subsistence Behavior Among the Western Desert Aborigines of Australia," *Oceania* 39(4):253–274.

————————, 1971, "The Archaeologist as Ethnographer: a Case from the Western Desert of Australia," *World Archaeology* 3(2):143–177.

————————, n.d.a., "Puntutjarpa Rockshelter and the Australian Desert Culture," *Anthropological Papers of the American Museum of Natural History* 54(1):1–189.

————————, n.d.b, "The Anthropology of Human Residues," *American Anthropologist*.

HANSEN, K. C. and L. E. HANSEN, 1969, "Pintupi Phonology," *Oceanic Linguistics* 8(2):153–170.

HIATT, L. R., 1962, "Local Organization among the Australian Aborigines," *Oceania* 32(4):267–286.

————————, 1966, "The Lost Horde," *Oceania* 37(2):81–92.

JONES, RHYS, 1969, "Fire-stick Farming," *Australian Natural History* 16:224–228.

————————, 1973, "The Emerging Picture of Pleistocene Australians," *Nature* 246:278–281.

————————, 1977, "Man as an Element of a Continental Fauna: the Case of the Sundering of the Bassian Bridge." In *Sunda and Sahul* (ed. J. Allen, J. Golson, and R. Jones). New York: Academic Press, pp. 317–386.

JONES, TREVOR A., 1965, "Australian Aboriginal Music: The Elkin Collection's Contribution Toward an Overall Picture." In *Aboriginal Man in Australia* (ed. R. M. and C. H. Berndt). Sydney: Angus and Robertson, pp. 285–374.

KIRK, R. L., 1965, *The Distribution of Genetic Markers in Australia*. Canberra: Australian Institute of Aboriginal Studies.

————————, 1971, "Genetic Evidence and Its Implications for Aboriginal Prehistory." In *Aboriginal Man and Environment in Australia* (ed. D. J. Mulvaney and J. Golson). Canberra: Australian National University Press, pp. 326–343.

LAWRENCE, PETER, 1964, *Road Belong Cargo*. Manchester: Manchester University Press.

LÉVI-STRAUSS, C., 1962, *The Savage Mind*. London: Weidenfeld and Nicholson.

LOMMEL, A., 1970, "Changes in Australian Art." In *Diprotodon to Detribalization* (ed. A. R. Pilling and A. R. Waterman). East Lansing: Michigan State University Press, pp. 217–236.

MADDOCK, KENNETH, 1969, "The Jabuduruwa." Unpublished doctoral dissertation, University of Sydney.

————————, 1972, *The Australian Aborigines: A Portrait of Their Society*. Baltimore: Penguin.

MARSH, J., 1969, "Mantjiltjara Phonology," *Oceanic Linguistics* 8(2):131–151.

MEEHAN, BETTY, 1977, "Man Does Not Live by Calories Alone: The Role of Shell-fish in a Coastal Cuisine." In *Sunda and Sahul* (ed. J. Allen, J. Golson and R. Jones). New York: Academic Press, pp. 493–531.

MEGGITT, M. J., 1962, *Desert People.* Sydney: Angus and Robertson.

——————, 1966, "Gadjari among the Walbiri Aborigines of Central Australia," *Oceania Monographs,* 14. Sydney.

MONTAGU, ASHLEY, 1974, *Coming into Being among the Australian Aborigines.* Revised ed. Boston: Routledge.

MOUNTFORD, C. P., and R. TONKINSON, 1969, "Carved and Engraved Human Figures from North Western Australia." *Anthropological Forum* 2(3):371–390.

MULVANEY, D. J., 1975, *The Prehistory of Australia.* Revised ed. Baltimore: Penguin.

MUNN, NANCY D., 1973, *Walbiri Iconography: Graphic Representation and Cultural Symbolism in a Central Australian Society.* Ithaca, N.Y.: Cornell University Press.

MYERS, F. R., 1976, "To Have and to Hold: A Study of Persistence and Change in Pintupi Social Life." Unpublished doctoral dissertation, Bryn Mawr University.

O'CONNELL, J. R., 1976, "Report of Investigations of Alyawara Land Claims." Department of Prehistory, R.S.Pac.S., Australian National University, Canberra. (Mimeo., 27 pp.)

PETERSON, NICOLAS, 1972, "Totemism Yesterday: Sentiment and Local Organisation Among the Australian Aborigines," *Man* 7(1):12–32.

——————, 1976a, "Introduction." In *Tribes and Boundaries in Australia* (ed. N. Peterson), Canberra: Australian Institute of Aboriginal Studies, pp. 1–11.

——————, 1976b, "The Natural and Cultural Areas of Aboriginal Australia: a Preliminary Analysis of Population Groupings with Adaptive Significance." In *Tribes and Boundaries in Australia* (ed. N. Peterson). Canberra: Australian Institute of Aboriginal Studies, pp. 50–71.

——————, 1977, "Aboriginal Uses of Australian Solanaceae." In *The Biology and Taxonomy of the Solanaceae* (ed. J. Hawkes). New York: Academic Press.

PIDDINGTON, RALPH, 1970, "Irregular Marriages in Australia," *Oceania* 40:329–342.

ROHEIM, G., 1945, *The Eternal Ones of the Dream.* New York: International Universities Press.

ROWLEY, C. D., 1972, *The Remote Aborigines.* London: Pelican.

SACKETT, L., 1975, "Exogamy or Endogamy: Kinship and Marriage at Wiluna, Western Australia," *Anthropological Forum* 4(1):44–55.

SADLEIR, RICHARD, 1970, *Animals of Australia and New Zealand.* New York: Hamlyn.

SERVICE, E. R., 1960, "Sociocentric Relationship Terms and the Australian Class System." In *Essays in the Science of Culture in Honor of Leslie A. White* (ed. G. E. Dole and R. L. Carneiro). New York: Corwell, pp. 416–436.

SPENCER, B., and F. J. GILLEN, 1899, *The Native Tribes of Central Australia.* London: Macmillan.

STANNER, W. E. H., 1958, "The Dreaming." In *Reader in Comparative Religion* (ed. W. A. Lessa and E. Z. Vogt). New York: Harper & Row, pp. 513–523.

——————, 1965a, "Religion, Totemism and Symbolism." In *Aboriginal Man in Australia* (ed. R. M. and C. H. Berndt). Sydney: Angus and Robertson, pp. 207–237.

——————, 1965b, "Aboriginal Territorial Organization: Estate, Range, Domain and Regime," *Oceania* 36(1):1–26.

——————, 1966, "On Aboriginal Religion," *Oceania Monograph,* 11. Sydney.

STREHLOW, T. G. H., 1947, *Aranda Traditions.* Melbourne: Melbourne University Press.

——————, 1965, "Culture, Social Structure and Environment in Aboriginal Central Australia." In *Aboriginal Man in Australia* (ed. R. M. and C. H. Berndt). Sydney: Angus and Robertson, pp. 121–145.

THORNE, A. G., 1977, "Separation or Reconciliation? Biological Clues to the Development of Australian Society." In *Sunda and Sahul* (ed. J. Allen, J. Golson, and R. Jones). New York: Academic Press, pp. 187–204.

TINDALE, N. B., 1974, *Aboriginal Tribes of Australia.* Berkeley: University of California Press.

TONKINSON, ROBERT, 1970, "Aboriginal Dream-Spirit Beliefs in a Contact Situation: Jigalong, Western Australia." In *Australian Aboriginal Anthropology* (ed. R. M. Berndt). Perth: University of Western Australia Press, pp. 277–291.

——————, 1972, "Ngaawayil: a Western Desert Aboriginal Rainmaking Ritual." Unpublished doctoral dissertation, University of British Columbia.

——————, 1974, *The Jigalong Mob: Aboriginal Victors of the Desert Crusade.* Menlo Park: Cummings.

——————, 1977a, Aboriginal Self-Regulation and the New Regime: Jigalong, Western Australia." In *Aborigines and Change: Australia in the '70s* (ed. R. M. Berndt). Canberra: Australian Institute of Aboriginal Studies, pp. 65–73.

——————, 1977b, "Aboriginal Community Autonomy: Myth and Reality." In " 'Whitefella Business': Aborigines in Australian Politics" (ed. M. Howard). Philadelphia: Institute for the Study of Human Issues, pp. 93–103.

——————, 1977c, "Semen Versus Spirit-Child in Western Desert Culture." In *Australian Aboriginal Concepts* (ed. L. R. Hiatt). Canberra: Australian Institute of Aboriginal Studies.

WARBURTON, P. E., 1875, *Journey Across the Western Interior of Australia.* London: Low, Marston, Low and Searle.

Recommended readings

PREHISTORY

MULVANEY, D. J., 1969, *The Prehistory of Australia*. New York: Praeger.
 The best overview of Australian prehistory. Unfortunately the revised edition
 (1975, Penguin Books) is not available outside Australasia.

GENERAL WORKS

BERNDT, R. M., and C. H. BERNDT, 1977, *The World of the First Australians*. Sydney: Ure Smith.
 The best general reference book on Australian Aboriginal culture, written in
 1964 and newly revised.
BURRIDGE, K. O. L., 1973, *Encountering Aborigines*. New York: Pergamon.
 This scholarly work attempts an answer to the broad question, Why Anthropol-
 ogy?, and puts the development of research on Australian Aborigines into a more
 general framework and perspective. Highly recommended for anthropology seniors and graduate students.
MADDOCK, KENNETH, 1972, *The Australian Aborigines: A Portrait of Their Society*.
 Baltimore: Penguin.
 A concise and insightful portrait of Aboriginal society that includes discussion of
 both traditional and postcontact elements.
ROWLEY, C. D., 1970, *The Destruction of Aboriginal Society*. Canberra: Australian National University Press.
 Republished in paperback by Penguin Books in 1972, together with two companion volumes, *Outcasts in White Australia* and *The Remote Aborigines*, this incredible trilogy first writes the Aborigines back into Australian history, then
 details in accurate, scholarly fashion the present plight of this oppressed minority. An absolute must for any student seriously interested in the place of Aborigines in Australian society.

ETHNOGRAPHIES

BERNDT, R. M., and C. H. BERNDT, 1970, *Man, Land and Myth in North Australia*.
 Sydney: Ure Smith.
 A detailed account of the culture of the Gunwinggu Aborigines of Arnhem
 Land, with particular emphasis on local and social organization and religion
 among these riverine people.
GOODALE, JANE C., 1971, *Tiwi Wives*. Seattle: University of Washington Press.
 An invaluable study which documents the important roles played by women in
 the culture of the Tiwi people of Melville Island offshore northern Australia.

Provides detailed data on subsistence, socialization, kinship, social organization, and the rich ceremonial life.

GOULD, R. A., 1969, *Yiwara: Foragers of the Australian Desert.* New York: Scribner. This extremely readable and entertaining account of the author's experiences in working with Western Desert Aborigines is currently out of print, but in the U.S. copies should not be too difficult to locate.

HART, C. W. M., and A. R. PILLING, 1960, *The Tiwi of North Australia.* New York: Holt, Rinehart and Winston. One of the earliest titles in the series of which the present study is a part, this study introduces the Tiwi (see Goodale above). It has proved controversial among many Australianists, and is best used in conjunction with Goodale's later, more detailed study.

HIATT, L. R., 1965, *Kinship and Conflict.* Canberra: Australian National University. This study of an Arnhem Land people provides the first detailed account of the dynamics of Aboriginal kinship and marriage, with a focus on conflicts and their management. Recommended for seniors and graduate students.

KABERRY, P. M., 1939, *Aboriginal Woman, Sacred and Profane.* London: Routledge. Now available in a facsimile edition, this is a classic study of women in Aboriginal society, set in the Kimberley area of Western Australia. Now, almost forty years after, its observations and contentions on women's roles remain valuable and relevant.

MEGGITT, M. J., 1962, *Desert People.* Sydney: Angus and Robertson. Now available in paperback in the U.S., this study remains one of the best ethnographies written on the Aborigines. It deals with the Walbiri, a central Australian group whose culture is in many respects similar to that of the Western Desert peoples.

MUNN, NANCY D., 1973. *Walbiri Iconography.* Ithaca, N.Y.: Cornell University Press. This is a brilliant structural analysis of the graphic forms of these central Australian Aborigines. The author relates iconography to sex role differentiation, social organization, and other symbolic dimensions. Recommended for seniors and graduate students.

SPENCER, B., and F. J. GILLEN, 1899. *The Native Tribes of Central Australia.* London: Macmillan. Now available in a Dover reprint edition, this early classic on the Aranda of central Australia is the first detailed account, complete with copious illustrations, of an Aboriginal religion in action.

TONKINSON, ROBERT, 1974, *The Jigalong Mob: Aboriginal Victors of the Desert Crusade.* Menlo Park, Calif.: Cummings. This is a study of Western Desert Aborigines living in a colonial, paternalist situation in a fringe settlement. It deals with the adaptive strategies evolved by the Aborigines in coping with whites, particularly missionaries, whose subculture is also described.

WARNER, W. LLOYD, 1937/58, *A Black Civilization.* New York: Harper & Row. A classic study of the Murngin people of eastern Arnhem Land, this work reveals the Aborigines in all their cutural complexity.

COLLECTED READINGS

ALLEN, J., J. GOLSON, and R. JONES, 1977, *Sunda and Sahul: Prehistoric Studies in Southeast Asia, Melanesia and Australia.* New York: Academic Press. The most up-to-date anthology of readings on the prehistory of Australia, with some important papers on Southeast Asia and Melanesia also included.

BERNDT, R. M., and C. H. BERNDT, 1965, *Aboriginal Man in Australia.* Sydney: Angus and Robertson.

Although the sections dealing with prehistory, physical anthropology, and linguistics are now somewhat dated, this collection contains some papers of major importance on marriage, law, religion and totemism, women's ritual life, and music.

BERNDT, R. M., 1970, *Australian Aboriginal Anthropology*. Perth: University of Western Australia Press.

A more recent anthology on social anthropological studies of Aborigines, containing some excellent papers on aspects of traditional religion, in particular.

KIRK, R. L., and A. G. THORNE, 1976, *The Origin of the Australians*. Canberra: Australian Institute of Aboriginal Studies.

Twenty-six contributors discuss environment, skeletal, and other morphological characteristics of the Pleistocene colonists and their descendants, and the genetics and microevolution of populations in Australia, New Guinea, and the neighboring Asian region. An up-to-date and valuable reference.

PETERSON, NICOLAS, 1976, *Tribes and Boundaries in Australia*. Canberra: Australian Institute of Aboriginal Studies.

Most of the 12 papers in this volume are addressed to aspects of the thorny problem of Aboriginal local organization, including the notion of "tribe" and its relationship to linguistic, natural, and cultural boundaries.

Films on Western Desert Aboriginal cultures

Following a film-making trip in 1965, in which I participated as scientific advisor, a series of films were produced by Ian Dunlop of the Australian Commonwealth Film Unit for the Australian Institute of Aboriginal Studies. The films were shot in 35mm black-and-white film, without synchronized sound; each has spoken commentary. They are listed as follows:

PEOPLES OF THE AUSTRALIAN WESTERN DESERT, PARTS 1–10

Part	Subtitle	Time
1	Seedcake Making and General Activity in the Camping Area.	21'
2	Gum Preparation (Spinifex Resin). Stone-flaking. Djagamara Leaves Badjar.	19'
3	Sacred Boards and an Ancestral Site (Restricted).	8'
4	A Family Moves Camp and Gathers Food.	48'
5	Old Campsites at Tikatika. Mending a Cracked Dish. Medicinal Use of Quandong.	11'
6	Spearmaking. Boys' Spear Fight.	9'
7	Spearthrower Making, including Stone-flaking and Gum (Spinifex Resin) Preparation.	34'
8	Fire Making.	7'
9	Spinning Hair-string. Getting Water from a Well. Binding Girl's Hair.	12'
10	Cooking Kangaroo.	17'

DESERT PEOPLE

This 51-minute film is made from material contained in Parts 1,2,4, and part of 9 above. It is more interpretive film, showing a day in the life of two desert families. To make the story, the actual sequence of filming was ignored; that is, the events as depicted did not necessarily happen in that order. A few activities were filmed as they actually occurred; most were initiated at our request—then the Aborigines were left undirected, except for stopping and restarting actions to fit in with film and lens changes, and such. Since we were filming people whose contact with whites prior to that time had been minimal (although they possessed some metal tools), we believe

148

that the activities filmed were carried out much as they would have been in precontact days.

There are some very important points to keep in mind when viewing these films. Because they lack synchronized sound, they convey no impression of the liveliness and chatter, the many noises and laughter that accompany much of the everyday activity of the desert people. Also, the films portray only one facet of the culture: subsistence activities—and then only a narrow range of the total possible (for example, the complexities of hunting are badly touched upon). Nothing is shown of the functioning of kinship or of local or social organization above the level of the family. Most notably, we did not film any of the religious life. In other words, the films show very little of what the Aborigines themselves regard as of fundamental and primary significance to their existence.

What the films do convey well, however, is a feeling for the physical environment of the Western Desert and for the routines of daily life among the people. Since the desert is now uninhabited, these films stand as a record of a traditional existence, relatively free of European influences, that is no more.

Film Availability   Anyone interested in seeing the films described above should contact in the first instance: Film Representative, c/o Australian Consulate-General, 636 Fifth Avenue, New York, N.Y. 10020. *In Australia:* Film Australia, PO Box 46, Lindfield, NSW 2070, Australia.

FILMS ON DESERT RITUAL

Several color sound films, made by Roger Sandall for the Australian Institute of Aboriginal Studies, are available in the U.S. (from Extension Media Services, University of California, Berkeley, CA 94720). All are rituals of the Walbiri of central Australia, whose desert culture and religion is in many ways similar to the Western Desert peoples.

Walbiri Ritual at Gunadjara
This film centers on a Dreamtime ancestor Widayiṅgula, who had a huge penis (cf. Nyiru, in this study).

Emu Ritual at Ruguri
In this film, an increase rite for emus is performed.

Walbiri Ritual at Ngama
A ritual concerned with a major snake ancestral being.

A Walbiri Fire Ceremony
This ritual is connected with the settlement of disputes; and like those listed above, shows the dual division into owners-managers in the organization and performance of ritual among the Walbiri.